TWENTY ACRES

Ozarks Studies

EDITED BY BROOKS BLEVINS

OTHER TITLES IN THIS SERIES

Hipbillies: Deep Revolution in the Arkansas Ozarks

The Literature of the Ozarks: An Anthology

Down on Mahans Creek: A History of an Ozarks Neighborhood

TWENTY ACRES

A Seventies Childhood in the Woods

Sarah Neidhardt

THE UNIVERSITY OF ARKANSAS PRESS

FAYETTEVILLE

2023

ISBN: 978-1-68226-227-6
eISBN: 978-1-61075-792-8

27 26 25 24 23   5 4 3 2 1

Manufactured in the United States of America

Text design: April Leidig
Cover design: Daniel Bertalotto

Cover photo: Sarah and sister Katy at the goat pen in 1977,
courtesy of the author.

♾ The paper used in this publication meets the minimum requirements
of the American National Standard for Permanence of Paper for
Printed Library Materials Z39.48-1984.

Cataloging-in-Publication Data on file at the Library of Congress

For Momma and Daddy
and Granminnow

I have only twenty acres. I cultivate them with my children; and work keeps at bay three great evils: boredom, vice, and need.
—The Turk in *Candide*

I'll call for pen and ink, and write my mind.
—William Shakespeare, *Henry VI*

CONTENTS

Acknowledgments xiii

Prologue
A Child's Work is Play 3

1

A Marriage 11

2

Reinventing the Wheel 33

3

To Arkansas 45

4

The Key Place 57

5

Visitors, Moonshine,
and Hard Work 65

6

On the Land 79

7

Pickin' and Grinnin' 105

8

Neighbors 115

9

In the Kitchen 133

10

Back on the Farm 147

11

Fauna 163

12

Arcadia 177

13

Rural Special 201

14

Progress 209

15

The End 233

Notes 243

Index 261

Some of the names in this story have been changed (a footnote marks the first instance of any pseudonym). There are no composite characters. Recreating a world that existed over forty years ago is difficult, and memory sometimes unreliable. The scenes and events described in this book were created by cross-referencing the details in family memories with information gleaned from old letters, photographs, and audiocassettes, as well as contemporary online resources, to create the most accurate record possible. All errors in quotes are original.

ACKNOWLEDGMENTS

In writing this book, it sometimes felt weird and unsatisfying to simply whittle everything down to quotes and trim memories. My intense memories of the landscape of Fox, Arkansas, are vivid and emotional, but I had to pore through the letters, photographs, interviews, and online research to build a full story, to collect the fragments, like shards of unearthed pottery, and make them whole. What is lost—except what little traces I could glean from the letters—is the real feel to each of those days: the stomachaches, headaches, tears, rage, melancholy, jealousy, irritation, lust, exhilaration, hunger, the bumps and bruises that ache while you work, the soft warmth of sun on a fall day, and the bitter chill and rattling cough in the dead of winter. The smells of bacon and wood fire, of body odor and shit on dirt. Gone is the grimy sweat, the palpable fear of wind and snakes and ominous clouds. And what did my parents really feel as they sat down with a book or in our tender moments as a family, babies and animals content, work done for the day? I can no longer really remember the deafening croak, buzz, and screech of frogs and cicadas and katydids in the dying light. Or what it felt like inside the cabin on a crisp fall day, in the middle of a snowstorm, on a first day of fall rain, of spring warmth. Did it smell of oak inside, did the Arkansas damp give it a thick mustiness?

I do have a few hundred mostly imperfect photos. There is no doubt they have cast their yellow-brown, hazy images over my memories. And I have the bundles of letters and the rambling cassette tapes we made. I have since copied them onto an iPhone. Miraculously it seems, I can now stream my old voice, small and twangy, anywhere in my home or car, that voice and the occasional crowing rooster following me through my days.

The photographs and tapes and letters were an archive I couldn't turn away from. I went through the photographs looking for clues like a detective, staring long into their depths to capture details I had forgotten or missed. My homemaking instinct wanted to conjure it all, to rebuild that home piece by piece just as it had been. I suddenly noticed late in working on the manuscript, a photo of the cabin in winter with an unpainted four-pane window in front, not the original six-pane white window. And

Daddy in front of the cabin in about 2003. (The air conditioner, deck, porch and posts, and concrete foundation are the only noticeable changes.)

I could see what appeared to be shims holding it in place on each side. I went back to earlier photos of the cabin and, yes, the original window was white with six panes instead of the four in this new window. It was probably an inconsequential repair, but I was determined to know why my father had changed it out. But he had no memory of it. I just couldn't know it all.

Daddy took a trip to Arkansas and out to our old land in about 2003. When he knocked on the door of the cabin—still standing and lived in after all these years—no one answered, and he left. Serendipitously, a woman ringing him up for a purchase later in a Mountain View store recognized his name on his check and said she and her husband were living in our old cabin. They had moved to Arkansas from Petaluma, California, a thirty-minute drive from where Daddy was then living. The cabin looked more pristine and romantic than it had in our day—the front grass filled in and kept clipped with none of the detritus we always had— but it was otherwise almost exactly the same. I've thought about visiting again myself, but something holds me back. I would be such an outsider there. And what if seeing the land again breaks the spell?

I have since communicated with the owner of the cabin on Facebook. She and her husband built a new house in 2004 but kept part of the cabin. I can follow the same familiar dirt road on Google Earth, still petering out as it reaches our homestead. The house and bare outlines of a garden and the dark pond are still there, and the woods still spread out into a dark green nubby mass, obscuring our endless playground.

Writing this book has been a long and often lonely process, and the intense feeling of navel-gazing was not always pleasant, but I have had many supporters along the way. None of this, of course, would exist without my parents, Wendy McPhee and Richard Neidhardt, who never tired of my endless questions and were open and generous with their answers (and my mother read many, many drafts). This is your book.

When I found the writer and editor Megan Nicole Kruse, it was a breakthrough moment. Megan, thank you for your invaluable editing, for seeing the value of my story, for the ability to ask just the right question, and for the confidence you gave me to keep going.

Thank you to everyone at the University of Arkansas Press. I feel there's no better place for my book to have landed. Thank you to the Ozark Studies series editor, Brooks Blevins, for being so enthusiastic about the book and giving such valuable input. I was a fan of your books (and relied on them) long before I saw your name in my email inbox.

And thank you to my sisters, Katy Dittmer and Miriam Neidhardt-McPhee, for your enthusiasm for the project and help confirming some of the weirder details of our childhood. And to my cousin Dave Roberts for your always funny insights into our cabin years.

Thank you to Ariel Gore for your thoughtful feedback and Literary Kitchen classes (and for sending me to Megan). Thank you to David Orr for reading and believing in the manuscript and for sharing details about Meadowcreek. And thank you to those of you who read earlier versions of the manuscript or parts of it or just gave constant encouragement: Betsy Boyd-Flynn; Susan Osborne; Tracy K. Smith; Jill Lepore; Leah Reznick; Jodi DeMunter; David, Nate, Nina, and Sasha Kagen; Aimee Kibbe; Ron Pernick; Dena Shehab; Sharon Colombo; Pete Dahlgren; and my dear aunt, Sarah McPhee.

And thank you most of all to my son, Lewis, who keeps me in the present and is proud of his mom, and to my wonderful, patient husband, Bryan Geraldo—you gave me the support, space, and time to write this book.

TWENTY ACRES

A CHILD'S WORK IS PLAY

During the whole summer poor little Tiny lived quite alone in the
wide forest. She wove herself a bed with blades of grass, and hung it
up under a broad leaf, to protect herself from the rain. She sucked
the honey from the flowers for food, and drank the dew from their
leaves every morning. So passed away the summer and the autumn.
—Hans Christian Andersen, "Little Tiny"

I was never athletic growing up, but on our farm I was a nimble
woods dancer. I climbed trees to the very top, unafraid and sure-
footed. I navigated through woods booby-trapped with branches
and holes and rocks with speed and confidence. I swam in cold
clear creeks and crawled through damp, cramped caves. I led my sisters in
dance performances in our tiny living room, pointing my toes and gazing
to the tips of my extended fingers. I felt full mastery of my place.

My sister Katy and I roamed the land freely from as early as I can
remember. We didn't have to venture far to find the nooks and crannies
of our woods. Our "yard" consisted of patches of stony dirt and weeds
and a pothole-studded gravel driveway under siege from the surrounding
underbrush. We played in the shaded back of the cabin where I imagined
the life and world of Thumbelina (Little Tiny) from our stories. That's
where she lives in my brain. Behind the cabin, in a half walnut shell, on
the gentle slope among trees and rocks and goldenrod. Just east of the
cabin, a narrow path worn into the woods ran alongside the garden and
Daddy's marijuana patch. There, in a tiny, sheltered clearing, Katy and I
started a log cabin of our own with fallen tree trunks. We stacked a foot-
high, haphazard square, like Lincoln Logs. The light was warm and soft,
and the undergrowth surrounding the logs was not a deep, overgrown
green, but a sparse, pale, worn yellow. The air smelled of sun on wood,
and the space felt like another, supernatural, realm.

Katy and me in front of the goat pen.

I would on occasion cross over into the strip of marijuana and finger the sticky buds, but once standing among the pungent plants, the magic seemed to dissipate, and I was just at the edge of our garden again. It was the logs and the light that created the aura of mystery, a bit of wood embroidered with a child's fancy.

When I asked Daddy several years ago about the path by the marijuana, he said that it petered out beyond the house and gave in to the woods. As Daddy recounted the story, I was reminded of our kinship, our shared incessant curiosity. These woods, he remembers, led to a glade and large bluffs suspended above a forest of ferns before moving south to Lick Fork Creek. As he described it all, I could tell he felt a little excited too and was grateful for the memory. There were remnants of a pioneer settlement in the woods.

"I used to go there all the time to look at it," he told me.

All that remained of the cabin were sill logs along the ground, but the old stone fireplace and chimney were still intact, with beautiful stone-work set with mud mortar. Next to it was a dug well lined with more artful stonework. A little further on near a field covered in small cedars growing like weeds, were bits of old split rail fencing and another dug well.

Homemaking was the central preoccupation of my childhood. I wish I'd seen this old homestead Daddy had found, but Daddy kept it to himself, and I was left to my own imagination. I was obsessed with any feature of the landscape—a canopy created by low-hanging branches, a space between boulders—that could be used for shelter. My parents were busy all around me turning a plot of land into a home: constructing walls, gardens, fences, and a pond, bringing in water and electricity, growing, butchering, cooking. I went to work creating my own little homes, my own corner of the wilderness to keep me dry and safe. Looking for just such a spot—a place where, like Little Tiny in the story, I could build a bed of grass and shelter under leaves—my sister Katy and I would often pack our small frog- and pig-shaped knapsacks and head off into the trees to eat cheddar cheese and saltines on mossy boulders with the fairies, surrounded by mayapple, the air pregnant with possibility.

Katy and I would chat and hike back miraculously unbroken and not snake bitten. Later, when I read *Heidi*, I was most intrigued when they took out their wrapped packages of bread and cheese on the mountainside. I paid so much attention to ritual, to the folding and unfolding of a carefully made lunch, like the wax-paper-wrapped sandwiches Momma tucked into Daddy's black-dome lunchbox.

Katy and I also made diaper bags, like good suburban mothers, stuffing them with scraps of cloth for diapers; plastic baby bottles; little wallets; and cigarette soft packs we collected from the trash left by visitors, with discarded empty matchbooks stuffed between the clear plastic and paper. We pulled cigarette butts out of the ashtrays of cars in the yard and drew long empty drags off them with the cool detachment we saw the adults use. We drew breasts on our chests with marker. Sometimes we lay down together and imagined we were husband and wife, but we were unclear on what that meant, still more interested in the structural aspect of home than the emotional. When our grandmothers both sent us Barbies, they just got incorporated into our homemaking—we made furniture and little houses for them too, and we dressed and undressed them, and occasionally experimented with them, cutting their hair down to its dotted roots, immersing them in water, and scribbling on them.

We built many playhouses over the years with the piles of scrap wood cluttering the yard from my father's carpentry work and the building of the farm. We used old trunks and nailed boards to trees. We dug holes for toilets, not so different from the old metal kitchen chair with a toilet seat that for years my parents kept in the woods behind the house and moved from place to place—the teeming sea of bugs on the forest floor could dissolve the shit in a day (dung beetles were childhood favorites), unless the dogs or other animals got to it first. And we set up little tables and shelves in makeshift kitchens.

I watched Momma make bread and beans and butter, as a toddler at her leg and then as a young girl who could have joined in. But Momma never had us help in the kitchen, where, after years of modern kitchens, she was learning to cook over wood and with all the parts of the animal. While she hauled water and stood over the wood cookstove, Katy and I went foraging to stock our own kitchens, picking shiny yellow buttercups and goldenrod and Queen Anne's lace for our mud pies and dried yellow dock seeds for our stews. We were practicing the small ceremonies of everyday life. We stirred and baked and organized our supplies just like Momma. In the heavy summer sun, we cracked eggs over metal scrap left in the yard and watched them sizzle.

When Katy and I grew bored with kitchens and home building, we pushed opened a big metal gate and skipped into the field across from the cabin, kneeling at salt blocks to lick along the massive grooves worn smooth by fat cow tongues. As we ran through the short grass and clover, crushing meadow mushrooms and giant puffballs, the air buzzed with the electric sizzle of insects, and a haze of humidity gathered near the forested edges.

We ran on to the small lean-to barn, the pigpen, the pump house, a hickory tree with wood planks nailed up its side for climbing, and, a little farther on through the trees, to the pond.

The pond was fed by a small wet-weather spring that met a low part of the bank from which we collected slippery frog eggs, tadpoles, and watercress. We marveled and grabbed at the hundreds of spring peepers and toadlets scattered along the banks. I climbed the hump of the pond's south bank to chase the minute amphibians down the other side through fitful bits of grass and a brown blanket of soft, leafy humus that led back into the forest's crowded maze of tree trunks.

Daddy tied fishing line and hooks to sticks for us, and we learned to push on the uncooperative earthworms. Or, better yet, we tied on sweet-smelling, fat rubber worms in Day-Glo hues from his tackle box. We never swam in the pond—it was too muddy along the bottom—but we waded in

By the pond, about 1978.

up to our knees, entering at a muddy, cow-dunged opening in the bank surrounded by the swampy mineral smell of pond water and mud.

Katy and I rarely ventured farther than the cutoff to the pond where the woods grew dense and dark, but the road to our cabin continued on, turning into not much more than a gnarled trail. The road narrowed under a thick cover of hardwood and pine trees and flecks of sunlight before opening onto Wolf Pen Ridge and a grand vista of the valley below, icebergs of rock in a clearing that seemed to look out on the whole world. It was down this dim road that Daddy took me for a ride on someone's dirt bike one day. A rattlesnake entered the road like an errant stick in front of us, and Daddy swerved, upsetting the bike. We crashed onto the snake, everyone unhurt as the dazed reptile slithered away. On another afternoon, we rode gleefully down the road on the belly of our dead fawn-colored Jersey cow Daddy was hauling behind the tractor. The cow had died, our hound dog Old Belle had begun to eat it, and Daddy was dragging her body into the woods to rot out of sight. We bounced up and down on the carcass, unimpressed by death or stench, simply relishing a novel ride.

When we returned from our daily amusements, Momma frequently picked chicken shit from between our toes (particularly when we came back from the outhouse where the chickens loved to feed), hosed us down to thwart the army of seed ticks marching quickly up our little legs, or checked in our crevices for bigger ticks. And sometimes she gave us sweet red worm pills too.

This book tells the story of that life, of a family tucked away in a log cabin of white oak on a mountain in Arkansas that gave me the formative years of my life and changed the course of my parents' lives forever, taking them on a journey from privilege to food stamps. It is the story of a home, an American era, strangers in a strange land, class, childhood, and memory. It is both a cautionary tale and an ode to an unconventional and pastoral life.

I was one of countless American children born of the counterculture revolution who spent some period of their youth living an impoverished rural life. Our parents went back to the land—a misnomer in that most weren't going back to anything they once knew, but rather to some archetypal, pre-industrial past. As many as one million Americans went back to the land by the end of the 1970s.[1] Daddy—twenty-eight, quixotic, impulsive, and headstrong—brought us to the Arkansas Ozarks in 1973, in a fever for adventure and rugged land, caught up in the zeitgeist of this back-to-the-land movement.

When you delve into the stories of other back-to-the-landers, it can begin to feel as though we were everywhere, passing each other on the road to rural America with our flea-market farm tools and woodstoves and goats. But I was unaware of that, feeling mostly that we were in our own little world. Although my family was part of this larger movement that now threatens to whittle the experience into cliché, then it was just home. It was on the farm that I learned to walk. To talk. To sing. To run in woods and swim in rivers. To read and to write. To make a home. It was where I lived at an age when my environment was making an almost biological imprint, the sounds and smells and experiences speaking to my very genes.

"What's that tree?" a visitor from Colorado asked a five-year-old me.

"A hickory," I said.

"How do you know that?" Momma asked with surprise.

"The bark," I replied.

It was probably a shagbark hickory, or scaly bark as it was known locally, and Daddy had taught me to recognize the long, gray strips of peeling bark. I couldn't count past ten, but I spent time with him in the woods, and he had clearly given me my taxonomy.

I have no memory of this time with Daddy, out walking or looking for mushrooms, as he has told me we did in the early years. But I do remember going into the woods as a family to fell trees. I was comforted by the familiar but sudden grinding roar of the chain saw.

"Timber!" Daddy would cry as Momma held us close, seconds before I heard the sharp crack and crash of a tree hitting the forest floor. Then the saw's buzz began again, and the air filled with the Daddy smell of cut wood. Perhaps it was then that he pointed to the trees and gave me their names and their telltale features.

The closely packed hardwoods that surrounded us list like a child's chant: red oak, post oak, blackjack oak, sweet gum, black gum, sycamore, ash, maple, sassafras, redbud, black locust, black hickory, white hickory, shagbark hickory.

Vivid images of our Arkansas land run like a half-ruined movie reel pulled out of an old box in my head—many of its parts degraded and moldy from time but others flashing clear: delicate Queen Anne's lace gracing the sides of roads; the Old Man's Beard tree covered in stringy, white pom-pom flowers along the winding dirt road out to our cabin, entrancing me with its name and beckoning us along towards home; and the old for-parts John Deere tractor we played on, its steel bones fading and rusting in the overgrown grass and weeds. In fact, I find I have an almost photographic memory of our land in my head: one distinct elderberry bush grew on the side of the main highway as it approached the tight curve at Devil's Elbow. A purple thistle grew along the fence on the last stretch of road to the cabin and a sumac a few feet away on the north side of the fence. The fruiting body of a shelf fungus anchored itself to a tree where the west path opened to the road. A rosebush heavy with hips was down a bit from the goat pen. A pokeweed grew by the compost pile.

I kept a sticky-backed photo album labeling leaves and other plant specimens I collected. I was paying close attention to the flora and fauna around me. We plucked stunned june bugs off the screen door, and Daddy tied their fragile legs to string and threw them into the air, turning them into tiny kites bobbing above our fingers. We smeared acrid, dusty, glowing firefly bellies onto our shirts. We dug up fat white grubs—the larval stage of june bugs and dung beetles—from their parallel universe beneath us. And we smashed blood-swollen purple dog ticks between rocks like ripe berries. Details as mundane as the empty husk of a molted cicada cling to my memory as emblems of that time, magnified by a child's ability to transform the ordinary into the extraordinary. My world was turning on one leaf, bug, conversation, and toy at a time, like lights coming on at dusk.

One

A MARRIAGE

I have been living in the past for over twenty years [. . .] a number
of pasts, a hodgepodge of pasts, a spider's web of pasts, a jungle
of pasts: my own past; my father's past; my mother's past.
—Joseph Mitchell, "A Place of Pasts"[1]

 I seem to have been born with a predilection for looking back. In the years we spent in the Ozarks, I was lively and intense, orchestrating the playacting of my sisters and me and selfishly absorbed in my inner thoughts but also listening carefully to my parents talk, capturing their stories like fireflies in a jar. I incorporated their childhoods in the Deep South and the West and their coming of age in the sixties into my own mythology. I cut out *New Yorker* cartoons—one of many incongruities lying about our tiny cabin— pasting them onto paper and writing my own captions that told the story of Momma and Daddy's marriage as I understood it—love, wedding, cabin, children. Even then, I was creating this story: making homes, reading of homes, thinking of homes. And the contrast between their tales and belongings and the life they built for us in the woods was like a soundtrack to daily life, playing quietly in the background, creating the strange mix that would make me WASP and counterculture and hillbilly.

When my parents moved us to a small plot of land in Fox, Arkansas, they abandoned their pasts; they left behind predictability and the world of country clubs and bookstores. It would not take long for my family to begin an economic cycle that would keep us for years, and in many ways forever, distant from the upper-middle-class world in which my parents grew up and even the counterculture that took them away from it. My childhood in the forest was cushioned with the remnants of their pasts, with books and paintings, heirloom furniture, silver spoons, and old monogrammed sheets. But we had wood heat and no indoor plumbing for years, and our world was made of miles of woods and dirt roads; old shacks and worn-out vehicles; salvaged and antiquated stoves, refrigerators, and washers; and country music played in overgrown yards. It would take me years to understand that the life that most defined me as once poor was in reality the very thing that most connected me to my upper-class ancestry—the ability to choose to check out.

As time passed, the life my parents created for us in Fox came to represent three things for me: the font of my richest, most poetic memories of childhood; the great mistake my parents made that would forever set us back economically; and the thorn in their marriage. But was this true? If I look through our family archive and my memories and those of my parents, how will the story look as a whole, rather than in the incomplete pieces of my memory alone? What was happening in the adult world on Fox Mountain? What will I uncover that is sometimes lost in the smaller pieces? Who are my parents? I wonder. What influenced them in their pasts? Why did they do the things they did?

Years ago, when Daddy and I still lived near each other in the small town of Point Richmond, California, he stopped by on a Saturday in October. He was walking an albino California king snake on R&R from a wildlife museum. He volunteered there every Saturday and occasionally took a snake home to give it a rest from the pressures of exhibition. My youngest sister, my then boyfriend (now husband), and I walked with him down to the park and all stood in a loose circle for half an hour watching the snake "walk," or rather burrow into the cool, deep grass. It would inch along, before doubling back into the pathways it had just created while flicking its pink tongue. I no longer remember what we talked about, just the white line in the lush, weedless grass and our casual closeness in the moment. Cars drove by, and a few drivers turned to watch our group staring oddly at the grass, the fat white snake out of their line of sight. Dusk and a chill began to settle in, so Daddy dropped the snake back into its bag, and we all parted ways. I watched him walk away with the bag in his left hand, his small frame slightly hunched, his butt saggy in his belted jeans.

Nowhere in this benign, aging image did I see the often abrupt, impatient man of my childhood, but I did see what had always softened

Daddy—his quiet love of nature and his desire to share it with others. I had begun years before this to jot down notes on our Ozark life in journals that never filled up. I wrote short and scattered thoughts on our Ozark public school; the homespun living-room church we attended; the live music at every gathering; the many images of plants and the lay of our land; and the countless names of people who came into our lives then, for however short a time. I sensed that I had to capture it all before it was lost. Not long after we walked the snake, I asked Daddy if we could meet to talk more formally about his life in South Carolina and our time in the woods. He seemed eager to talk about his past and those now idyllic-seeming years and met with me on a couple of weeknights. I turned on a small cassette recorder, and we settled into the couch in my living room.

Daddy was born a first son in a hospital surrounded by the rustle of palmetto fronds on Easter Sunday 1944, in Columbia, South Carolina, into an upper-middle-class, conservative, provincial world, a world that primed him for rebellion.

Daddy was wild and undaunted by his conservative surroundings. His parents tried to tame him. Mammy and Pappy, as we called them, whipped him with switches; washed his mouth out with soap; and, at the table, rapped his knuckles with a sterling knife. Pappy backhanded him, a ringed finger making contact with Daddy's cheek. "Think, think, think!" Pappy chanted as he helped my father with math homework, hammering his bent middle knuckle against the crown of Daddy's head leaving him with a lifelong aversion to math, and his father. Despite (or because of) Pappy's help, Daddy still flunked eleventh grade, a fact that added to his rebellious mystique when I heard him laugh about it when I was a teenager. I first thumbed through one of his high school yearbooks when I was a teen too. I was astounded to see his name printed boldly under the photo of an eager, smooth-faced young man with a flattop, in loafers, heavy black glasses, and a cheerleader's uniform. These bits of his conservative background were more surprising than the roguish stories I had become accustomed to (tying his brother to a tree over a pile of burning leaves, getting a B on a term paper he stole). He had been a cheerleader! But he was more often, he admitted to me recently, skipping class to hunt and fish and "generally not giving a shit." He was skinny and short, but

Daddy cheerleading in high school.
COURTESY OF RICHARD NEIDHARDT.

his personality was large with humor and enthusiasm and mischief—part nature, part compensation for his stature.

As Daddy grew into himself, he soured on Columbia. His college fraternity at the University of South Carolina had a white-Christian clause that got him in trouble on account of his Black and Jewish friends. A ducktailed co-worker at a local barbecue joint turned out to be an aggressive Ku Klux Klan recruiter. Daddy wanted out.

It was also a love of music (first stoked in the pews of his family church) that drew Daddy away, to the guitar and new ideas and the bohemian fringes of Columbia, where he played folk and blues at local cafés and socialized and marched with Black students from the segregated colleges.

My grandparents did not forbid popular music. They were Episcopalians, not Baptists. Like Daddy, Pappy had a beautiful voice and loved to sing; Mammy had been a swing dancer in college in the thirties and was known to love a good time. Daddy and his older sister turned the radio to rock 'n' roll and soul music and soaked it all in. At (segregated) church camp and city park dances, Daddy was one of the few young boys who could dance to hits on the radio. In high school, he discovered bluegrass and folk through the Kingston Trio and other albums played at parties.

I spent hours with friends flipping through albums in record stores at that age, looking for New Wave sounds that voiced my own young angst, lust, and excitement. I entered thrilling foreign worlds through reggae and gangsta rap and punk. I was toying with rebellion too, but for Daddy it meant a real split with the past, his albums like a wardrobe to Narnia.

Just shy of twenty-one, Daddy dropped out of the University of South Carolina, packed what little he owned into boxes, and shipped them to himself at the Port Authority Bus Terminal in New York. With a toothbrush and a clean change of underwear in his guitar case, he hitchhiked to New York and, at least psychologically, never looked back. Following in the path of the Beat generation, Woody Guthrie, and Bob Dylan, he was reinventing himself along with thousands of others from across the country. He walked the streets of New York in suede desert boots; a collared, button-up shirt over his slightly slumped shoulders; a pair of straight-leg, khaki corduroy floods; and an old, olive marine field jacket of his father's. He traded in his black horn-rimmed glasses from high school for a wire-rimmed pair and made a conscious effort to lose his southern accent, only embracing it occasionally to get folk music gigs. He partied at the Factory with his gay roommate, posed nude for an artist, and experimented with drugs for the first time.

His New York debauchery was cut short in 1965 by the Vietnam War draft and a notice from the Selective Service System to report to 39 Whitehall Street—made famous in Arlo Guthrie's draft protest song, "Alice's Restaurant Massacree." That summer in Vietnam, US General Westmoreland had made his infamous request for forty-four battalions to begin the United States' most active years in the war. Daddy attempted to use an injury from a motorcycle accident and tales of rampant drug use as a way out, but it didn't work. So he moved back to South Carolina to prepare for induction. While waiting, he attempted to enlist in the navy and the air force, but they had waiting lists. So he enlisted in the army in the hopes of getting the best deal possible—he had high test scores and was told he could have most any job he wanted. The language school in Monterey, California, required a four-year enlistment, so he chose instead to be a communications center specialist or crypto operator with duty in Europe.

Daddy in Germany during his army years.

He spent the next three years in the army never seeing the front lines of Vietnam. But his mortality made clear under the specter of war, he rushed into a short, doomed marriage to a South Carolina girl during basic training. Isak Dinesen, in her short story "Tempests," wrote about the father of a young girl, a man who married "in haste and with a will, such as he did everything." I can think of no better description of my own father. This marriage was also perhaps the most surprising revelation either of my parents ever made about their pasts. I no longer remember when I first learned of it—I've known as long as I can remember. I have a vague memory of betrayal on first hearing it, as though it had been an affair, but then the woman's name just became another marker in the family stories. But I never stopped feeling a sense of surprise: How could Daddy have been married before Momma?

He and his wife were sent off to Germany where he smoked weed in the cryptographer room on overnight shifts, and his superiors overlooked a pierced ear and just-too-long hair in exchange for his efficiency and warm body.

Long nights of work and Daddy's (by his own admission) insensitive, explosive nature made for a poor marriage. His wife left him for a close friend. And then another drama turned fortune in his favor. After narrowly avoiding a court-martial over a minor hashish scandal, he was instead given a disciplinary transfer to Colorado. No longer would he sit up late into the night watching on a teleprinter the decrypted names of men being called to Vietnam, praying his name wasn't among them.

He was sent through South Carolina on his way to Colorado. After a few days in town enjoying friends, he went home to his parents. He walked up to the large front door ready to push it open without announcing his presence, but it was locked. He knocked, and Pappy pulled the door open to the alarming sight of my father, his neck bare in a Nehru jacket, his hair shaggy around the ears and a rough beard grown in while on leave.

"My Lord," gasped Pappy with contempt, towering above my father at over six feet tall, "you look like hell."

I wish Daddy remembered what he said to his father then, but he doesn't. Perhaps he chuckled nervously and fired off some slangy quip, but more likely he turned red-faced in cartoon rage as I would see him do growing up.

Daddy does remember very clearly what Pappy said next.

"You're not my son," his father declared as he slammed the door shut with one strong arm.

Daddy turned from his childhood home and drove to see his quiet maternal grandmother who took him in. She pulled out old family photos of all his nineteenth-century ancestors with thick beards and long hair to console him. Within a day or two, his mother brokered a cool truce of sorts between father and son, but Daddy knew more than ever that this would never be home again. My birth, four years later, would be the next white flag in their relationship.

Daddy stayed in Colorado Springs when his military service ended, fully immersing himself back into the counterculture. He became an avid mountain climber, opened a craft guild with friends, and continued to play guitar and sing at local bars.

As I went through all the piles of letters Momma had given me—all the years and places jumbled together—I was particularly pleased when I came across a handful of long letters with Daddy's return address, in his neat cursive script. They were letters he had written to my mother over the summer of 1970 while she was in France, and they gave me a rare glimpse of his young self. They describe a very different man from the one who would be standing shorthaired and dirty on the manure-soiled floor of an Arkansas cattle auction in just a few years. To the world outside—or at least to one female customer at the bookstore where he worked who refused to be helped by him one afternoon with "that hair"—he was, in his paraphrasing in one of the letters, an "insidious long-haired, weirdo hippy peace queer."[2] (My mother's grandmother would describe him in a letter the following year: "He has bright little eyes that peek out from masses of hair—How do girls stand those hairy animals?!"[3])

But though Daddy's days were often viewed through a pot-smoke haze, they were more often quiet days of work, music, food, and reading. The letters show a softer, less rebellious side of him. He wrote to Momma that summer about his reading and, with excitement, about singing bass with a chorus at Colorado College for a performance with the dancer Hanya Holm.[4] (He named the Maine coon kitten he brought with us to Arkansas Kitty Hanya. We had her until I was seventeen.)

He wrote to Momma about food too, a lifelong interest. In the last week of June, he wrote that he was planning meals for the summer, and "By the time you return I'll be such a fantastic gourmet cook that you'll never want to leave again." He reveled in his dinners: "a huge sirloin, fresh asparagus, salad and for desert fresh raspberries & sour cream" followed the next night by "filet mignon, corn soufflé and a marvelous salad."[5] The following week, he wrote of an evening of sauna and beer at the Finnish consulate in Denver preceded by a Japanese meal at a friend's family restaurant. He listed each item he had eaten with palpable pleasure, "mushrooms & abalone," "bean sprouts & turnips," "trout and vegetables," etc.[6]

These were the words of a bon vivant, not a mountain man, but he didn't see the two as mutually exclusive. Daddy would soon experience the woods and the people and the odd delicacies of the wild with the same enthusiasm.

When my son started kindergarten six years ago, I suddenly had more time on my hands. Ever curious about family history and ephemera—my childhood had been filled with stories and photos of family, increasing over the years as people died and their belongings were dispersed—I dug through Momma's boxes of old papers and rounded up all the photographs from our cabin years. There were photos I had seen many times, just like the stories my parents told again and again, and there were photos I had never seen. There were also two cassette tapes we had recorded in the woods for Granminnow—as I christened my beloved grandmother

Minnow (from Miriam) when I was two—which Momma got back when Granminnow died. (My Aunt Rhett, my father's sister, sent me two more we had made, found in her father's things when he died.)

What I found most intriguing were several manila envelopes filled with letters my mother had written to her own mother, among other relatives, from Fox and during the years preceding, and the letters from my father when they were dating. I had seen some of the letters before and, even read a few passages, but hadn't had the time to give them more attention. This trove of letters—read for the first time fully and sequentially—drew me into the minutiae of daily life on the land, into the daily struggle of building a home.

Momma's handwriting—a rapid cursive punctuated with dashes—was remarkably similar to my own. Granminnow had saved most of them. Momma saved the rest, surprising to me, since I felt I'd never seen her do anything but divest of possessions during the many moves of my childhood. It's unclear how some of the Fox letters came into my grandmother's possession; I can only guess that other relatives must have seen the value of them even then. They were often my mother's only means of communication, handwritten at a time when we were a mile from the nearest neighbor and had no home phone much less a cell phone or a computer.

In with the tapes and photos and other letters, was also a handful of letters that Momma wrote home to her parents from California as a teenager. She had told me of this summer years before. Driving along winding back roads on the Northern California coast one afternoon, Momma casually mentioned to my now husband and me that she had spent the summer of 1962 in nearby Tiburon and St. Helena caring for the three-year-old daughter of wealthy family friends. She said she spoke French one evening at the dinner table with a Polish count on whom she had a crush. Why, I asked, would a sixteen-year-old girl at an American dinner party speak French with an English-speaking Polish count?

"Oh, well, we were all speaking French," she said plainly.

Her nonchalance was striking. She had slipped back seamlessly into another life, a life in which learning French was expected—a lingua franca among the educated and upper class. Little details of this sort have leaked out since—her childhood neighbors were the sculptor Jacques Lipchitz, whose chauffeur drove her to school sometimes, and the psychologists Kenneth and Mamie Clark, famous for, among other things, expert testimony in *Brown v. Board of Education*; she took a helicopter from Los

Angeles International Airport to Disneyland that same summer. I am regularly struck by how different my own childhood memories are from hers and by how far a life can meander from its source.

Momma—Caroline Wendell McPhee, known as Wendy—was born two years after Daddy, on September 21, in Denver, Colorado, to parents who struggled financially but had all the right connections. The Depression had wiped out their immediate families' wealth but not their social milieu, their Harvard and Yale educations, or their silver spoons.

There are two photographs of Momma that have always particularly captivated me. In both, she is strikingly beautiful. In one, her kinky black hair is brushed straight into an elegant upsweep. Her red lips, frozen by the camera in a toast, match a long red satin dress with spaghetti straps. With a coy look in her kohl-blackened eyes, she holds out to the camera a glass of red wine. Cupped around the bowl of her glass are the hands I know well, because I have them too. In the other photograph, she is Cleopatra in a college play. With nothing but dark shadows framing her figure, she is in movement and midspeech, her hands blurred, and her cheeks hollowed dark to form the word on her lips. Her figure is a slender form dressed in marbled orange fabric, a golden cobra crown encircles her forehead. She *is* Cleopatra, and she is my mother, my mother who by my teenage years was overweight and tired with three kids and a full-time job and never enough money.

Momma's parents were both from Colorado, but she spent her childhood in Hastings-on-Hudson, New York, while her father studied and taught sociology at Columbia. Although she and Daddy were both Episcopalian by tradition, they were from very different worlds. Momma's home was liberal and academic, and discipline was progressive even by the standards of today. (Her mother started a cooperative nursery school that still exists.) Daddy was the descendant of over two hundred years of enslavers; Momma the great-great-great-great niece of the famous abolitionist, Wendell Phillips (hence her middle name).

Momma's family returned to Colorado when she was fifteen, to Colorado Springs and its big sky and mountains. She soon moved in with her maternal grandmother in Denver to attend a private school for girls, where her classmates were from the top echelons of Denver society.

Momma (left) and her brother, Jock (center), in her aunt and uncle's (Chuck and Janey Emery) backyard in Colorado Springs.

She moved back home with her parents (and their unraveling marriage) to attend Colorado College. She majored in history but spent most of her time escaping reality in the theater department where she was often the lead, donning the gowns, heartache, and names of other women: Ninotchka, Estelle, Barbara Allen, Cleopatra, Jennet.

My grandfather (Granpa Will) meanwhile was drinking bottles of whiskey through the night while he wrote his sociology books.[7] I was moved, in a letter I found that Momma wrote to her mother years later, to read how openly and almost warmly she spoke of him in those years, drunk "in his office, you in the kitchen, me in the living room. He passed out and fell against his filing cabinets. I thought for sure he was dead, but he revived in a few minutes and was back at work."[8] She suspected he was a lost cause but couldn't help showing her pride. And she could intellectualize his drinking until it carried no surface emotion for her. I still see her do this in the midst of crisis. She is slow to react and condemn; her emotions don't bubble over till much later, if at all. She learned to accept from a young age that families were imperfect and that men, in particular, could be difficult.

Over the Summer of Love in 1967, the streets of San Francisco buzzed with bacchanalian, psychedelic excitement. Momma was in Colorado

Momma as Cleopatra in 1968,
Colorado College.

Springs mostly oblivious to it but experiencing her own summer of love. I discovered when I was in high school that I was not my mother's firstborn. I found a hospital vital statistics record book from my birth in a file folder of my old drawings and report cards. On it was a handwritten "1" in the box next to prior births. I remember feeling at the time that it was surely a mistake, but when I asked Momma, she told me it wasn't.

Momma was still in college, living in the town where her prominent family had a long history, and no longer dating a man who refused to marry her when confronted with the news (he mailed her ten dollars later). Although she had broken up with him and hadn't loved him, she assumed they would marry once he knew she was pregnant. She was caught in a confusing borderland between pre- and post-sexual revolution and couldn't quite make the journey across.

She met with a doctor who would perform an illegal abortion, but she left his office too frightened to go through with it. Her mother convinced her that another woman would love to have her baby, and to spare her the shame and awkwardness of the situation, my grandparents made plans for her to continue the pregnancy in New York City and give up the baby for adoption. In the last days of December 1967, her father typed a letter to her from his college office on department letterhead, expressing his happiness in her decision:

Dear Wendy:

Contrary to what you must expect, I am delighted with the final outcome.

Your life expectancy is about 80 years, and you'll look back on it as the best thing that ever happened to a 21 year old who was about to be bogged down in diapers before she had even got out of her home town.

At exactly the same age, I was picked up and sent to China with every rational expectation that I would be killed.

Instead I found about 400,000,000 Chinese in similar circumstances, and we had a good time not letting it kill us.

I think you'll find the numbers about the same.

In any event, China was the first and last time I ever got a sentimetal letter from my father, who couldn't spell it either.

William N.[9]

Momma moved into a brownstone in Chelsea with the ex-wife of a business colleague of her father's, into a household in turmoil—the husband had left his wife for a younger woman. In her fifth month of pregnancy, after a sleepless night of pain, Momma woke bleeding. On February 22, 1968, in a delivery room of Beth Israel Hospital, she had a stillborn boy.

Her maternal Uncle Chuck typed out a discreet letter to her the next day that I found slipped in with all the others at her apartment. It was one of the few references to the episode and an insight into the forbearing world in which Momma was steeped, and which gave her strength, or at least the appearance of it, in the woods.

"Needless to say . . . etc.," Uncle Chuck opened the typed letter with, his ellipses carrying the weight of the scandal, "Here I postpone other than the mildest sort of emotional expression on the ground that nothing should appear on paper [. . .] as far as we know, you continue to have pneumonia in New York City."[10]

The night before my grandmother had driven up to the mesa to see Uncle Chuck. She had gotten the call that Momma had lost her baby, and she needed a good cry. They sat in the modern home on built-in, low wooden couches covered in cushions surrounded by paintings and books and Calderesque mobiles, looking out on the sagebrush blanketed in snow and the twinkling lights in the valley below. Granminnow couldn't hold back her tears. But "[Your mother's] good cries are like mountain rainstorms," Uncle Chuck wrote to Momma, "here and gone in about as long as it takes to tell about it. [. . .] In good Puritan fashion, [she] turned them off and drank some scotch."[11]

Despite the Puritan stiff upper lip Momma was born to, the loss of her baby boy, however unplanned and unwanted, was a crushing sorrow. The months that followed were a blur. She stayed in New York until just after Martin Luther King Jr. was assassinated. Within days or weeks, she was back in Colorado Springs and attending Colorado College. And then in the first week of June, Robert Kennedy was also assassinated. She has never spoken to me of this time with much emotion, but all the trauma of the preceding months—shame, isolation, loss—combined with her father's spiraling alcoholism and the violent death of two public figures made for an acutely unsettled time in her life. She would briefly sum up those months in a letter that summer to a cousin (who was herself secretly pregnant and unmarried), Momma's only mention of it in writing:

> At the moment I am totally recovered from my "experience" [. . .] and I am working at the Chinook Bookshop and looking forward very much to returning to college in the fall. "Totally recovered" sounds a little cold—and it reminds me of all the doctors, guidance counsellors, and self-appointed welfare workers who have been hovering around me for so long with their well-meant, but so, so horrible cliches along the lines of "it's all for the best dear". Well, the fact is though when things hurt very much, there is a certain refuge in cliches.[12]

A year later, she was on the move again. It was the summer of the first moon walk, the Manson murders, and Woodstock, and Momma, having graduated from college that January, moved to Boston for three months with a childhood friend from New York to see if a life there could stick. But Colorado and the outdoors were on her mind.

"*Every* day I think of mountains + mountains + mountains," she wrote her mother from Boston in July 1969.[13] She was aching for Colorado and restless again: "I'm still changing plans daily + I may have a new one tomorrow—if I seem unsettled, it is because I definitely am unsettled—I have nothing that I am sure I wish to do—but I am absolutely determined to be somewhere that I wish to be—so I may have to perform several environmental experiments before I'm through."[14] She wrote the next month, "I definitely do not want to artificially create a satisfied life in some corner of the world like Boston."[15]

She returned to Colorado at the end of summer. She began applying to graduate schools and worked for a short time as a substitute teacher in Denver before returning to Colorado Springs to work again at the Chinook Bookshop, alongside Daddy, still just an acquaintance and coworker.

The Chinook was a bookstore owned by friends of my mother's family, where Daddy and my great aunt Janey—wife of Uncle Chuck—worked. Many of the employees were like family to my parents, and we always visited on trips to Colorado Springs. We would walk to the small downtown from my grandmother's house and through the Chinook's huge Mexican wood doors to find walls and tables and imaginative displays of books and a cozy white house for children with painted vines winding up the front and big stuffed gorillas waiting inside. Our world at home in the cabin was so tiny, but here people who seemed important and sophisticated hugged us and admired us and spread pretty books out around us. *Town & Country* magazine called it the best bookstore in America in 1975.[16] The store's brown-wrapped books with gold foil stickers—a cow skull logo on them—were the staples of birthdays and Christmases in the cabin and after. I recently found, stuffed between yellowed pages, an old Chinook bookmark, the bookmark that came in each book we received, until its quote from *These Thousand Hills* by A. B. Guthrie Jr. had taken hold of me:

> The warm wind kept blowing
> . . . like a low chant from the land
> or like the flurry of far wings . . .
> lapping up the snow . . .
> until the whole body of earth
> lay brown and breathing
> except for the topknots of buttes
> and, away and away,
> the high float of mountains . . .
> Chinook . . .
> Promise of Spring.

There were no Chinooks to promise spring in Arkansas, but the ideas and worlds Daddy would find on the store's shelves did offer the promise of a new start on the land. It seems fitting that it was where my parents' life together began.

In June of 1970, almost a year after Momma returned from Boston and began working with Daddy at the bookstore, her aunt and uncle had a big gala for their twenty-fifth wedding anniversary, and my parents both attended. They had become increasingly drawn to each other at work, and that night under a big tent, Momma in a simple flowered sundress, they danced to fifties music, the heady sound of their adolescence. Their short courtship had begun.

In the second week of June—just after this first "date" at my aunt and uncle's party—my mother left the Chinook and Colorado to attend a summer theater program in France. My father sat down to write her a letter the very evening she left:

> Just escaped from a party up at the Manitou house & came down to stay at Kathy's house to read & get some sleep. I'm no longer able to even breathe up there. Tonight was especially bad because there were 25–30 people there—stoned, drunk or merely fucked up—and they were screaming & making things generally unpleasant. Also I was thinking a lot about you having left this morning. I looked at the clock at 9:40, said, "Well, there goes Wendy," and was a bit sad for the rest of the day. Already I miss you.[17]

The letters Momma wrote to Daddy from France are gone, but I have those she wrote her parents. Her letters home were filled with traces of homesickness but mostly wonder at France, the rose and green French countryside bringing the history she had studied alive. Between theater courses, she studied art and rhapsodized over the bread and butter and jam served for breakfast each morning and the beautiful fashions and people: "I don't think hippiedom will ever really catch on in France, because I think most Frenchmen would find it inconceivable to purposefully dress like a bum (it is pretty inconceivable, anyway—when one examines it from this distance)."[18]

I read Momma's letters vigilantly for any clue to her real feelings about Daddy, what was perhaps hidden between the lines. I read into this comment from France a hint of disillusionment with my father and a growing interest in a Frenchman she wrote of named Claude. Momma did not dress as a hippie herself. She had a simple, college-girl look: she wore her curly hair straight and drawn back neatly or in brushed-out, shoulder-length waves, and she dressed in knee-length skirts, turtlenecks, cardigans, and classic button-up shirts with rolled sleeves or in short sheath dresses or in her standard Colorado gear of jeans, hiking boots, and thick wool sweaters. But Daddy's small frame was weighed down under the garb of a hippie—bell-bottoms, rings and bracelets with polished stones and brass, beads dangling from his neck, long hair, full beard, a thick mustache.

Momma could ignore Daddy's hippie dress, though, because it was mostly surface "hippiedom." It was the outdoorsman in him that she was most attracted to, and it's not hard to see why when I look at an old photo of him at the very pinnacle of Mt. Massive in Colorado in 1971, a man appearing to walk on a sea of craggy peaks.

Momma wrote from France that she was working on the play *Électre* by Jean Giraudoux, proud because "the whole class is in French and I really feel I have accomplished something, to *act* well at the same time that I manage to remember and pronounce correctly my French."[19] And, stunningly to me—having never heard this before—she wrote that she had been accepted at the University of California, Berkeley for graduate school. "I am *so* delighted to be going to Berkeley—I can't *believe* it!"[20]

Momma hadn't just let go of a more glamorous life in going to the woods, she had walked away from real opportunity. And she had planned to go: "I have a lot of money to earn between Sept + Jan in order to pay for Berkeley. I really don't want to work at Chinook, because I know I'll be harried and nervous all the time if I work there—but—I thought I might piece together a living from various odd jobs [. . .] I can't bear the thought of returning to a steady 9–5 boredom."[21]

She seemed to have so much ambition and forward momentum, but the allure of love would be greater. Marriage was still the ultimate prize to her

Daddy on Mt. Massive, Colorado ca. 1971.
PHOTO BY JAMES M. BRANTINGHAM.

in 1970. A comment in a postcard to her dad from France also stood out to me: "I always thought being in a new culture would be terrifying—but it's exhilarating—and only makes me hunger for even more exotic parts."[22]

Meanwhile, Daddy's letters continued to arrive. "I know that I've fallen in love with you," he wrote one day, and then in the days that followed:[23]

"I have about 2 weeks' worth of memories to draw strength from until you come home."[24]

"Nothing to look forward to today but loafing—and thinking about you."[25]

And then—as if reading my mind:

"I hope I'm not coming on too strong too soon."[26]

But he couldn't help himself: "I love you and I want you and I'm god-damned glad of it."[27]

Daddy's letters are so remarkably feminine, chatty, expressive—not the father I know now or remember from childhood, who alternates between complete immersion in the book or task at hand, jocularity, and irritability. But that man does creep into the letters. In late June, he wrote of his day at The Craft Guild, the arts-and-crafts shop and studio space he'd opened after leaving the army. He worked there on days off from the

Chinook, barely managing to keep it open, entrusting it to a friend to run most days. Perhaps he had woken up that morning with one of his headaches or spells of vertigo. "I got very up tight at my employees today and did a bit of ranting + raving," he wrote.[28] A week later, he went to see the movie *The Adventurers* and wrote her that it had been "the most absurd, ludicrous, poorly done, disgusting movie I've ever seen. Just amazing how much money can be spent to produce such unmitigated horseshit."[29] Two days later, he lamented, "Today was a singularly miserable day. [. . .] The customers were low grade morons."[30] Daddy is and was an absolute expert at the expletive and the coarse description.

Perhaps some of the openness in these letters was a side of himself he was exposing for my mother's sake—she was a sophisticated local college girl. But Daddy's letters feel completely raw, like a diary, maybe coming at a time in their relationship, and his life, when he could more easily tap into and expose those inner anxieties, thoughts, and kindnesses.

Most poignant are the moments of youthful angst and ennui in his letters, as though they were torn from the pages of one of my own diaries, particularly those when I too was pining over someone:

"I've been generally depressed for a couple of days."[31]

"It seems that when one thing goes wrong everything does. SHIT! I am in a blue funk."[32]

"Miserable rainy weather since yesterday. Nothing to do but sit indoors & mope, too bored even to read."[33]

It stunned me to peek into the workings of his brain, to read sentiments of lethargy and depression I can't imagine emanating from his lips.

His very earnest homemaking also struck a nerve for me as I read on. In mid-June, he wrote, "my little house should be ready for me this weekend. That will give me a lot to do while you're gone, & by the time you return it will be beautifully done and ready for you."[34] The next day, he went shopping during his lunch hour "for pretties" for the new house and wrote, "it's becoming obvious that I'm going to spend a lot of money on toys & goodies. When you get back it should really be beautiful. So beautiful that I hope you'll want to live there."[35]

But while Daddy was pining away for her, my mother had fallen momentarily for France and Claude, and she wrote my father a breakup letter. Claude was with her in the flesh, and, I suspect, Daddy had come on too strong. In a July letter home, she included a postscript to her mother: "Perhaps you should know that I wrote Richard Neidhardt and told him I just couldn't possibly be his true love or whatever as much as I liked him—thought I should tell you to avoid any disastrous faux pas. I can explain why better in person."[36]

Momma returned to Colorado in the fall of 1970, with her mind on Claude and Berkeley. But, not surprisingly, once separated by half a continent and a large sea, she and Claude soon lost interest in each other. The push and pull of my father's exoticism—he was from the South (a foreign country in her mind) and adventurous—now pulled her fully in his direction. She was unimpressed by the culture of drug use and casual sex that surrounded him, but she was attracted to his guitar playing, mountaineering, and what seemed like maturity. Daddy had his own store; he had been in the army; his life was his own. And he had appeared romantic and vulnerable and charming. There was something intrinsic to her personality that propelled her toward someone as different as she could find, the magnetic south to her north pole. On New Year's Eve 1970, she pasted to white paper a cutout of Maurice Prendergast's postimpressionist painting of women outdoors, *Acadia*, with a poem typed out "To Richard" below:

> Whom do you love now, Sweet Richard?
> I threw your love away like paper,
> Want to open it again, unfold
> You in the darkness of your room.
> Ah! Pale suitor, since I left you,
> See my emptiest self reflected in your eyes,
> This sullen heart an only mirror to the past.
> Whom do you love now, Sweet Richard?

By the end of January, things were serious between them. My mother remembers telling him she had dreamt they were married. He asked her again to move in with him, but she told him she couldn't live with someone in the same town as her parents, still caught in that strange cultural lag between freethinking and convention.

"Then one day down by Monument Creek he asked me to marry him," she told me.

On March 20, 1971, in a small adobe chapel at the Fountain Valley School in the foothills of Pikes Peak—where I would marry thirty-five years

Momma and Daddy on their wedding day, 1971.
PHOTO BY JANE ZWINGER.

later—they were married. My mother carried a simple bouquet of stepha-
notis and wore her great-grandmother's 1883 silk dress, and my father
wore white leather pants; a long, dark suede jacket; beads; and a brown,
green, and pink silk scarf.

Ten months later, I was born. Twenty-two months later, Momma and
Daddy were ankle deep in mud and hard work.

Two

REINVENTING THE WHEEL

Today it is not communities or groups who seek to lead the
'good life' but isolated individuals. [. . .] Starting anew, for this
type, means leading a vagrant's life, tackling anything, clinging to
nothing, reducing one's needs and one's desires [. . .] these individuals are not concerned with undermining a vicious system but with
leading their own lives—on the fringe of society. [. . .] For the
man who wants to lead the good life, which is a way of saying *his
own life*, there is always a spot where he can dig in and take root.
—Henry Miller, *Big Sur and the Oranges of Hieronymus Bosch*[1]

When I tell friends stories from the woods, they almost always
respond with the same question: Why? Some, particularly certain white-collar men, are almost hostile in their incredulity. My
mother's aunt Janey once retorted, "Why reinvent the wheel?" I
frequently explain it with a lazy shorthand of "my parents were
hippies." But Daddy was only sort of a hippie, and Momma was not one.
They were politically progressive, even radical, but there was no flower
power sentiment in our household. My sisters and I were not Krishna,
Sunshine, and Rain, we had old family names, biblical names. But as long
as there have been cities, people like my parents have been wanting to
leave them. The agrarian ideal goes back to at least ancient Rome, where
Virgil's old man with a scrappy plot of land in *The Georgics* "fancied himself a king in wealth."[2] Marie Antoinette had the Hameau de la Reine for
her milkmaid fantasies. Thoreau had Walden. Victorian England had a
back-to-the-land movement.[3] Even Louisa May Alcott's father took her
and her family in the 1840s to a vegan farm commune he co-founded
called Fruitlands.

Now in polished urban shops, one can find tools for a new agrarian
movement, expensive hand-forged axes from Sweden, fermentation

crockery, stacks of glossy magazines like *Modern Farmer,* and accessories for backyard chickens. There are blogs and Instagram feeds of earnest young homesteaders making and doing. An article about modern homesteading caught my eye in a *New York Times* article in 2017. A few hyperlinks later, I was scrolling through pictures of a "homestead cabin" on Airbnb. For one hundred dollars a night anyone can rent a 1950s desert cabin with its original green paint, a dirt road, folk music, and an outhouse (and air conditioning and organic fresh-squeezed-juice delivery).

Back-to-the-landers of the 1970s, like their predecessors and perhaps their modern counterparts, "possess[ed] an ingrained sentimentalism in favor of family and spiritual and pastoral values," Jeffrey Jacob notes in his book *New Pioneers,* what he calls "superficially conservative" despite their push against the mainstream.[4] A back-to-the-lander in Eleanor Agnew's book *Back from the Land* said they "yearned for psychic rewards and spiritual wealth, not money, so we planned to generate mere trickles of cash flow from our cottage industries, manual labors, and crops. The payoff was to be freedom."[5]

They wanted freedom from claustrophobic mainstream mores and demands, but there was also a real sense of nagging fear, of needing to find a way to survive a societal collapse. What is known as the Great Inflation occurred between 1965 and 1982. Inflation rose to over 14 percent during the 1970s (it had been a little over 1 percent in the decade before; in late 2020, it was 1.2 percent, and it reached 9.1 percent by the summer of 2022), interest rates went as high as 20 percent, the Arab oil embargo of 1973 led to shortages and skyrocketing energy prices, and unemployment rates were some of the highest in recorded history.[6] And much like Americans now—inundated daily with images in the media of a pandemic, an economy in free fall, climate change, civil discord and a divided populous—in the late 1960s and early '70s, the papers were covered in catastrophe: news of Vietnam, riots and police shootings, economic disaster, political corruption, and widespread pollution. There was a real sense among young people in particular that American capitalism had failed, that the modern world had corrupted humanity and that the way forward was to return to handiwork and self-sufficiency in place of mass production. Meanwhile, songs and literature and the American identity glorified the sanctity of the rural, which had never been more than myth till now for the mostly white, college-educated, urban and suburban youth who took to the hills. They would purify themselves, through fresh air and hard work. Bookstore shelves filled with books for the new movement.

My parents' move began as a literary adventure, with Henry Miller and Walt Whitman and Daddy's childhood reading of *The Swiss Family Robinson* and with books shelved and sold and bought at the Chinook Bookshop, books with titles like *Five Acres and Independence, Stalking the Wild Asparagus, Living the Good Life, The Whole Earth Catalog,* and *A Reverence for Wood.* Daddy was in many ways a boy going to the land, to the movies and stories he'd seen and read as a child. But I imagine there was something desperate in his desire too. Daddy has told me he wanted peace, from a fractured world and from his own recent years of family strife—his overbearing parents, his father's disowning of him, his cheating wife and the rage he felt when he found her with another man, the life-and-death pall that hung over his military service and its conservatism pressing in on him, and the chaos of the drug-fueled partying around him. He would create his very own self-sufficient world. The country could fall apart, but he would have milk and meat and vegetables, a roof over his head, a forest of wood for heat and shelter and adventure, and nothing but his wife and children and stars and animals and woods to answer to.

Although Momma was not so interested in wilderness or farms, she had read *I Married Adventure* by Osa Johnson as a teenager and had thought then that she wanted to be the kind of woman who didn't drag her husband down in his pursuit of adventure. And both of my parents, like many of their generation, traumatized and invigorated by war and social upheaval, were drawn to explore the edges of society and experience something different, to escape the inertia of a bourgeois existence.

A young leatherworker named Larry drove into Colorado Springs in the early summer of 1972, a year after my parents were married, from a seemingly far-off place called Fox, Arkansas. He and Daddy met through mutual friends at a leather shop near the Chinook. Over beer and joints, Larry extolled the glories of the Arkansas Ozarks: the caves, the music, the swimming holes. Daddy had looked at land in southern Colorado—

all he could afford in the state, and the location of the first commune in the US, Drop City, among others—but it was dry and grim. He only knew of Arkansas as hillbilly country, but, according to its license plates at the time, it was the Land of Opportunity and anything but dry. And Larry painted a back-to-the-land utopia with his stories.

A few days later, Larry's car was stolen; in Fox fashion, he had been leaving it unlocked with the keys dangling from the ignition. He now had no way to get back to Arkansas. Seizing the chance to observe Arkansas's bounty for themselves—again, "in haste and with a will, such as he did everything"—Daddy and his climbing friend, Ray Connor,* drove Larry back home in the summer of 1972 with a reticent Momma and six-month-old me in tow.

We spent a night with a folksinger and dulcimer maker, Judy Klemmedson, the first back-to-the-lander to come to Fox, in her old, run-down farmhouse in the woods. She had no electricity, and only candles lit the night. A deafening cacophony of night creatures emerged in the utter blackness and spooked Momma as she lay me on a sleeping bag on a rough wooden floor. I woke in the middle of the night screaming inconsolably. Momma groped for me fearfully in the dark, unable to see even her own hands. She was terrified. She reminds me of this story several times—"I really was frightened. I couldn't even see you, Sarah."

We stayed in a tent for the next few nights, and Momma recoiled at the wet heat (the Ozarks are a humid subtropical climate). Beads of sweat covered my face and neck and chest like blisters, and Momma feared something was wrong. But I was happy, and we sweltered on in the buggy sauna of an Arkansas heat wave while Daddy and Ray looked at land.

A few days into the trip, Momma sat nursing me in our car in front of a real estate agent's office on Main Street in Mountain View, the agent a heavyset local woman in her sixties with a round, high puff of neatly coiffed hair. Daddy walked out of her office, opened the car door, and told Momma he and Ray had decided on a piece of land.

She stuttered that it was a bad idea. She hadn't believed it would really happen and had no interest in living in that remote sweatbox.

"You want me to give up my dream?" Daddy protested, already lost in his plans.

* Pseudonym

Momma fell silent, looking out on the town's sparse collection of stone facades, waves of heat haze blurring the road.[†]

We returned to Colorado the shared owners of twenty thin-soiled acres on a stony Ozark ridge. It cost $2,200, our half paid for with money borrowed from Granminnow. Granminnow had written to her sister the year before about something she may still have been feeling: "At the moment I'm just making sure Richard thinks I'm gods gift to the world + he seems to accept that."[7] She wanted to preserve her closeness with her daughter, who she knew would follow her husband.

The twenty-two months since my parents married had been very hard. After marrying, Momma moved into Daddy's small cottage on a mountainside between the Garden of the Gods and Pikes Peak and set up home. But, once married, my father was not the chatty friend and great romantic he had seemed in his letters. Momma had woken up from their whirlwind romance more alone than ever. Daddy was content with her by his side for life but drawn more to his friends and music and climbing. Momma's plans for UC Berkeley had disappeared, the reasons lost to time, except that she remembers deciding quietly on her own that it was too expensive and that she didn't tell my father.

She felt unhinged by emotion during the first months of the marriage. She was raw from the tensions of the prior years—the loss of her baby, her parents' divorce—and now faced a difficult husband and the hormonal changes of early pregnancy. Granminnow wrote in that same letter to her sister not long after my parents married:

> I can't decide whether to talk with her or keep quiet. [. . .] I regret to say she reminds me so much of myself I want to scream. She's so tired she's lost her sense of humor as well as her perspective—but she never could

---

† In the trailer for the 1975 back-to-the-land movie *The Adventures of the Wilderness Family*, the couple had a different version of this story:
"You really want to stay, don't you?" she says to her husband.
"Only if you do," he replies.
"Well, if this is gonna be our home, we better clean it up," she says.
"We're staying!!" the two young kids scream with glee, and Mom and Dad kiss against the backdrop of a gleaming lake.

break down and tell me anything 'till things hit rock bottom so I'm just sitting here and waiting. I'm sure she's pregnant which would ordinarily be a happy occassion but she works all day at a job that she hates and then has to go home to cook for two men (they took in a boarder so they could continue to pay the rent) [. . .] She did say to me she was surprised Richard was so much like Bill [her father]—lordy—love is blind isn't it? [8]

By the time the land was purchased and that adventure set in motion, Momma was twenty-six years old, in love, had me, and was pregnant with my sister Katy, so she stayed—perhaps she thought a change of scenery would bolster the marriage. Daddy has since admitted to me that he knew Momma was merely resigned to it. "Because I just sort of never bothered to consult her," he told me, with a repentant honesty I found comforting, "Just sort of did it, you know, and said this is what we're going to do."

But how much did Momma actually disapprove of the move? I suspect she felt a frisson of excitement herself. She's always portrayed the woods years as having been against her will, but the letters she had written to her parents while she was in Boston in 1969 had shown me how hard she was looking for a place to settle, "environmental experiments" she had called them. She still remembers having been moved by a book excerpt she read in the *New Yorker* in September of 1970, "The Greening of America" by Charles Reich. Reich wrote of the cultural revolution sweeping America that brought with it young men and women more in touch with their humanity, with society and nature and the land, and to Reich, "who thought the world was irretrievably encased in metal and plastic and sterile stone, it seem[ed] a veritable greening of America." [9]

Momma had also grown up roughing it in the Colorado mountains during summers. As a young woman, she most often daydreamed of an apartment in New York City, but she also knew the taste of trout fresh from a mountain stream dipped in cornmeal and cooked in bacon grease. She's touted the virtues of this trout to me many times over the years, one of those talismanic stories we carry with us.

In her extended family "everyone wanted a cabin in the woods," she told me. Various branches of the family had come West in the late 1800s, looking for land or clean air. Her paternal great-grandfather left his affluent New York life with his brother to start a cattle ranch in Colorado in the 1870s before moving on to build railroads and towns in New Mexico. And by 1974, his grandson, Momma's father, was living in Allenspark,

Colorado, a small village in the high Rockies, in a cabin he had literally built into the rocks of Deer Ridge. He told her when she was growing up that he had fantasized, on returning from the war, about living in the woods rather than being the academic he became, maybe running a small version of a company like Abercrombie & Fitch (in its original incarnation) that supplied outdoorsmen.

I have a photo of Granminnow from the forties, standing on the rocky shore of a river in tall rubber waders and dark lipstick, fly rod in hand, flies in a carrier on her hip. I have digital copies of 16 mm silent movies filmed in 1930 of my gamine young grandmother and her siblings running through mountain fields and evergreens, swimming in lakes, fishing, and cooking tiny fish on sticks over a smoky campfire. The summer beauty of that mountain and their youth is as fresh as if left frozen to thaw out all these years later. The very breeze is visible in the movement of leaves as my grandmother and her siblings are captured setting off with their mother on a mountain path under sunny skies. Granminnow told Momma in my first year that the peace of the woods would be good for me. She must have been thinking of the woods of Momma's and her own childhood summer idylls.

"The rural South is a very different place from the Colorado Rockies," Momma told me when she and I spoke more recently. And subsistence farming is very different from summers in a vacation cabin—bugs, snakes, humidity, raising animals, and gardening were all anathema to my mother.

As soon as we returned to Colorado from Arkansas that summer, Ray and Daddy began to prepare for the move. To save money, my parents and I moved in with Granminnow, then divorced and living alone, into Momma's light blue bedroom with its built-in desk and bookshelf and the mahogany bed and bureau she'd had since she was a girl.

Daddy left the bookstore and got work as a carpenter. The fresh air and physical work was invigorating—it was the best thing next to climbing, and he was creating something. He began salvaging building materials and buying tools and equipment at flea markets and auctions, including an old Centennial woodstove, that he would take to Arkansas. These early finds were a fixture of my childhood: the hand-cranked butter churn, the cone-shaped metal strainer and wood pestle, the wooden farm table (years of crud between the boards), the washboard, and the old electric washtub with rollers attached. Daddy gained general construction knowledge from the carpentry work and read books about log cabin building. While not conscious of an actual movement—something discussed more in retrospect—Daddy was well versed in the popular literature of the time. The subtitle of the first *Foxfire* book, one of many books back-to-the-landers relied on, says much about our life to come: *Hog dressing, log cabin building, mountain crafts and foods, planting by the signs, snake lore, hunting tales, faith healing, moonshining, and other affairs of plain living.*

Daddy loved Walt Whitman too—his books were always on our shelves—with his divine sense of the natural world, his odes to labor. Daddy had written to my mother in 1970, "I think tomorrow I'll go get my book of Whitman short stories out of hock and spend tomorrow evening reading them—if I'm allowed so to do. The prospect of reading some new Whitman is exciting. I've read *Leaves of Grass* so often that it's become totally familiar."[10]

Daddy has been drawn to the wild his whole life. No matter where he's lived, he's never stayed away from the woods or its creatures for long. Even before Arkansas, I knew he had spent much of his time in Colorado climbing red sandstone boulders and 14,000-foot peaks.

"I *always* wanted to live in the woods," Daddy told me recently, as if it were just occurring to him.

His love of nature began in childhood, in the wooded areas near his grandparents' home in suburban Columbia, South Carolina: the Little Woods with deep, dry creek beds; thick vines for swinging; and a cool pond; and another pond deep in the heart of the Big Woods further out. When he was thirteen, his family moved into a long, brick ranch house with a large daylight basement opening onto an expansive backyard. As a child visiting my grandparents, I was in awe of the street lined with broad magnolias and stately homes, the upstairs laundry chute to the basement, and the green sweep of lawn in back that led to a small dock on a man-made pond. By the time I dipped my body into this suburban water hole, it was overrun with algae and only good for frog gigging by night with a flashlight. In Daddy's time it was paradise. The neighborhood was on the outer edge of the city then, and there were miles and miles of woods beyond to play in. He found snakes—eastern hognose, banded water, green, and eastern king—that he kept in his room. He hunted and fished instead of doing schoolwork. He spent a high school summer at a friend's family farm in upstate New York hauling hay, trapping woodchucks, and cleaning out barns. He spent time with an assistant minister from the family's church, an amateur archeologist who took boys out on digs by the Congaree and Broad Rivers in Columbia. And he went to summer camp every year at the church's Camp Gravatt amid cedar bogs and pine woodlands.

Remnants of southern plantation life gave Daddy a taste of the land too. Some of his mother's family still lived in one of the old plantations in Oxford, North Carolina. At big family reunions, his great uncle made Brunswick stew in a giant pot. Daddy picked ears of golden corn to roast in the tobacco barn, where oversize tobacco leaves were cured on wood fires, and he ran around the fields and farm buildings with his cousins. Although a far more casual and genteel introduction to a life on the land than he would later encounter—his great uncles Joe, Reeves, Bilikin, and Archibald were by then doctors and lawyers and other professionals—the family was still growing tobacco and corn as a side income.

I found myself digging though Google for Daddy's ancestors, as though I would find something of Daddy in them. There was a long family history of agriculture, mostly tobacco, back to the 1600s with early Tidewater Virginia planters. Daddy's great-grandfather, "Daddy Tom"—whose plantation he had run around as a child—owned the Oxford Smoking Tobacco Company. The *Oxford Public Ledger* had at least ten mentions of Daddy Tom's famous watermelons between 1894 and 1901, the "prize watermelon raiser in this section."[11]

But theirs was far more than subsistence farming, and enslaved and ex-enslaved people did most of the work. There was no tradition in the family of doing anything more than playing at manual labor, and the farms were tainted with the tears and broken flesh of other humans. Momma wrote to her mother from the cabin in July 1975 that Mammy, Daddy's mother, had visited and told her about the Taylors and her grandparents Daddy Tom and Miss Mill "who had umpteen 'colored' people running in and out to do all the things that us ordinary mortals must do for ourselves."[12] As a child Mammy had known once-enslaved people who still lived on her family's land. I have a very small, turn-of-the-century photograph of one

Daddy with me in Colorado.

woman, Laura, who, old and wrinkled with a slim hand to her chin, is thoughtful looking under a fedora.

But, Momma added in her letter, "The family place burned down recently and the old days are gone."[13] I have always thought Daddy got rid of his southern accent to avoid being seen as a hick—but that never occurred to him, he's since told me. He didn't want to be seen as a racist. Daddy was running from that version of the past as fast as he could.

While Daddy worked and planned and gathered what he needed for Arkansas, we were still living in Granminnow's house. Momma was immersed in her own preparation of sorts. She was no longer working or studying but nursing me and plying me with eggs and applesauce on orders of my doctor (who worried about my tiny frame), grocery shopping, and making meals for everyone.

We flew to South Carolina for Christmas, to show me off to that part of the family. Shortly after our return, in late December 1972 or early January, in a long-forgotten whirlwind of packing and goodbyes, Daddy and Momma and I left Colorado's cold, dry winter bound for Arkansas mud. Daddy drove a moving van towing an International pickup, both vehicles filled with the paraphernalia collected for our new life. Our co-landowner, Ray Connor, followed in a station wagon with his wife,

Susan, and their baby Sunshine.‡ We drove away from 1973 into a fac-simile of the past, leaving behind wars and oil embargoes and pop culture and the nine-to-five life. The United States was in the midst of an energy crisis, and the Colorado college town we lived in was too close to subur-bia, but Arkansas lay in front of us with the rising sun and a promise of country roads and a bountiful farm.

‡ Pseudonyms

Three

TO ARKANSAS

I've met with ups and downs in life,
and better days I've saw;
But I never knew what mis'ry were
Till I came to Arkansas.
—Folk ballad, "The State of Arkansas"

Our caravan travelled down into New Mexico, turning east onto I-40 at Albuquerque, on across Texas and Oklahoma and into Arkansas. After leaving I-40 in Conway and heading north, we entered rougher terrain. As Daddy steered the heavy moving van with the towed pickup down the steepest incline of the trip, he and Momma could see a sprinkling of buildings ahead in Mountain View, sheltered in a valley between the sheer cliffs and rolling hills of the Ozark Mountains. It was three hours north of Little Rock, the county seat of aptly named Stone County, and our new temporary home. My parents no longer remember what they felt in those minutes of arrival. Perhaps they were buoyed by the beauty of the valley and the adventure of their road trip. Daddy most certainly felt anxious to touch spade to dirt on his own land as soon as possible. I was a baby, rooting for breast and comfort and crying for my mother, as yet unaware of my new home.

The Ozarks are the highest region between the Rockies and the Appalachians—a giant uplift of land carved by erosion into deep valleys and bluffs between not-true-mountain plateaus.[1] Geographically, they cover most of northern Arkansas and southern Missouri, a small chunk of northeastern Oklahoma, and a tiny sliver of southeastern Kansas. Arkansas itself lies inside two famous American borders—its northern border is the dividing line between the Confederacy and the Union, its eastern border the Mississippi River, once the line between the

establishment and the mythical Wild West. Arkansans are both western-
ers and southerners at the same time.

When white traders first came to what we now call the Ozarks, there
had been no year-round inhabitants there for hundreds of years, but the
Osage Indians controlled the land as a hunting ground.[2] The French
established a riverside post south of Osage lands in 1686 in southeastern
Arkansas (not part of the Ozarks) and named the local Native Americans,
and the region itself, the Arcansas, taking a native word for "people of
the south wind." The area became known as "aux arcs" (at the land of the
Arkansas) by the French, which British traders later turned into "Ozark,"
a name that slowly spread north and into the interior.[3] Control of the
area turned over frequently in the early days—from Osage to French to
Spanish, back to French—and many groups moved in and out, including
Native Americans slowly being pushed west from their tribal lands by the
relentless push of the Americans. In 1804 the United States took control
under the Louisiana Purchase.[4] They gave a group of Cherokees land in
Northwest Arkansas to free up their native lands for US expansion before
later forcing them to Oklahoma in advance of the Trail of Tears group,
and the Osage continued with little success to use their hunting grounds
into the 1830s, but none of these groups could compete with the flood of
westward-migrating Americans that continued to come.[5]

The Ozarks is the child of Appalachia; the white settlers of the Ozarks
were the "western branch of the upland southern family."[6] They were
from Kentucky, Tennessee, Virginia, and North Carolina: largely Scots-
Irish, English, and Germans—although American by this point, having
mostly shed their earlier ethnic identities—looking for more land and
opportunity, so they too could have a piece of the so-called American
dream.[7] By the end of the nineteenth century, the region was fully settled.
Steamboats and railroads and general stores arrived. Our Stone County
had 2,000 more inhabitants in 1910 than it had in 1970.[8]

It wasn't until the early 1900s that geographers defined the boundaries
of what we know of now as the Ozarks.[9] The Ozarks as a cultural con-
struct rather than merely a geographical region was also born at this time,
primarily through one book, in 1907—Harold Bell Wright's *The Shepherd
of the Hills*, which centered around an outsider come to the Ozarks, a
charming place of strange people and strange customs, of vigilantes and
dolts. The book was a national bestseller, and tourists flowed into this new
"Ozarks." (To this day you can go to The Shepherd of the Hills Outdoor

Drama and the Shepherd's Adventure Park—with the Vigilante Extreme ZipRider—in Branson, Missouri.) Books and films continued throughout the twentieth century to capitalize on this image of utopia and moonshine and hillbillies.[10]

The Ozarks were mythologized as a place where time stood still—just what back-to-the-landers were seeking—even if in reality most of the Ozarks were in tune with modern America. Arkansas has never been seen as the bohemian mecca of Maine or Vermont or Northern California, but the state attracted many back-to-the-landers who were as much a part of the movement as those in these more visible areas. What my parents and others in the 1970s were mostly unaware of, however, was that the road to their vision of the Ozarks had been paved for them long ago, in the early twentieth century. *Shepherd of the Hills* played its part, but Teddy Roosevelt's Country Life movement and the arts-and-crafts movement both exalted the rural and handwrought, and thousands flocked to rural life, including the Ozarks, for "moral rejuvenation." In the first years of the 1900s, educated professionals and artists flowed into the hills of northern Arkansas, hiring local guides to take them to their mountain idylls and even build them one-room cabins.[11] Donald Harington worked these early back-to-the-landers into the story of fictional Stay More in his classic novel *The Architecture of the Arkansas Ozarks*: "During the pastoral age symbolized by our barn, there was an influx of new homesteaders, not farmers but people from the cities [. . .] people suffering from 'city fever' who wanted to get back to the land. [. . .] There appeared on the newsstands of the cities a rash of new magazines [. . .] extolling the healthful benefits of a return to the soil."[12]

When we drove our laden vehicles into town, we were following in the spiritual wagon ruts of this long tradition of American pastoralism in the Ozarks. Stone County, where we landed, was only half a county away from the southern border of the region, but it was the sort of place in which the Ozark stereotype was born. The most prosperous areas of the Arkansas Ozarks—like Fayetteville—are in the Springfield Plain, which is easier to plant and develop and therefore more populated. Our cabin was in the Boston Mountains, one of the most isolated and rugged regions of the Ozarks, a place ill-suited to agriculture and transportation and economic development and most closely resembling the Ozarks of myth.[13]

Mountain View was a small, isolated town twenty miles down the mountain from our land in Fox. (Technically our land was in Mozart, but only Fox had a post office, so the address was Fox, and Fox was all we ever referred to.) In Mountain View our group rented a small white, clapboard house for fifty dollars a month for all six of us, a place to stay while Daddy and Ray built the cabin on the land.[14] Mountain View had enough commerce to keep us in food and simple goods—a hardware store, a Ben Franklin five-and-dime, a grocery store, a bed and breakfast—but it was a sleepy town of small stone buildings, accessible only by a few twisting state roads. There wasn't a single traffic light in the whole county. Daddy and Ray drove over seventy miles to return the moving van.

I celebrated my first birthday there on January 25. The one photograph from that day shows me standing in front of two uneven layers of sheet cake with white frosting smeared crudely across the top. Daddy's romantic ambition—a busy woodworking shop in the woods where he'd craft objects of utility from the hills of timber—was evident in the IOU I received that day in lieu of a gift:

TO SARAH TAYLOR NEIDHARDT ON THE OCCASION OF YOUR
1ST BIRTHDAY.

I.O.U.

one wagon, all wood, 1 father power (or mother), and large enough to haul around a bunch of blocks and other nifties. This wagon must be built by your father as soon as possible after his workshop is operational

Signed and attested to
24 January, 1973 in the town of
Mountain View, Arkansas
Richard F. Neidhardt, Jr.
Father

With my birthday celebrated, the moving truck returned, and our living quarters arranged—our life in Arkansas began in earnest. Our rental house quickly became a health hazard; the plumbing backed up, and the bathroom sink and tub were unusable.[15] Momma—four months pregnant—was at least happy to have Susan's company, even if she sometimes seemed too young and high-strung and flaky, the archetypal dope-smoking hippie in flowing dresses. Momma was pragmatic and unfussy and dressed for the woods in jeans and boots, but she needed Susan. "I'm lonely," she wrote Granminnow, "Richard must spend several days to a week up on the land with [Ray] in order to get all the work done (they are twenty miles away) so we 'homestead widows' are home with the kids."[16] She and Susan both had babies roughly the same age and could share the daily joy and stress of motherhood (and bad plumbing). When we babies were healthy and the weather cooperated, they could make the winding drive together up the mountain to see the men.

Daddy and Ray put up tents on the land, twenty rugged, rocky, heavily wooded acres—"up Fox Mountain" in the local parlance—1,400 feet above the sea on the northeastern edge of the Boston Mountain plateau. Branching off the state highway—just before it hit the edge of the ridge to descend the mountain along Devil's Elbow, a treacherous hairpin curve down to the Great Timbo Valley and Mountain View—were three miles of unpaved road that led to our plot of trees and meadow.

Daddy and Ray camped on the land most of that winter and spring, clearing brush and trees and trying to improve the old logging road enough that we could use it; it was only passable in dry weather. Their time was swallowed up in breaking down large rocks in the road and hauling the rock and dumping it into mudholes. The older locals called our land Tucker Field and had no memory of anyone ever living on it—people had farmed and logged it but never lived there—so the road was not meant for year-round access.

"This is the worst winter here since 1917, which means chiefly that it rains one hell of a lot and there is mud everywhere—worst of all too much mud on the road up to our property," Momma wrote.[17]

Progress on the land was slow without a good road. It would be another year and three months before we lived there full time. Daddy built a toolshed out of hickory poles and salvaged sheet metal siding, but he and Ray had barely started the cabin.

This put Daddy "in a fit," Momma continued in her letter, "for as you know when he decides to do something . . . it must be done A, B, C and absolutely no waiting. So [his] patience has been tenuous especially with two crying babies around and too many people and cats—But he is definitely doing well under the circumstances, as are we all."[18]

Momma's relatively mild complaint probably alluded to nights and mornings filled with shouting and cursing and sharp criticism.

"God damn piece of shit!" Daddy often barked at an errant tool or chair or piece of news, "son of a fucking bitch!" But his anger usually dissolved quickly into laughter or singing or talk of the day, and Momma could ignore her singed nerves for the moment. I sat nearby registering this discordance, harsh and jarring, an unsettling rhythm that would become familiar over the years.

The endless rain and mud and what Momma called "cold, cold, cold," was interspersed with seventy-degree weather and blue-sky sunshine, a mercurial climate to match Daddy's temper.[19] The countryside was painted with early blooms, daffodils, forsythia, azaleas, peach, plum, redbud, and flowering crab, a welcome relief to the relentless brown of winter.

"[Sarah is] having a wonderful time playing on *her* land," Momma wrote to her great aunt Ruth, a retired child psychologist.[20] I was toddling over dirt clods and clutching at the grasses, weeds, and insects on sunny-day visits up the mountain from town. The first logs were finally up for the cabin, and the garden land was turned and cleared.

"How proud we feel of our small accomplishments!" Momma continued in her letter, "How I do admire the pioneers—and yet nothing has ever been more fun to me or rewarding than the work of building my own house and helping to plant our own garden—And the peace and quiet of Fox Mountain is so far removed from so many horrible things in modern life—How I hope our children + ourselves will prosper there."[21]

What does it mean to prosper? To succeed, to be fortunate or prosperous, to thrive, to make gain? For a certain twentysomething in the 1970s like my parents, it was reasonable to think it could be found in the land, with your own sweat and suffering, if the payoff was peace and quiet and clean living. I was raised in that world; it's in my blood to have at least some reverence for these ideals. But if I scratch a bit below the reverence and my own mythical longing for this original home, I find I struggle to understand why my mother did this at all.

Two years before we went to Arkansas—a year before it was even a concrete idea—she had planned to go to UC Berkeley for grad school. What if she had just told Daddy of her Berkeley plans? Just let those simple words out. She never said a single word to him about it—even, I've discovered, gave him what she'd saved for grad school to pay off some of his debts. She never looked into financial aid, she never asked her mother or her professor father or her like-parents aunt and uncle for advice or help. After months of work on the application, she just gave up and turned to the security of marriage instead, and then, she tells me now, stewed over it off and on for the rest of her life. What if Daddy had liked the idea of Berkeley and California, especially then before the seed of Arkansas was ever planted? Of course, I might never have been born. But what if I had, and Daddy and I had followed Momma instead of the other way around?

I might have been turning one in a little rented bungalow in Berkeley, sun streaming through the windows, while Momma worked on a paper and Daddy played the guitar. There would be chickens and vegetables in the backyard, perhaps we'd walk to the local co-op for cake-making supplies and stop to chat with neighbors along the way. There would be students to come in and watch me while my parents worked, or they'd take turns during the day. There would be mild weather, the beauty of the local hills and sea, good schools and doctors nearby.

I was a nervous wreck the first year of my own son's cosseted life, worrying over his sleep positions, his breathing, the quality of our indoor air, whether he was warm enough or cool enough at night. I was overwhelmed by his care, even with running water at every tap, central heating, and a diaper service that whisked away the soiled diapers at the door. Then later when the exasperating world of close-pressed neighbors and video games and playdates came, my thoughts often went rushing back to these days in the woods. What if we could just be free to pick blackberries and feed goats and walk under the trees, to work with our hands and forget all this technology and complexity?

After school one afternoon near the end of my son's first-grade year, I cleaned out his blue take-home folder. There was, among the many uninspiring worksheets he'd completed that week with a fraction of the effort he gave to Lego creations, one from his class farm segment. He had written one line to sum up the experience: "I wood not like to be a farmer because I lik the city. I wood not like to be a farmer because it is a lot of work and it is very tiring."

The road to the cabin continued to be a serious setback to the adults' plans, and Daddy and Ray soon gave up on the idea of building it themselves.

"We have realized that quaint country roads are fine for weekends in the country," Momma wrote in May, "but excellent roads are essential for living in the country."[22]

Ray sold some stocks (a not uncommon back-to-the-lander irony), and he and Daddy hired a local man to build us a mile of road with a bulldozer across our neighbor Dalton Moody's land. It was the shortest route, and Moody suggested it. He was a stocky, balding man with a warm, open nature, and he became a mentor to Daddy. Moody was from the area but had worked out west for years as a sawmiller before returning to Arkansas to retire on his small farm. He accepted our family from the first day, and taught Daddy at least as much as his back-to-the-land books.

The road they built was a narrow dirt ribbon through the woods. It wound gently uphill as you approached the land, up Rattlesnake Hill, curving sharply to the right and up again over rocky ruts past a vast patch of blackberries, before bisecting a narrow meadow. The right side of the road would be fenced and become pasture. On the left, an old John Deere would eventually sit buried in the grass, then a little farther on the toolshed, then a small chicken house. The woods on the left opened a bit after that into a patch of dirt and grass backing into the trees where the small cabin would be built facing the pasture.

These early months of labor were stressful for Daddy, but fun and exhilarating, a life's work. He recognizes now that it couldn't have been as fun for Momma and Susan mostly housebound in Mountain View with us babies. Susan was particularly nervous and tense, worrying about her daughter's stomachaches and sniffles, but there was nothing to do but wait and care for the children, to sleep, cook, wash, feed, and nurse.[23]

All that spring, I was sneezing too, and coughing, with enlarged glands behind my ears, a coated tongue, and heavy congestion leading to eye and ear infections.

"Sarah on the other hand is part disaster area and part joy to behold," Momma wrote.[24] When my head finally cleared, I woke with a rash, which Momma was convinced was German measles—a grave danger to her unborn baby—although she would never know. She wrote, "Last Friday we drove the sixty or so miles to see the doctor, and he was so busy (not his fault, but damn it, what a pain) that we waited six hours and never saw him."[25]

Momma was also trying to put together the things she'd need for a newborn. She asked her mother to find old discarded cloth diapers from the Colorado Springs' diaper service. "No matter how ragged, they would

*The cabin building begins; Daddy in background
with Kevin Klemmedson.*

be worth it to me when the new baby comes," she told her in a February letter.[26] She also asked for clothes hangers, castile soap, books for me, diaper pails for soaking, and, strangely, "extra large opaque panty hose." She even hoped a sandbox or wading pool could be sent "so that things won't be too hard."[27]

Meanwhile, my nineteen-year-old aunt, Sarah, wrote from Paris. Her airmail letter found us somehow, the envelope's classic red, white, and blue onionskin addressed to "Mme Richard Neidhardt," in "Fox, Arkansas, Etats-Unis."

"Oh, how I find the name of your home romantic," Aunt Sarah wrote, "I am so jealous of you even tho mother says you're poor and it's raining and the babies are sick. Your lives could be so exciting and so clean and pure and Sarah might just grow up without too many hang-ups and you'll all be so healthy and tired at night, always able to sleep."[28]

My parents' move can now seem too precipitous, haphazard, even irresponsible, but my aunt's letter highlights the tide of thinking they came in on, the feelings that made it all at least fathomable. Throughout our years on the land, a trickle of visitors who were mere acquaintances or friends of friends would come just to admire our chunk of earth and see the dream. Momma had less romantic concerns.

"We are using up our money quickly," she wrote that March, and then again later in the spring, "We have never had to worry about starving, although I've had some worrisome moments."[29]

Momma's letters regularly refer to small infusions of money from her family and at times Daddy's parents, a scaffolding of family help by which they must have been at least subconsciously emboldened. A generous donation of $400 from Aunt Ruth in April helped us pay for "hog wire, chicken wire, barbed wire, tin, and enumerable building materials." "Thanks to you the cabin building can continue," Momma wrote, "and equally important we can now afford a chicken coop for all the chickens we have been given."[30]

Nana, my mother's maternal grandmother, sent twenty-five dollars.[31] My parents bought a used sixty-dollar truck. On credit. They put twenty-five dollars down and financed the rest.[32] Ray used more of his money to buy a mule for log hauling and garden plowing. (Daddy had been cutting logs and dragging them out of the woods on his shoulders.) And my parents also anticipated a small income tax refund and had their hopes on agriculture classes down the mountain at the Timbo School, where Daddy, for a few nights a week of total boredom, could earn $200 a month through the GI bill.[33]

Every dollar was being squeezed from somewhere, often for our most basic necessities. We could not truly live off the land, at least not on a true farm, until the animals and people had food, fences, and shelter, and all of this cost money. My parents were extremely naïve and young, and neither were economic planners. They went to the woods with presumably a small bit of money saved while living with Granminnow (no one remembers) and the assumption that there would always be work—Daddy was ablebodied and willing—and that since everything was relatively cheap in that life, there would be enough money. Daddy was excited, and Momma was resigned, and they had no rules about how they would do it, but a sense of doing it on their own. They would have a simple but comfortable home and a thriving farm, built with their own hands.

But random checks in the mail and other small cash sources were never enough. Daddy had to find jobs to support us while he worked our land

Progress continues on the cabin.

on the side, a factor he and Ray in their youthful hubris had never considered in all their planning back in Colorado. Momma wrote Granminnow that Daddy had a few hopes for some piece work in carpentry that would help.[34] And we would soon leave Mountain View and find a free place to live while the cabin and the farm were being built. But, as they say, you get what you pay for.

Four

THE KEY PLACE

I have no money, no resources, no hopes.
I am the happiest man alive.
—Henry Miller, *Tropic of Cancer*[1]

 My first memory in life is of a heap of trash. Just a pile in a small room, barely visible in my memory, an inconsequential image. Momma told me recently that when I was very young, there was in fact a mound of dirty cloth diapers and trash in a small room off our kitchen. I was more excited that the memory could actually be real than I was dismayed to have had such a foreboding first window on life. The kitchen was in a dilapidated farmhouse we lived in for free before the cabin. We had no garbage collection and no washing machine, and diapers piled up too fast to keep up with washing them in a tub of boiling water. Momma shook off what she could and threw them in the closet.

Three months after moving to Arkansas, my parents loaded all their belongings back into cars and trucks and moved us up the mountain closer to the land. We moved into this farmhouse of my earliest memory on a cattle ranch outside Fox that the owners called the Key Place; we've never referred to it as anything else. Ray and Susan were to move in with us, but there was a last-minute, diplomatic change of plans, and they found their own house even closer to the land.[2]

"Everyone was just on the verge of losing their tempers from living at such close quarters," Momma wrote her mother, "[Susan] is a bit of a bitch, so we are glad not to have to aggravate anyone, since we must all share somewhat and [Ray] is a great guy, so we wouldn't want to hurt his feelings—sigh!"[3]

The Key Place.

The owners of the Key Place, Earl and Bobbie Morris,* let us live there for free in exchange for my parents fixing it up and keeping an eye on some Brahman bulls ("Brimmers" in local lingo).[4] "It will take a bit of cleaning up to be livable," Momma wrote but it "[has] 3 enormous rooms, with back porch, attic + basement and a beautiful view of the mountains."[5]

It is hard to separate Momma's true excitement from a tendency to stifle feelings and facts that might worry or agitate others—or her—and from a dogged determination to prove she could handle matters on her own. I've always admired this quality, ashamed by my own opposite inability to see the rosy side of shit, but her eternal optimism bordered on mania, or, in some passages I suspect, propaganda. She had to convince her family back home that she hadn't lost her mind.

The Key Place was not much more than a leaky shack built in the 1930s, surrounded by bulls, with no bathroom, no hot water, missing

* Pseudonyms

windows—the heaviest rain in years fell that spring—and only wood-stoves for heat and cooking. But Momma wrote with her suspect optimism that "having plenty of water + refrigeration makes old timey living a real pleasure."[6]

In its halcyon days, it must have been some farm wife's dream home, a huge wood cookstove in the kitchen, a potbellied heat stove in the living room, and each room's walls papered long ago in a print of beige squares. In photographs, there are two large oaks in the front yard, a stray white car door leaning against one. Across the worn grass and dirt road and another stretch of grass is a billowing expanse of bushes and small trees, like a storm cloud of vegetation.

Momma did her best to put lipstick on the pig. She put out an orange Moroccan pouf, threw an Indian paisley bedspread over the secondhand couch, and hung goldenrod sheets on windows that did, in fact, look out on a lovely wide pasture abutting dark green woods and blue hills in the distance.

Perhaps the hardest aspect of the house was the lack of bathroom facilities, of any kind. The outhouse had long ago fallen down, and, because the land was cleared for pasture, there were no close-by woods to offer privacy. We had to find a place to relieve ourselves in sight of the dirt road and near the potentially dangerous bulls. "So sometimes we have to stay in the house for safety's sake in spite of the call of nature," she wrote Granminnow after we moved in, never bemoaning the complication of being pregnant too. They made partial do with an old-fashioned "adult potty chair."[7]

The new landlords and neighbors, the Morrises, were originally from New Mexico. They were "about as leathery and weather beaten as anything I've ever seen in Colorado," Momma described in a letter, "and they are wonderful people with lots of knowledge about country living."[8]

Of course, along with their sun-worn faces and ranch know-how came a country attitude that was utterly foreign to Momma in particular. She didn't always know what to say or how to act in this strange new world. The role of women on the ranch confused her. Bobbie Morris did all the cooking and cleaning *and* worked out on the ranch with the men.

On a visit to the Morrises' one day, only Earl was home. He stood in the yard in jeans and a button-up, collared shirt and cowboy hat. He asked my parents if they wanted coffee.

"Sure," they both said.

"Wendy," he responded, "coffeepot's in the kitchen."

She stood there in embarrassed silence and let the moment pass. She couldn't bring herself to walk in that house and make them all coffee.

Another day, Earl got to talking about how women in cities were lazy and made their money on their backs. Momma again stayed wide-eyed and quiet with a wan smile.

Earl added new words to my parents' lexicon too. His oft-discussed heroes were the great "Abagonians of Australia," and he frequently mentioned a variety of things in the world or on the ranch that had "run ramparant."

"Boy, it come a real harpoon last night!" he declared when a summer storm ripped through the hills.

But Earl and Bobbie were kind and protective of our family. In a series of old photos, Earl rides horseback with a cloth-diapered me in front of him on the saddle, my tiny hand resting with his on the reins. And there were words of wisdom to calm a frazzled ex-urban mother. I pulled away from Momma's side one afternoon and stepped boldly into the tall grass by the Morrises' house. Momma ignored me, absorbed in her conversation with Earl. Once in the soft grass, I was unburdened and ran tottering till my small body was obscured by the waving green sea. Momma gasped when she realized I'd disappeared from sight, picturing rattlesnakes and copperheads weaving through the same verdant shoots.

"Don't worry, she'll come back," Earl chuckled.

In June of 1973, the heavy rains of spring had moved on, but the heat was now too great for long days of work. Heat and disabled trucks and rain continually hindered progress on the land. "Richard absolutely has to build houses and a barn before winter," Momma wrote, frustrated by the Sisyphean task ahead of them.[9] (They planned to build a cabin for each family.) But Daddy had to spend the productive part of the day earning a living. He got a building job and woke in the cool, fading black before dawn and worked until 2:30 p.m. each day to avoid the late afternoon swelter.[10]

The Arkansas heat was often unbearable for my parents, so they were both surprised later when a co-worker of Daddy's donned long underwear as soon as the temperature dropped into the sixties, right when my parents were finally comfortable. When winter came, locals kept their houses blazing hot with the free wood fuel all around them. They had grown accustomed to the heat. Daddy had been raised in the heat of Columbia— "built over hell" as his mother always said—but he hadn't been earning a living doing hard labor there.

"It makes me breathless to think of working outside in this sweatbox weather. On the other hand, I have a hard time keeping my temper *cool* with Sarah when the [wood] stove starts heating up," Momma would write to her great aunt Ruth that summer.[11]

Despite whining and mucous and a seeming chronic, low-grade cold and crying for a bottle at midnight, I was thriving. I was seventeen months old and could say "do-do" when there was something in my pants and "empty." "She understands when things are empty which seems astounding to me," Momma wrote.[12]

In mid-June, Momma and I moved back to Mountain View to wait out the last weeks of her pregnancy in the home of a local woman, Ray Aberli. This put Momma forty paved miles rather than seventy partially unpaved away from the hospital in Batesville, and Ray could watch me while Momma was away. (Momma never considered finding a midwife or having a home birth.) Ray was a local thirty-five-year-old mother of five who lived across from the Mountain View rental we'd lived in. "And a mother and a friend to all who cross her path. One of the many friendly Arkansas people who have saved our skins," Momma wrote Granminnow.[13] Momma and I stayed in a spacious extra bedroom in the Aberli house trying to cope with the oppressive heat. We slept together on top of the sheets, and I woke regularly in the night and clung to Momma throughout the day. Momma and I had never been separated, but I would stay with Mrs. Aberli and her house full of kids for a day or two while Momma gave birth to Katy.

Daddy was too busy with work and the land to care for me, but someone got a message to him when Momma went into labor, and he made it to the hospital for Katy's birth on June 23. The nurses wouldn't let him in the delivery room, but from the hallway outside he could hear Momma "hollering like she was being killed." She was struggling on a steeply angled table in the delivery room with a doctor who said he knew all about natural childbirth but knew nothing. No drugs, and a nurse's arm to hold while she screamed and pushed, was the best they could do.

Momma and Katy remained in the hospital for a day or two. Daddy had been busy building a 10,000-square-foot chicken house for Johnny Whitcomb[†]—a tall, blond, extraordinarily handsome man as Momma remembers, part of a large local family. While Katy and Momma enjoyed a few days of rest in the hospital, Daddy and I stayed with the Whitcombs, and Johnny's pretty, young Pentecostal wife watched over me while the men worked.[14]

As a nurse wheeled Momma out of the delivery room to a waiting Daddy, the nurse's young daughter—inexplicably hanging around the hospital hallways while her mother worked and, perhaps, noticing Daddy's full beard and mustache or the cut of Momma's hair—leaned into her ample mother and proclaimed loudly, "They're so hippified!"

My parents took Katy home to the Key Place. Fleas jumped from cat and dogs to floor to couch to nursing baby. Momma lay Katy to nap in the kitchen near her but the wood cookstove created pockets of blistering heat in the summer air, and Katy broke out in a heat rash. Momma moved the crib to the bedroom under a mobile of bright paper butterflies someone had sent.

Daddy took over waking with me in the night, and the upset of childbirth and a new member of the family soon settled back into routine. Nana reached Daddy by phone at a neighbor's house where he was working a week after Katy's birth. She wrote her other daughter, Cooie, of her exasperation with our situation. "Richard said everything is fine which it always is when he is doing as he D[amn] pleases," she lamented, "So—I will now assume that 'Everything is Fine' + just send a check in a week or two. We are supposed to admire this back to nature way of treating new mothers. If you go through old graveyards you will see that one man usually wore out two or three women!"[15]

Aunt Ruth, the child psychologist, ignored our substandard housing and wrote only with advice about me:

† Pseudonym

I hope in your busy and so *hot* life you can still find time for my first law of child care! That is, and especially when a child has a problem with which to cope, that time can still be found for Sara to be alone with you or Richard—competitor out of sight and you are not busy with household tasks. You don't need to *do* anything with her—just relaxed and receptive, perhaps in a chair, perhaps just watching her play but responsive *only* to her. Fifteen minutes of such "whole time" three or four times a day, should get it over to her that she still counts. Maybe! Of course![16]

Alone time with me was a tall order, but Momma now had two children to help keep her company in that "lonely old place" by the dirt road and the bulls.

Five

VISITORS, MOONSHINE, AND HARD WORK

The carpenter singing his as he measures his plank or beam [. . .]
The delicious singing of the mother, or of the young wife at work [. . .]
—Walt Whitman, "I Hear America Singing"

"Now I can't wait to have visitors, since we really have a comfortable place for them to stay," Momma wrote that spring, pleading with Granminnow to come help with my new baby sister before or after my grandmother's planned trip to Europe.[1]

Granminnow arrived in July. Two photos of her from that trip survive—small squares bordered in white taken with our Polaroid Square Shooter like so many of the others—one in which she's holding me and one holding Katy. She is standing on the side of the Key Place, its windows crudely covered in sheets of plastic, in a grassy field with a haze of distant trees and blue hills behind her. If not for her outfit and the color film, it could be some old dustbowl photo—with the shack, the expression. She stares sternly into the camera with nothing but the slightest flat hint of a smile on her face, wearing a beautiful orange dress à la Chanel with pockets and brass buttons, a choker of pearls, her neatly combed grey hair swept back in a black ribbon. It was presumably her traveling outfit, and she had come straight from her trip to Europe by way of her sister's apartment on Fifth Avenue.

Granminnow wrote home to her own mother, Nana, during the visit:

Dearest Mother,

I'm certain you're wondering if I'm dead or alive and unfortunately I'm alive. As Wendy said, "You've come at the best time for us, but the worst time for you." I suspect things are like this a good part of the time,

Granminnow and me outside the Key Place.

but certainly I got here just before Wendy collapsed. For the first time since I arrived both the children are asleep and it's a blissful moment indeed. Neither of us dare speak for fear of breaking the spell.

Well, to go backwards a bit—Cooie + Paul departed for a business weekend at Fischer Island on Friday—Lou [. . .] had come up from Baltimore to see me—Cooie made us a delicious lunch + then we took off to get my penicillin shot and then to do whatever seemed fun. We found a good movie "The Heirling" and then went back to the apartment. Charlie was about to entertain three girls for dinner so Lou + I went on to a restaurant Cooie had suggested—then back to the apartment to watch Watergate and pack.

My trip here went very smoothly—that is for once all planes went on time and there was no need to dash from one place to another. Richard + a friend met me in an old car and off we went—the car had to stop every half hour or so for water but otherwise everything went smoothly until we were stopped by a State Patrol. Since liquor is illegal in this county Richard had stocked up on beer and I had gotten my evening

Bourbon (actually I didn't know it was illegal but I knew they were out).
One head light on the car was broken + the state trooper proceeded to
check the rest of the car—he not only fined Richard $60 but took all the
liquor.

When we got here the heat was overpowering and (it was a three hour
drive from the airport) I admit it was a shock to find the state they're
living in. I guess everything is relative—apparently no one lives in a
much better fashion here so they're not only content but continue to be
full of enthusiasm. Why—I can't imagine?! Arkansas is not unlike New
England—hot—sticky—and if you live in a "Grapes of Wrath" house the
flies, mosquitoes, snakes, mice—oh—Lord knows what all—overpower
you—or at least me. I do seem to be getting used to it myself. I do not
like going to the bathroom with the cows, but there seems to be no other
choice.

Wendy has done a magnificent job of making everything look as nice
as possible but there's just so much you can do when the ceiling is falling
down and rain spits all over ancient wallpaper—in fact, she obviously
doesn't see the dirt—I remember well how one can blot it out—she's
hung pictures attractively over holes in the wall, etc. but when there are
a hundred flies hanging over the dinner table it's hard to enjoy much of
anything. I decided if the children could live through it I could. They're
both adorable and well in spite of all the bugs. Kate really looks all
Emery—sometimes she looks so much like Jake it's comical—maybe
she looks like my baby pictures—in any case, she's chubby—placid—
smiling already—rolled over yesterday and is learning quickly she needs
to speak up if she's going to be noticed. Sarah is an absolute pistol—cute
as can be—a great comic—we've had fun walks down the road while she
points out "cow"—"pretty flower"—"doodie" (cow pies—there are at least
a million of them)—in any case, she's quite willing to leave Wendy so
we now spend the morning in the front yard together. Yesterday, I did
36 diapers—today I'm trying to work through twice as much—Wendy is
two weeks behind on laundry + both trucks have broken down—we're
also very low on food but Wendy is a master at putting things together.
Richard did manage to bring home a few goodies yesterday but he had
to walk twelve miles in the rain for it. Susan and Ray have decided to
leave + Richard is now trying to arrange a loan so that he can have all
the property for himself (I still haven't seen the land since the trucks
are broken down)—I will say Richard does seem to be holding down

two jobs but obviously the demand will always be bigger than the supply. I do think Wendy will be better off when she can move up to the
land because at least Richard will be there off and on—now she's totally
alone—what she would do if anything went wrong I have no idea—and I
must say I prefer not to think about it. In spite of all she's happy—has a
good + happy pioneer spirit, and is full of enthusiasm. Not I! I just hope
to live through it all + at least get her off the ground on laundry—well—
Sarah is eager to go out and I must get on with the laundry—it takes
hours since not only does it have to be scrubbed by hand but boiled on
the wood stove (not to mention all water has to be heated on the stove)—

I'm going to try to get a ride to Little Rock on the 7th and spend one
night in the Holiday Inn—for a bath if nothing else—and then will fly
into Denver on the 8th! Have a basket ready for me!

Do pass all this news on to Cooie + Aunt Ruth. There's little time for
writing letters + heaven knows if they'll ever get mailed—

Much love,
Minnow[2]

As Granminnow wrote in her letter—perhaps written while sipping stove-
top whiskey Daddy had procured from the local "shiner" Os Compton—
Ray and Susan had decided to leave in July. With the mid-summer air
engulfing them in swampy heat, Daddy and Ray began to realize they
had opposing philosophies. Their plan on the land was to divide respon-
sibilities—initially at least, Ray would be the gardener and Daddy the
builder. The first cabin would be for Ray and Susan so that Ray could
get a garden going to feed everyone. But Ray's ability to garden was hindered by an inability to cut down a tree. He preferred to plant in dispersed
natural clearings, which Daddy felt was too inefficient for a sustainable
food supply, particularly on land constantly plagued by the reclamation
efforts of pine and sumac. Ray agonized over every tree and bush Daddy
cut down. He was gentle and passive, a college graduate who painted
phantasmagorical images signed Leprechaun. Daddy was a pragmatist
and quick to temper.

But the partnership stayed friendly enough, and Ray's garden efforts weren't a complete failure. They did finally plow a garden plot in the field south of the house, and Momma had written in early May:

> [Ray] has managed to do an excellent job and so far very little has been ruined in the garden (most people don't even have their gardens planted, so we are very proud of him). But poor fellow, every day he carries 2 buckets of chicken litter a ½ mile into the land to get enough manure for his garden—since no truck can get up there with a load.[3]

Even as Ray carried those heavy buckets and worked harder than ever, he and Susan began to grumble about Arkansas and its climate. Smothering wet heat and biting insects were too much on top of hard work and mean housing and incompatible personalities.

In July 1973—six months into our Arkansas adventure—the couple decided to leave. My parents arranged to pay them one hundred dollars a month through a lawyer for their half of the land until they could secure a loan.[4] (Which they got a year later from Mammy and Pappy, Daddy's parents, to be paid back at twenty-five dollars a month.[5])

"It was a great relief for me to have them leave," Daddy told me, "I could then get on with the work of feeding you all without having to debate every sumac bush I needed to remove."

My parents were now the sole owners of the twenty-acre property, if very little else. They never saw or heard from Ray and Susan Connor again.

Katy turned two months old in August, a fat, dark-haired, ruddy, happy baby to take Momma's mind off her troubles. I was nineteen months old, charming and "irritat[ing] the hell out" of Momma in equal measure, she wrote, and learning new words daily.[6] I could look out the window and name the wandering cows, chickens, ducks, dogs, cats, and horses. There was beauty around us, and Momma had moments of joy. But there was no time for the sort of pastoral endeavors one might dream of in that life. There were no long walks on country roads or picnics on a blanket in the grass. Momma and Daddy were deep in the drudgery of rural life, Momma lost in a hot woodstove, diapers, and tearful children, Daddy in backbreaking labor and long days and continual setbacks due to weather.

At the end of August, Momma complained yet again about the slow-down in work on the farm on account of heat and lamented to her grand-mother that "for every pretty tree, I'm afraid God sent a little pest to go with it—sigh. Life in the country can get awfully defeating at times."[7] She reached for a potato and found it crawling with maggots, the first she'd ever seen. Day after day the low, sawing buzz of flies and mosqui-toes played like a tiny, winged orchestra. She wrote Granminnow that the "mosquitoes were destroyed by a spray of poison and oil on the water in the basement. But, now it is ticks again—millions—but the flies are dying down—sigh again."[8] The proximity of the cattle at the Key Place brought Biblical fly infestations. Momma hung sticky brown coils of flypaper and placed a small bucket of poison on the kitchen table. A dead mole then appeared on the living room floor. I squealed and danced around its body as if caught in the throes of an animal rite.

Momma opened a short note from Nana that summer and read, "I have some little flannel jackets that were worn by the Washburn babies + the Emerys—they are not just another hand-me-down—they are heirlooms— Tell your mother if you would like one and I will send it along."[9] Heirloom jackets were not a pressing need, and Momma doesn't remember if they ever came, but it is not hard to imagine Katy propped up in the dirt wear-ing fine, late nineteenth-century flannel at that old farmhouse. There were strange juxtapositions in every corner of this house and later the cabin. My parents had brought their Colorado furnishings with them: various pieces of antique furniture; a small lithograph of a prince in par-adise; a framed reproduction of Van Gogh's *Night Café*; a large litho-graph in shades of gray of a Mexican woman draped in her mantilla done by family friend Ellen O'Brien; and a rapid charcoal scene of houses on a rise, *Las casas de los olvidados*, bought by my parents together in Colorado.

But the hot flannel of our forebears would have to wait. By the end of that unusually dry August, we were all, Momma wrote, "parched and dusty and praying for rain and fall."[10]

Daddy started a new job in late August with Earl Morris, our landlord, at the sale barn, a livestock market and auction in Conway and Clinton. He left every Tuesday morning at 6:00 a.m. and worked for twenty-four hours. He slept most of Wednesday (if he could through the noise of two children) and left again Thursday morning at 8:00 a.m. and returned about 8:00 p.m. that night. "Exhausting work and smelly, since he spends most of his time standing in cow shit," Momma wrote, but the condensed schedule left him more time to spend on the land and with us.[11]

Daddy worked with a surveyor to mark our land's boundaries on his days off. Along the property's northern perimeter, he strung two lengths of barbed wire between standing trees. He fenced the livestock pens in the pasture directly across from the cabin with hog wire and a strand of barbed wire, all hung between gnarly, unpeeled black locust fence posts. The same locust poles were used to fence the rest of the pasture and the chicken pen. It was a time-consuming endeavor of felling small trees, cutting them, hauling the logs and wire around the property, digging post-holes, and attaching the wire, but by the time we moved onto the land, all but the garden would be fenced.

Daddy was also now enrolled in agricultural school one night a week at the Timbo School, sitting in a classroom taking turns with his classmates reading paragraphs from a textbook. It was a disinterested crowd of local veterans—all there for the monthly GI Bill stipend of $200 for two and a half years—under the tutelage of a local farmer who'd gone to college.

In the first week of September, rain finally broke the drought, but it fell "all day every day" melting the dust into sticky puddles and stopping all work. "One can only be pleased with a snail's progress and hope that ten years from now we will have gotten somewhere," Momma wrote her grandmother.[12]

Amidst all the toil, Momma at least pretended to find contentment. She wrote her mother, "Arkansas seems a better and better choice every day." "I know we couldn't do what we are doing—or *wouldn't* do what we are doing in Colorado" because life there, a local, Flossie Lee, had told her, was "jest too fisticated."[13] Later in the year, she echoed this with, "Life in the country seems harder but it is actually so much easier since you are free from so many external silly tensions."[14]

For all the difficulties of this life, as a modern, urban, financially stable mother myself now, I do see its advantages: no stuffing biting, hitting, crying toddlers into car seats and off to restaurants or playdates; no decisions on where to go to school or which car seat to buy; no pressure to drag children to every activity known to man. But Momma acknowledged parenthetically in her letter, "of course, there are always tensions!"[15]

While Momma praised our clean life to her mother, she complained to Daddy.

"I don't see how people like us who know almost nothing about farming can live off the land when all these people around us have been trying for a lifetime and still can't do it. They all have other jobs and are still barely making it," Momma remembers saying as they drove slowly along a dirt road.

"Horseshit!" Daddy exploded, "Dammit. Let me do this!"

Momma continued to push her argument but finally let it go. "Why is this not obvious to him too?" she thought, "Why can't we just discuss it without his losing his temper?"

Daddy was impatient and explosive and insensitive. And Momma had two children under two in appalling circumstances. On an early morning after Daddy left for his overnight at the sale barn, Momma was alone in the kitchen with two crying children. Her inner resolve failed her in that moment. She grabbed a metal chair and threw it with fury. It bounced back from the floor like a rubber ball and hit her in the head, drawing a small trickle of blood. Still not thinking clearly, she was seized with the terror that she would faint and leave us alone, so she packed us into the car and drove to the Morrises' for help. The wound was minor, and she was left only with embarrassment and the fear that this was her unraveling. She tried to express this to my father, but he was distracted and unmoved.

Although Momma and Daddy had to delay moving onto our property again, we already had pigs, rabbits, chickens, and at least one goat living on the land. Every Tuesday or Thursday, Momma drove with me and Katy in the truck to feed and water the livestock while Daddy was at work. "It is not half as complicated as it sounds and a welcome change for me," she wrote, "I get out of the house and I feel useful for a change!"[16]

A photograph shows the four of us on the front porch of the unfinished cabin. There is no door; the upstairs dormer window, poking through the tin roof, is still glassless; and a fragile-looking, handmade log ladder leans against the right side. The deciduous forest closes around the sides of the house almost immediately. Daddy is standing with me in his arms in a cowboy hat and thick dark mustache. Momma, with baby Katy, is seated at his feet in a peasant blouse with a red bandanna around her dark hair, looking strained and slightly amused for the camera's sake and so very young.

Daddy, Momma, Katy, and me at the unfinished cabin.

Momma's frustrations won out again as fall set in—maybe sparked by a letter her sister had sent the month before about warm Spanish beaches and grand European cities—and the honesty she sometimes found too hard to contain spilled out into a letter to Granminnow:

> I am definitely feeling rather desperate—However [the girls] both con-
> tinue to be as cute as bug's ears—and as Mrs. Junior Price says (a local
> lady with 6 kids who wants more), "Kids is company"—And if you stop
> to think about it, I would be terribly lonely up here if it weren't for Sarah
> + Kate—As it is I just wish like Sarah that I could "Go, Go, Go" (her new
> complaint instead of "side, side, side").[17]

A few weeks later, Momma's sense of isolation had grown even more. "Richard did *all* the dishes for me last night," she wrote, "I was in such a bad mood he said he couldn't stand it any longer."[18]

Mammy, Daddy's mother—four feet, eleven inches tall, with dark eyes and dark brown, wavy hair—came to visit us alone in late October of that year. I remember her gaunt, bony body; her Carolina accent from another time; her deep, throaty cigarette laugh. She was kind, but I was careful and restrained in her presence. Mammy was smart, sharp-tongued, a grammar hawk (she'd been an English major in college), an expert with needle and thread, a good dancer. She was a proper southern belle.

"I enjoyed her visit but R. did not," Momma wrote to Granminnow after she left, "she can be an awfully nice person when she isn't *drinking*—she peed (pissed) & shat outdoors without any complaints, cooked on the wood stove, and helped us fight a small fire without any hesitation. She is a good, hard worker but of course she prefers the suburban life."[19]

Mammy annoyed Daddy during the visit with a constant stream of minor criticisms about his every movement. But despite her sometimes sharp words, Mammy was mostly patient and silent about our life—except about the poison set out on the kitchen table for flies, one small act that encapsulated all of our squalor for her. "I'm glad your father isn't here to see this—he couldn't bear it!" she cried.

The small fire Mammy witnessed nearly burned the Key Place down. A pipe from the heat stove burst into flames in the attic. Daddy worked to put the fire out with the hose while Momma ran down the road to our nearest neighbors, screaming their names as she ran, hoping to rouse them faster. But Daddy put the fire out before the neighbors could be summoned.

"You overreacted!" he said, "You were panicking."

"I screamed so they'd hear me sooner! That fire was moving fast and could've burned the whole place down! Don't tell me I panicked, Richard!"

The fire was alarming, but the whole life was more so. The anxiety of her days, of what she'd gotten herself into, overwhelmed Momma in these moments. Daddy never told me a single story about things Momma had done wrong (despite his regular criticism of her at the time), but so many of Momma's stories surround these incidents between her and my father, partly I suspect because she had less control over their life. The stovepipe fire reminded her that just that summer, Daddy had left her with green cedar for the cookstove, which makes boiling a pot of water an all-day affair, and she had been angry. Daddy, with his usual impatience, threw a cup of kerosene on the smoldering slab wood later that day, blowing open the stove's iron door and terrifying Momma. Richard obviously doesn't know what he's doing out here, she thought, and left me all day to battle green wood. But the green cedar had been free at Mr. Peachy's home saw-mill. Daddy had been on his way home from a long workday and spotted it, and what did he care how long it took to burn? He had no babies cling-ing to his legs.

Momma told Granminnow in October that we wouldn't be able to travel to Colorado for Christmas, "no money + no vehicle."[20] But by the end of November she had changed it to a mere delay, "Nana writes she will pay for our trip, so we will come at the *earliest* opportunity [. . .] I will come by myself if it seems that R. cannot get away—but would rather come with R."[21]

I found myself hoping we would make the trip as I read the letters, hoping my parents got a respite, so it was depressing to read in an early December letter that it was again a firm no. Daddy had a new job in con-struction and was making a decent wage, Momma wrote, so there was no time for a vacation.[22] And she made no mention again of the possibility of coming alone, having decided subconsciously that she would not be sepa-rate from my father for fear that he would stray, so unsure she was of his affections. He had chased her in the beginning, but once they were mar-ried, he was flirtatious and free with his compliments of other women, and she was never able to shake the suspicion of his infidelity. Despite a lack of any evidence, Katy and I would eventually feel this worry too, fearing that Daddy would find another woman.

Momma went on in her letter to say,

> But I do wish you would have Jock [her brother] bring you for Christmas—
> Jock promised us a visit now anyway—If you want an old-fashioned
> Christmas, this house couldn't be better. I don't know when we can
> interrupt to visit—but presumably some time will come when we are
> free—However, we are awfully involved and it is getting harder and
> harder to just take off—so I think everyone will have to come see us.[23]

Momma would try to lure her later with the immensely unappeal-ing exclamation, "We actually have a sofa bed that works—got it for 2 dollars!"[24]

My great uncle Chuck and aunt Janey, like second parents to Momma, never visited us. But Momma never gave up trying. In 1975, she would write with the carrot, "we have a decent vehicle so if we need liquor or a trip to the swimming hole or the laundromat we have transportation." She knew it was probably a losing battle with Chuck and Janey, admitting in the same letter, "I don't imagine them feeling adventurous enough to come here until they are well assured of tennis courts + liquor—both quite unavailable here as you know."[25]

The first year in Arkansas closed on a quiet and relatively content note. We were still not in our own cabin, but Daddy had his new better-paying job, and he and Momma were able to go to sleep and rise early together. It meant an earlier start to the day for Momma, but Daddy was now there to help get the fire started in the woodstove. "The mornings + evenings are very cold in this old house, but the days are so sunny and bright and clear that we can't complain," she wrote.[26]

The house did have electricity, more than she would have in the cabin at first, but with no insulation or furnace, it was also bitterly cold. We slept all together for warmth on two twin beds pushed close. Wet diapers left out overnight froze on the floor. Momma, accustomed to the cold being tamed with central heat and insulation and real windows, felt that she had never been so cold in her life. It was, she wrote later, "a little more pioneering than Richard or I had bargained for, but my theory is that wherever you find a pine tree [her shorthand for wilderness], you find a little misery."[27]

Christmas was celebrated in the Key Place with a plentiful supply of clothes and books and small toys from grandparents. Momma wrote to Granminnow three days later, admonishing her for too lavishly spending on gifts, "We'd far rather have you save your money for visits and stick to one present apiece—We are grateful, of course, but I think Xmas has become too much—especially for little children who don't need it all!"[28] How pious a young mother she was! We had very little, and Granminnow's presents were so modest.

We in fact did have a visitor that winter. My uncle Lewis, Daddy's younger brother, had come to live with us for a short time at the Key Place in the last months of 1973. He was taller than Daddy, with wavy long hair and a voice still carrying its pronounced southern drawl, but also slender with the requisite beard and mustache and the same wire-rimmed glasses.

"He is a big help to Richard but not much to me," Momma complained to Granminnow in February, "although he is pleasant and good with the kids and I appreciate the wood splitting. Otherwise, however, he is a typical bachelor—totally under the assumption that women can work day + night without help."[29] Her temper had simmered in the heat and wasn't fairing much better through sickness and freezing cold, and she had no more patience for what she saw as "laid back, pot smoking hippies," like my uncle at the time, who was only twenty-five and in over his head. He had stumbled into a world of grown-up problems with which he was ill equipped to cope.

Momma had a rundown Chevy sedan that she drove to the market about seven miles away. It was big and drove well, if a little rough to start. She drove with Katy in her lap and me in the seat next to her, oftentimes both of us wailing; or she nursed Katy while maneuvering the steering wheel. Most of her driving was slow, methodical work over rough roads, so she felt safe. One morning, the sedan was broken down, and Lewis drove Momma in our temperamental truck to Mountain View, twenty miles away, to the bigger grocery store and the laundromat to wash clothes and cloth diapers. The truck couldn't be turned off or it would stall, which required a push start, so she needed Lewis's help. But with two babies and Momma and a stalling truck, Lewis lost his temper, and she never went with him again. She watched him sit by the warm stove while she worked all day. He would wait for her to put more wood on the fire, not thinking to do it himself. Daddy grew tired of coming home to Momma's complaints about Lewis each day and blew up at his brother. Daddy had his issues but seemed to have a core understanding of a certain equality between the sexes, even if he struggled to master the concept on a daily basis, and he could no longer afford the luxury of sloth.

Lewis moved into the unfinished cabin for a few weeks of roughing it without family demands and then left town. Momma, however, was up in the night with Katy in the cold and again overwhelmed by the weight of our needs:

You ask what we need—I hate to tell you since you have the least money—
but since you ask—Everything—R. brings home a good paycheck and
seems to have pretty steady work—but groceries are outrageous—We
may have to get food stamps—Basically we are still in a struggle to finish
the house or build a new one—and we don't have the large amt. of cash

necessary ($500–$1000) to do the job—Thought of a loan from Aunt Ruth, but chickened out since we can't pay back for awhile and have already taken so much money from her—Sarah needs great big blocks + clothes—(size 2½ or so). Katy needs clothes (1 yr. old size). We need millions of other things I guess but I can't think of them now with Sarah in my lap and me in an early morning daze.[30]

ON THE LAND

There's thirty thousan' acres, out west of here. Layin' there.
Jesus, what I could do with that, with five acres of that!
Why, hell, I'd have ever'thing to eat.
—John Steinbeck, *Grapes of Wrath*[1]

"We're to start an early garden, the weather is so good," Momma wrote in February 1974.[2] We were still living in the Key Place, but after the Connors left, Momma took over the garden duties on the farm. She listened to the advice of locals and read the *Old Farmer's Almanac* and *Organic Gardening* magazine and learned to plant according to moon cycles. She tried planting as the moon waxed and waned, as it grew lighter and darker, as lunar gravity supposedly pulled moisture up into the soil like the tides. She was also following the astrological stages of the moon, each sign either fruitful (moist, watery, earthy) or barren (dry, fiery, hot, airy). One day was good for tilling or plowing, another for weeding, another for planting. Some phases called for leafy, above ground plants, others for root crops, others for plants with seeds outside the fruit, others for seed inside the fruit. When Momma strived to plant in Cancer, a watery sign of abundant growth, rain would fall all day and she stayed inside. She would be pulled into town for laundry when the moon passed into Scorpio or Pisces. A free day for planting would finally arrive on the first day of a new moon when no planting should occur. The system was too difficult, and she abandoned it.

Momma planted her first garden in a new plot close to the cabin that Daddy had just cleared of small trees, weeds, and overgrown sumac, exposing fertile, long-fallow soil. (Tucker Field, as the locals called our land, had been long ago planted with crops.) Daddy used a walking plow he'd bought at a local farm auction hitched up to our mule, Liza. She was disgusted with his artless efforts to direct her and would stop and refuse

79

Momma admiring her sunflowers
in the summer of 1975.

to continue every few minutes. (Years later, he bought an expensive Troy-Bilt rototiller on credit and, at some point, a cheap tractor with a disc harrow to break up soil for seeding fescue in the pasture for the cows and a Bush Hog to mow it.)

The garden was initially spectacular, and vegetables burst forth as though trapped beneath the meadow grasses and weeds all along. The first season after plowing up the overgrown meadow was the most abundant—compost and chicken manure never proved as fecund as years of biodiversity rotting away undisturbed—though Momma still managed to get a sufficient harvest from the garden every year to feed us. But she never came to love it, admitting to her mother in the same February letter, "We have inexperience and lack of interest (and time) to contend with."[3] While many other women in the area got excited reading seed catalogs in January, Momma dreaded it, despite the immense satisfaction she felt in a row of ripe vegetables. "Who knew that potatoes and watermelons were so easy to grow?" she wrote.

Despite its rapid early growth, Momma's first garden would eventually succumb by summer to equally prolific weeds and ignored plants gone to seed in waves of flowers. And Momma didn't always heed the advice of locals or her books. Locals warned her not to touch blister beetles, but she figured this was an old wives' tale she could ignore. They were garden pests, and she went about smashing them freely, wiping the sweat from her brow. Her now rough and calloused hands escaped the poison the bugs excreted, but a blister grew on her cheek, and she popped it. It drained and more serum-filled bubbles formed, a weeping line of painful blisters that took weeks to heal. She was reading Ruth Stout's book *How to Have a Green Thumb Without an Aching Back* but missed Ruth's advice as well: "If you cover a bush with lime or anything white (flour will do) the beetles won't go near it."[4]

Momma's next letter home was on real stationery. Granminnow—either determined to maintain a certain level of propriety or, more likely, just being practical and knowing no other way—sent Momma a box of embossed stationery and envelopes that spring with small, blue serif capital letters at the top: Mr. and Mrs. Richard F. Neidhardt, Fox, Arkansas 72051.

The irony of such a gift was not lost on Momma. "I do feel a little silly with such an impressive letterhead and no plumbing," she wrote.[5] Any feminist concerns she may have had over the moniker surfaced only meekly. She complained just once, several years later, when my grandmother sent some cards printed with the heading "Mrs. Richard Neidhardt." Momma requested that she have them printed in the future with either "Mr. & Mrs. Richard Neidhardt" or simply "Wendy Neidhardt."[6]

By the end of April 1974, my parents had begun the slow process of moving onto the land, and Momma wrote on her new, stately letterhead in her now familiar refrain,

This is taking time because Richard leaves for work at 6:30 a.m.—comes home at 5 p.m.—except 3 days a week he goes to agricultural school until 7 or 8—plus he must feed the pigs which we had to move to the land—and I'm stuck with 2 babes, so we move slowly—Our garden is really looking good this year [. . .] plus we have pigs, rabbits, chickens (8 or 9 eggs a day) and a goat who will be giving milk in a year or so—Perhaps we will be semi-freed from the supermarket—what a joy![7]

In June, we finally moved onto the land, in heavy rain, the cabin still unfinished. Daddy had grown tired of driving the many slow miles between work and farm and Key Place. It was time to live on the land.

We moved into a small pup tent while Daddy worked to finish chinking inside the cabin. The Federal Emergency Management Agency (FEMA) declared a major disaster in Arkansas that month because of flooding and severe storms.[8] It rained day and night for three days, and Momma feared the lashing wind and water would carry us away like ants.

I was two and Katy had just turned one. Momma was stuck with us in the claustrophobic, damp stuffiness of the tent while its thin walls vibrated in the wind and pounding rain. The tent walls collapsed in the night. A fast stream of water ran down the slope of the land. The clouds were violent shades of black and blue and gray, and there seemed no respite from their relentless dumping. But we remained on solid ground, if a bit waterlogged.

Daddy must surely have been moved to sing Dave Van Ronk's folk tune "Mr. Noah"—a favorite of his throughout my childhood—begging we be allowed to ride in the Ark of the Lord.*

The cabin was secluded at the end of a long dirt road. It was a small eight feet by ten feet of unpeeled white oak logs—and one log of black gum, as Daddy is still quick to point out—resting on a foundation of dry stacked stone piers, thick flat stones Daddy and Ray Connor had found on the land and stacked in precarious-looking columns of varying height as the hill sloped. It had saddle-notched corners Daddy cut by hand with an axe, each log resting on the curved hump of the one below it like a saddle on a horse's back. The log ends were left sticking out in uneven lengths until a later addition. The cabin was built as a temporary living solution, so no time had been spent peeling the logs for longevity. In the chinks, Daddy and Ray applied heavy masonry cement on top of hundreds of finish nails salvaged from a condominium project in Colorado and hammered in about an inch apart. They framed the loft with two-by-fours and plywood with a steeply sloped roof in front and a shed dormer in back that ran the width of the cabin. Three square white windows peered from it into the woods behind.

---

* The 2013 movie *Inside Llewyn Davis* was partly based on Dave Van Ronk's life.

A crowded wood of mostly oak and hickory with a smattering of locust, maple, dogwood, redbud, pine, wild azaleas, and sumac surrounded the cabin. The heavily wooded terrain was bookended by Fossil Rock Bluff to the north and Lick Fork Creek to the south. Through the tight curtain of trees behind the cabin, the ridge descended the bluff in steep benches to the valley below. (Daddy considered clearing trees behind us to open up the view of the valley, but it was too great a task, the trees too dense.)

Inside the cabin, the floors were rough boards milled from trees on our land, as were the treads on the ladder staircase against the east wall and the two shelves fit under it. The staircase led to the sleeping loft, from which a shed dormer window—with a space just big enough for Katy and me to curl up in with blankets when we got older—framed a view of the front yard and the pasture beyond.

A white-enamel Centennial wood cookstove was downstairs against the wall opposite the stairs with its tall backsplash and shelf. Momma used the stove, an old dresser, and a metal folding table for preparing food and washing dishes, in two metal washbasins—one for rinsing and one for washing. "Just like Aunt Minnie taught me, glasses first, then plates and cutlery, then the dirtiest pots and pans," she told me years later, as though we were discussing a suburban wife's first blissful months of marriage in her new bungalow.

The window dormer in the loft protruded from a corrugated tin roof perched on three timber support posts over a front porch of wide planks. There was a small, six-paned white window to the left of the board-and-batten front door—the only window downstairs—that filtered in the sky and a small square of pasture and visitors and passing weather. The neat horizontal lines of the cabin logs ran perpendicular to the boards of the door in pleasing geometrical contrast. Stripped in early photographs of the usual debris and equipment that would soon cover the porch and spill out onto the surrounding dirt—cardboard boxes, fuel cans, red Maxwell House tins, climbing ropes dangling from hooks, a washing machine, tools, wood—it was picturesque.

The fierce June wind ripped through still missing chinking in the logs. Daddy had realized too late that the cabin faced the prevailing south winds. A robin's-egg-blue propane refrigerator sat on the porch, its pilot light protected by a sheet of scrap plywood and a square of plastic nailed up between two porch posts. For a week or so, a blanket hung in lieu of a front door with rocks at the edges securing it from the wind's firm grip. When Momma lifted the blanket to step outside at night while washing dishes, the kerosene Aladdin lamp blew out. She relit it again and again. Daddy fixed the door after she broke down in tears.

But, Daddy and Momma told themselves, at least we are in the cabin, not in a rental surrounded by bulls, and not in a tent or a camper like so many other homesteaders in the hills. Daddy had planned to build another more substantial house for us to live in, but as the cabin neared completion after hours of work and sweat, it seemed the best and only affordable option.

Granminnow and Uncle Jock drove from Colorado to help with our move. After driving through thunderstorms that nearly drove them off the road, they arrived under calmer skies and awoke in their tent on the land to sunshine. Granminnow grabbed a few minutes to herself inside the tent to write her own mother back home:

> It's great to have Wendy + Jock together but frankly this operation is so repulsive to me four days will be more than enough. Don't mention my feelings in front of Jock—I suspect he feels much the same as I do since he's working so hard to amend the evils—but it's like pouring water into a si[e]ve. Why anyone is healthy is beyond me (actually I don't think Sarah is but how does one do anything about that?).[9]

Jock—a tall, muscular Zeus with a large head of brown curls and a beard—is in a series of pictures with us, sawing wood, holding Katy and me in his massive arms, leading a resistant goat through tarp-covered mounds of furniture in the grass. In one set of photos, he is picking through a litter of items, our belongings spread out through the under-growth in the dappled sunshine of a stand of trees. In the foreground, Katy and I sit with Momma in a stained, worn armchair, the tangle of woods and weeds threatening to swallow us all up at any moment.

Another missive arrived from Aunt Sarah that summer. She wrote that she'd had the "'*meilleur pot de Paris*' and plates of *Jambon blanc* to make you die. We sat on the terrace for three hours turning over intellectual and metaphysical queries and pondering Antibes for the summer."[10] Momma read Aunt Sarah's words, perhaps as she stirred beans and waited for her corn bread to rise. She too had been pondering intellectual queries in France just four years before.

Uncle Jock with me and Katy.

Momma with me, Katy, and Uncle Jock.

Inside the cabin on the stairs to the attic,
about summer of 1974.

Aunt Sarah again lauded our lifestyle and relished the bragging rights she'd gained through my parents' adventure:

> I loved the photos that you sent and I show them avidly to my French [friends] even straight Americans and they can't believe it. That's why I'm tired of Europe—people are so civilized [. . .] And they don't dare anything—there is absolutely nothing perilous about life in Paris except trying to keep one's sanity.

Momma's first inclination in rereading her sister's and her own letters a few years ago was to say that they were "both full of shit." But she, even now, agrees that there was something vital in that perilous life. It kept her in the moment, away from petty thoughts and apathy.

June had been rainy and cool enough for us to sleep under blankets, but July "came on with a bang and a crush of heat."[11] Momma wrote that Daddy was suffering more in the summer heat than he had in winter's cold: "He says his head aches + he feels faint by the end of the day."

The woodstove was also a drag in the warm weather, but with the cover of trees and that south wind that bedeviled us in winter's chill, the cabin was cool.

"I can rest myself and the girls between forays into the heat," Momma wrote.[12] Daddy cleared out the undergrowth on the east side of the house for a place to eat under the shade of trees and hung a swing for me.

Momma was downstairs at the stove, maybe stewing in anger about something Daddy had said or done, or frazzled by waves of heat from the stove, or enjoying a moment of quiet. Looking up from her work, she realized Katy had disappeared and, in the same moment, heard, she wrote her mother later, a "dull thud and baby cries."[13] She dashed out the front door just steps from her place at the stove towards the muffled wailing. Her chubby baby lay crumpled in the dirt. Katy had pulled her way up the ladder staircase and crawled out the still windowless loft dormer and fallen ten feet to land between the stone foundation of the house and a tree stump. She cried like a dying goat, went glassy-eyed and pale, and began to doze off in Momma's arms. Momma had no working car that day. She grabbed both us girls and walked-ran to our neighbor's house a mile down the road for help and a ride to Mountain View.

Tucked in the middle of a letter to Granminnow a few days later, Momma wrote with the casual calm of afterthought: "Richard wasn't able to get the upstairs finished before Katy fell out the window onto the ground. About a 10' fall." We made it to Mountain View, "probably within a ½ hour of her fall + had x-rays," she wrote.[14] It is impossible that all of this could have happened in half an hour—a bit of optimistic storytelling to manage my grandmother's worry no doubt, who would not have been fooled.

Katy recovered from a concussion, but Momma was deeply shaken. She was angry with my father for not having finished the window, but she knew the accident was her own fault. "Katy's not fearless," she wrote, "but she does run around and I never have watched her as nervously as I did Sarah."

In mid-July, after a night lit by the flickering bulb of heat lightning from distant thunderstorms, the hot spell momentarily broke with claps of earthshaking thunder and rain. Momma penned a long letter to Uncle

Chuck and Aunt Janey summing up what was happening on Fox Mountain
that summer, now that we were officially residents of our very own cabin:

To others it seems pretty but small—or just pretty small—To us, at least
on good days, it seems a palace—since we remember when there was
nothing here at all—*and* we know the blood, sweat + tears that went into
it—It is full of mistakes—But the general impression (to me at least) is
every bit as nice as the beautiful homes in "The Woodbutcher's Art"—
Many thanks for that beautiful book [. . .]

We have been feeling pretty proud + smug these days—since moving
to our land and being fairly comfortable here gives us the impression of
having "made it"—of course pride goeth before a fall—and God knows
it's still no bed of roses, but we have heaved several sighs of relief—since
struggling to get out of that farmhouse + survive was really hard times—
But now we look forward to a winter with a freezer full of meat (we
should have electricity by the end of summer)—our own meat—(goat,
pig, calf) if not vegetables—Our garden was only passable this year—
due to neglect since we didn't have much time for it—we may be
cramped into this little cabin this winter, since I doubt Richard will be
able to finish the addition before the cold sets in—But at least we can
heat it—I can't spend another winter like last one—We thought we'd
freeze in that drafty old house—And the kids are so much more comfortable here—There are so many more places for them to play—safely—

I finally got to read the books you sent—The Auchincloss was a
pleasure—I only dabbled in Mary McCarthy's book, but enough to hope
I'll get time to finish it someday—Richard was really hooked by it +
finished the whole thing + thought it excellent—It certainly adds to my
respect for Gene McCarthy to say nothing of my respect for her—What a
great love she must have for him, to write such a book *after* their separation (why did he leave her?) Next time you are in a book sending mood,
(my birthday?) How about some paperback Colette? Maybe in French,
though I can't say whether I'll be up to it or not. By the way, the Adelle
Davis is wonderful—They are a revelation to me. [. . .]

It is time to put this letter to a close—I wish I could help you imagine us here—and see all the trials + tribulations as well as the joys of
Arkansas—I can only say that tonight after a rain the forest sounds
alive with life—as you would imagine a tropical rain forest to be—the
other day, after a morning of excruciating heat, we went swimming in a

natural pool and were surprised by a downpour—Climbing up from the
pool to the cars through the rocks + underbrush along the forest path,
I felt like a jungle girl in one of those 30's movies—However usually we
feel baked to death + dry as a popcorn fart (Richard's phrasing) since
our land and much of Stone Co. is high + dry—We have never worked
so hard or been so frustrated in our lives but we are slowly beginning to
feel a sense of accomplishment and a confidence in our new abilities.[15]

Despite the heat and the daily labors, there was still time to read, to feel
inspired by it all, and to experience moments of satisfaction at the end of
the day. "Since the children are in bed early, the dishes are done, house is
clean, water is drawn, the weather is cool—perhaps tonight I can write,"
she had begun the letter.

The dawning of a new day started the long list of chores again. "I pray
for a pump before winter," Momma wrote in another letter, "Drawing
water + hauling it is a pain in the heat. It will become almost impossible
in ice + snow."[16] Until we got electricity and a pump and pipes for running
water, my parents got all our water directly from the well. They (mostly
Momma) pulled the water up by hand with a long, cylindrical galvanized
metal well bucket and carried the water across the pasture in big five-
gallon plastic containers back to the cabin with Katy and me in tow.

Daddy had our neighbor Dalton Moody, a water witch, dowse the property for the well. Moody walked the land with two lengths of coat hanger
wire—a common witching tool—one in each hand pointed forward, waiting for the spontaneous crossing of the wires to signal a vein of under-
ground water. He found a spot about 500 feet from our house near the
southern edge of the pasture. There is no scientific basis for water witching, and our land may very well have had water throughout, but Daddy
felt the wires cross with his own hands. I was surprised that my very
rational father had never questioned the legitimacy of the process, but
he hadn't. And nobody else on the mountain had as good a well as ours,
which "was excellent, 30 gallons per minute," Daddy still remembers.

In the last week of July 1974, Momma wrote to Granminnow, "We will
have electricity by the end of the week at *considerable* cost + hassle—But
it will be awhile before we have lights, etc.—*Hopefully* our pump will be in
quickly (I drew + hauled 18 gallons 1 day)."[17] The lines for electricity were
staked out in July, but a right of way still had to be cut and poles put up.[18]

Recently, Momma reflected on this time before they got running water and electricity. She told me they were both engrossed in how to do things without those comforts and that "it was an exciting challenge." It wasn't pure drudgery for her. She too was reading the manuals of that life; the *Foxfire* and Nearing books, *Organic Gardening* magazine, Ruth Stout's *How to Have a Green Thumb Without an Aching Back*, and her idol Adelle Davis's book *Let's Eat Right to Keep Fit*. Granminnow and Uncle Chuck and Aunt Janey were sending books from the Chinook Bookshop, and my parents were by then well aware that a significant number of young people were moving to the country—to Stone County even—building their own homes, eating organic foods, and trying to find alternative sources of energy. Momma wrote in her July letter to Uncle Chuck,

> *Five Acres + Independence* is an excellent book that we will really be using—*How to Make It on the Land* is *not* an excellent Book—The *Foxfire Books* are constantly useful—and the Gibbons [*Stalking the Wild Asparagus*] too if anyone has the time for such lollygagging in the woods—I say all this in case you wish to advise any customers— also the Eric Sloane books [*A Reverence for Wood*] are helpful.[19]

"Don't worry so! I am actually on occasion enjoying myself + the children are the best part—not the worst!" Momma added as a postscript to her late July letter to Granminnow. The unbearable heat of July was upon us, and Momma's tension practically leaps off the page in the body of her letter:

> I was a bit irritated that you bent over backwards *not to* irritate me in your words about Sarah—You've got to learn to be a little less timid or you'll drive me mad—I know you are much more of an expert on 2½–5 yr. olds or on any age for that matter than I am—That doesn't necessarily make you right, but I certainly need + have sought your advice on occasion— As for what you said, I couldn't agree more. However, I know from expe- rience with the C. Spgs. doctors + all doctors that they are of *no* help—I think that the doctors—Dr. D—— and Drs. T—— and L—— may actually have *caused* Sarah to have allergies. You can laugh or whatever, but Adelle Davis has really helped. [. . .]
> Also—I'm not about to leave Richard for a gay vacation in C. Spgs—

If I got desperate, I would—but meanwhile—we *are* in this together and we can't pop off whenever we like—*But* we both want to come when we can—But who knows when that will be—At the moment, we don't even have time to go to Little Rock to visit Lewis—

Well—I don't mean to be harsh + I know you'd like to have the girls around, but you must realize that we have a big job to do here that can't be interrupted.[20]

Later I discovered in another batch of family letters (between my maternal great-grandmother Nana and her daughter Cooie) that Granminnow had feared I had rickets that summer. She was desperate to convey her worries to my mother and get help for me.[21] Momma was also worried about me, "*so* skinny [. . .] I hope she'll survive it all," but wrote, "I know Richard + I are doing the best we can by keeping her here + feeding her up as the farmers say."[22] Momma happily shared the colorful, hardscrabble details of country living, proud of her unorthodox circumstances. But, despite occasional lapses in which her frustrations leaked into the letters, she was determined to hide from her mother, and to an extent herself, how truly difficult she found my father and how lonely and overwhelmed she felt.

In the fall, we were living on Daddy's GI Bill check for agricultural school, food stamps, and his various jobs. He began building a commercial-size chicken house for our old landlords, the Morrises, and he hoped for various odd jobs through the winter until construction work could start up again in the spring.[23] Ubiquitous in my life then, and in my memory now, are chicken houses and sale barns. Someone in Fox once told Momma that chicken houses were a "Cadillac investment for a Volkswagen income." They could also be a trap. Corporate poultry processors controlled everything: the loan process, feed, required upgrades, and final meat processing. The farmer provided the land and labor and then just did what they were told. Many locals took out loans to build them anyway, in the hope of partnering with these big poultry companies to avoid leaving home to harvest crops or work in sawmills all over the Midwest and California. Almost no local resident could make a living from farming alone. They worked at the livestock sale barn, Blanchard Springs Caverns, or the shirt factory. Or there were a handful of entrepreneurial endeavors available, like the chicken houses or "peckerwood sawmills," portable, small-scale saws set up in the woods. Or people could catch chickens for the trucks from the processor or haul hay or cut stave bolts—chunks of straight-grained, knot-free white oak split in half and sold to a local stave mill for making watertight wooden barrels—the last two of which Daddy did for a time. There were few opportunities for the educated beyond a small number of positions as schoolteachers or nurses or county employees. But, according to the US Census Bureau, in 1980, only 42 percent of Stone County residents over twenty-five had a high school diploma and only 7 percent had a college degree; 42 percent had stopped going to school before ninth grade.[24]

Momma has repeated over the years that the only jobs available to her in Fox were in a chicken house or the shirt factory. The shirt factory always sounded ominous to me, like hundreds of women lined up and sweating in a long chicken house–like structure making sleeves and collars with steam rising from big irons. The Blanchard Shirt Factory had opened in Mountain View in 1967. Women in particular went to the factory so their husbands could maintain the farm, bringing home steady paychecks and health insurance and paid holidays for the first time. "Retired from the Blanchard Shirt Factory" still appears in one local obituary after another.

Many of the locals were too proud to get food stamps, but my parents still defend their occasional use of government assistance. Daddy believed he paid for that right by working and later by employing locals on his construction jobs. The farm had become our life, one my parents couldn't just walk away from. There were jobs started, animals accumulated, structures built, a garden sown. There was, at least for Daddy, an emotional obligation to finish what they'd started, and financial assistance had become a necessity.

But Momma had her limits. She told me she was sure she wouldn't have mentioned it to her mother (she did, on several occasions in her letters). Momma also didn't like to use food stamps at Ticer's Market in Fox, because Mrs. Ticer was a known busybody, "Tele-Ticer we called her, so one didn't want to give her any reason to gossip." (At least once, Mrs. Ticer rubbed her fingers quickly along Momma's back to ensure she was wearing a bra.) Momma was leery of gossip, because she was actually embarrassed, but she was more ashamed of her own shame than the handout. Welfare was something she believed in, a government program rightfully earned. And she felt she couldn't advocate for it in theory and be too good to accept it for herself. On the other hand, when Earl and Bobbie Morris cooked thick steak dinners for us on their ranch, Momma felt ashamed of their charity, since they themselves were struggling. Our lives were full of these quandaries: my parents hated snobbery but couldn't always shake it. Bad grammar in their own children was cringe worthy. Thank you notes must be written. The ancestors were important.

Daddy's sister, Aunt Rhett, who would move to our woods in the late seventies, used public assistance for a time too, but gave up due to the hassle or embarrassment or both. I remember a red, unmarked, Costco-sized block of American cheese in her kitchen that I somehow knew was a government handout, and Total cereal in our house, packaged foods that were like colorful sculpture to my sheltered eye. This food was unusual in our life then and gave food stamps a bit of glamor. Many years later, the fact that we'd had government assistance seemed another strange chapter in our story to me, particularly considering the worlds my parents had come from. But now I find—to my relief *and* disappointment—that government assistance was just another cliché of the counterculture. In *After Kathy Acker*, Chris Kraus writes that "Acker, apparently, saw no correlation between the catastrophic municipal debt and a well-educated twenty-eight-year-old Jewish white girl availing herself of social welfare services . . . but at the time, nobody did. Throughout the 1970s, welfare, unemployment insurance, and disability SSI were the de facto grants that funded most of New York's off-the-grid artistic enterprises."[25]

But there were more permanent aspects of self-imposed poverty. In later years, when a tooth became too painful to ignore, Momma found a cheap dentist in the county who used no anesthetic. She was desperate with no funds and too proud to ask my grandmother for more. She entered the dentist's small waiting room and passed a large table of fliers proclaiming that Jews and Catholics were destroying the world. She considered walking back out the door. The dentist was white-haired and stooped, and his wife was his assistant. He mentioned nothing of his nutty ideas about the world as he examined her teeth, and she endured. But his dental work was a sham—didn't "know his ass from a lock washer" as Daddy would say—and she lost the tooth and wouldn't feel she could afford a replacement until the nineties. The black void it left was somewhat hidden on the side of her mouth, and only her father was ever rude enough to mention how bad it looked. But it was a mark of poverty, a kind of emblem of what Fox took, a hole in her mouth that was like the hole in her work life and their finances and her dreams.

In answer to Momma's summer prayers for a pump before winter, we had electricity by September 1974, and an electric pump was set up over the well in place of the manual galvanized tube.[26] But Momma and Daddy still had to walk to the pump house, fill the water cans, and lug them back to the house.

I wish I could remember the days before we got electricity, the light of the kerosene lamps flickering in the night and the shadows that must have swept the corners. I don't, come to think of it, remember light flooding any rooms with the flick of a switch either. It is always day in my memory of the woods. I recall the buggy sounds of darkness, but the black of night is oddly gone. As is the cloudy glitter of the Milky Way that must have spread out above us on clear new moon nights. But Momma remembers the impressive glow of a full moon. It comforted her to have the outdoors alight when she was up late alone washing dishes.

Mammy and Pappy arrived in September to spend two weeks with us, at least in theory to help with the wood chopping, water carrying, dish-washing, and baby tending.[27] And to help Daddy build an eighty-square-foot, wood-framed kitchen addition onto the back of the cabin.[28] Pappy had a resonant, smooth voice and smelled of shaving cream, but there was a trace of impatience on the edge of his words, always keeping us both charmed and apprehensive as children. He was a veteran, a churchman, and an insurance man—straitlaced and conservative—and he saw our lifestyle as "harebrained" but grudgingly developed respect for the work my father had accomplished.

With his short-sleeved, collared pocket shirt tucked trimly into his belted polyester pants, Pappy did his best to help collect rocks for the foundation, and he wired the original cabin and addition for electricity (he learned how from a book). In his job as an insurance agent for MONY of New York, Pappy had by court order been made trustee of a bankrupt electrical supply firm in South Carolina and had to liquidate the assets of the company. He found piles of electrical remnants—wire and receptacles and switches—that couldn't be sold that he brought out with him to use for the project.

Pappy on the porch with me.

*Momma and Pappy with Katy and me at
the door to the new kitchen addition.*

Between jobs, Daddy and a few friends ripped through plywood and
two-by-fours and got the basic structure of the kitchen up quickly, and by
the end of September, we could spread out a little. We were all still sleeping in the loft, but there was now a living area downstairs and a dedicated
kitchen space instead of a stove and table in a corner. There was a sink

Katy and me in our Lions Club shirts
from Mammy and Pappy.

Momma and Daddy during
Mammy and Pappy's visit.

(but no running water), salvaged cabinets, and electricity. The cookstove now sat against the west wall of the new space, a sink to the north below a small window, and the blue propane fridge—which we always called an icebox because that's what Momma called it—was brought inside to the south wall.

"We have modernized slightly," Momma wrote her grandmother, Nana, who was herself surrounded by the gold-leafed frames of ancestors and plush floral couches and thick drapes. "We feel at the height of luxury— And really we are! We have 20 acres of yard, a house of our own—food + warmth—what more could we ask?"[29]

Health was ever present in Momma's mind, and, where Daddy had the building up of the land to drive him, this—in addition to childrearing— would most often be the focus of her zeal and enthusiasm. An early September letter to Granminnow included one of Momma's very detailed vitamin requests:

Can you get me some vitamins for my birthday? I know it sounds mundane, but it's what I need and can't get—*Vitamin C* (*natural*, not ascorbic acid)—try to find a large quantity on sale (500 mg. size) if possible— get it as cheap as you can. I need a B vitamin syrup for Sarah in these proportions (approx): for every 3 mg. B, 3 mg. B_2, 3 mg. B_6, 18 mg. Pantothenic acid, 18 mg. niacin amide, 18 mg. PABA, 600 mg. cholin, 600 mg. inositol, 9 mcg. vitamin B_{12}, 15 mcg. biotin, 0.1 mg. folic acid— or some brewer's yeast in these proportions—if the vitamin syrup also has iron—all the better (this damn pen is slowing me down)—if you would prefer, we need more good peanut butter, oil, and sunflower seeds for snacks—If you find Vit. E (*d*-alpha tocopherol) in cheap form—get some—or you can be really mundane—but also *really* kind and get me a new brassiere—(34 B)—Take your pick—as usual, my needs are endless, my finances null.[30]

She wrote again at the end of the month: "If you use vitamin E, please note that Adelle D[avis] recommends D-alpha tocopherol, not the *mixed* tocopherols."[31] Momma admitted that she didn't do everything Davis said, but "I *idolize* her, since she saved Sarah's life, if not her physical life at least her emotional life. Since Sarah is no longer a potential sickly child, but a blossoming, beaming almost 3 yr. old."[32]

There were never-ending requests over the years to my grandmother for vitamins with these very specific instructions and advice based on Momma's bible, Adelle Davis's *Let's Eat Right to Keep Fit*:

"*Please* read Adelle Davis cover to cover carefully. It is more than *Vit. C* +
liver—If you don't, you deserve to be *sick*—If you have iritus, take Vit. A
+ Vit. E as well as Vit. C in large quantities—also milk, liver, etc."[33]

In another long letter waxing on about the benefits of Adelle Davis,
Momma recommended that Granminnow eat for breakfast "½ lb. liver,
orange juice, milk, vitamin C (5–10,000 mg if you felt sick)."[34] The name
Adelle Davis has been uttered so many times in my life she feels as familiar as family, becoming one word, *adelledavis*, that means wheat germ
and wellness and Momma.

She got carried away at times, caught up in near proselytizing, but her
preoccupations are still relevant. She wrote Granminnow again that fall
of 1974, "almost all beef + milk cattle are fed antibiotics *routinely*—many
beef cattle eat chicken litter (shit) for feed (yum, yum)—chickens (the
ones that supply the shit) are fed adrenalin to make them grow faster—If
you yell at them or scare them, they have heart attacks—chickens that lay
eggs are fed methedrine (SPEED)."[35] She wrote to Uncle Chuck that same
month on the growth cycle of plants: "Beautifully simple and elaborate
too. Too bad we can't put plastic + BHA + BHT in the picture."[36] She wrote
this forty years ago, but her words could just as easily be from a twenty-
first century conversation (or more likely a Facebook post). It was her generation that began the movement towards cleaner food, and it's only just
begun to go mainstream. But as much as I agree with her and appreciate
that she has instilled in us her concern for these matters, these sections of
the letters irritated and impressed me in equal measure as I read. She can
still trigger my internal eye roll with her endless health facts and diets.

In a 1975 letter to Granminnow, who was in the midst of problems with
her then boyfriend (later husband), Momma took her earnest rhetoric too
far, closing a letter with: "I wish I could be more helpful to you in getting
through your troubles. Time will heal all I guess. I hate to be a bore, but
the best health food for crises, is liver—and then yogurt + wheat germ +
fruit mixed—very good."[37] A bore indeed.

Granminnow sent a Merck Manual to help Momma with diagnoses.[38]
We had less access to health care than she had had in the 1920s when her
heart was permanently damaged by rheumatic fever. Momma also did her
best to keep up with our vaccinations, about which she had no qualms—
this was before any pervasive anti-vaccine movement. But my maternal

great-grandmother, Nana, had expressed fear that Momma would forgo them, for lack of money or access or will.[39] Momma promised her she would not. She had us vaccinated sporadically when roads and health allowed, read her Adelle Davis and, when we got old enough, plied us with spoonfuls of cod liver oil and vitamins E and C the size of horse pills crushed with a bit of honey.

By the middle of October 1974, Daddy was working six days a week on the chicken house for the Morrises.[40] While the weather was still mild, he knew he needed to be cutting wood and finishing the barn and the house (livable but perpetually incomplete), but he had to earn a living. Work on the cabin and land crept along.

Paid work gave the promise of future funds, though, and my parents went into debt to buy a cow and a calf from the sale barn in the weeks before Thanksgiving. "So we don't buy our milk at the store anymore," Momma wrote Granminnow.[41]

The cow was a black Angus-Holstein cross with a white belly and feet that Daddy named Mama Cow. He milked her each morning before work and spent his Sundays off doing as much as he could on the land. "Winterizing the house, building a barn, working on vehicles, etc., etc.," Momma wrote Uncle Chuck, "The load is tremendous, so I must help as much as possible."[42]

Momma wrote with palpable fatigue in this letter to Chuck, "Tonight as I started your letter I realized I had to feed the dogs, change the sheets where Sarah had peed, and find some wood for the fire, split it, etc., etc." She went on in a long letter on feminism and frustrations that were clearly weighing heavily on her:

> I was most interested in your reflections on male-female relationships. I am often thinking about such things and find it pleasurable to be a woman (children, home, etc.), but difficult to accept a secondary role—which nevertheless occurs quite naturally, especially when you have children. Richard is in some ways a male chauvinist pig—not intentionally, but unconsciously—most frustrating to deal with—Anyway, Pat Schroeder (a wonder woman from what I hear) is right about the

frontier—This is not so much true of the modern frontier, although it
is still partly true.† However it is quite clear to me from studying atti-
tudes + customs around here that a man + a woman stuck off in the
woods alone together naturally will share all burdens—especially when
all labor is hand done + time consuming—Most men here of 40 and
over remember helping with the wash—a hand wash being a gigantic
chore. They know how to cook—and of course the women work in the
fields, split wood, haul water, tend animals, etc. The modern day equiv-
alent is women working at the shirt factory in order to keep the men at
home working the farm—Anyway, one does often see women nowadays
around here taking over a lot of the man's work—leaving the men to plan
+ bullshit—But it would be unfair to apply that role to all the men [. . .].
Life is hard for everyone around here without much money—Richard
now works construction 6 days a week, leaves the house at 7 A.M.,
home at 6 or so except 3 days a week he has school from 5 to 7 or so.
[. . .] Meanwhile, however, I am equally overloaded—and Richard is
not patient with womanly confusion in male matters so it is difficult
for us to work together—But we try—This sounds grim, but mostly (not
always) it is quite pleasant since we now live on our own land and feel
fairly assured of our position here. Last winter we still felt pretty shaky
and we lived in a dump, so life was hard. When I see what we have built
for ourselves in just the past (almost) 2 years I feel proud and sure that
all the misery was worth it—also I look forward to what we *will* do in
the future. Anyway—back to man vs. woman—Ms. Schroeder should
realize that for centuries in civilized citified cultures women + men have
lived separate, *not* equal lives—*But* I imagine primitive life always gives
the woman a certain—although not a perfect—equality. I must add
that watching the barnyard society I see equality but strong differences
between the sexes—The male is the *stud* or the *meat*—valued in his stud
capacity—expensive—*But* no more important than madame who gives
milk, eggs or whatever (+ meat). The male is much more *aggressive*
always—and stronger + bigger—The male is the vessel for the semen—
The female the vessel for the child—They are separate, but equal. It

† Patricia Schroeder was a Democratic representative for Colorado in the
House of Representatives from 1973–1997, the first woman to represent Colorado
in Congress and an advocate for family issues and working women.

seems inevitable to me that the male will retain the governing edge in any human or animal society—But we are equal in function in the eyes of creation I am sure. Hard to face a secondary role when for years in school + at home, we women nowadays are trained to think of ourselves as men—have careers, etc.—But no one says *how* it can be possible to raise a happy family + work too.

Momma considered herself a feminist at the time but in an informal way; she was unaware that she was writing this in the middle of second-wave feminism. She'd read a little of Simone de Beauvoir, but none of Betty Friedan's *Feminine Mystique* (1963), the book that in many ways ushered in the new movement. When I asked her what she'd thought at the time of feminism, she told me, "I remember sometimes being annoyed with the arrogance and attention seeking of the male leaders of [the civil rights] marches. [. . .] [And] in my own case, I certainly expected to be treated equally, but I hadn't been out in the world enough to see the worst abuses. I ignored the fact that my own mother lived a really difficult life with my father taking every male privilege. However, she was also an example of a liberated woman even before her divorce. She worked, started a school, and was in charge of every aspect of our lives, given that my father was so absorbed by his work."[43] And Momma was in France when fifty thousand women marched down Fifth Avenue in New York on August 26, 1970, for the Women's Strike for Equality March, followed shortly after by her marriage, childbirth, and the cabin. She did think twice about taking Daddy's name after marriage but did it because she was afraid to offend his parents. But this letter to Uncle Chuck showed that she would have recognized and aligned herself with the idea then popular among second-wave feminists: "The personal is political."[44]

Uncle Chuck was a gifted letter writer and an English teacher, so Momma was giving him her all in this letter and presumably relishing the chance to flex her brain a bit, to prove her inner thoughts had not changed along with her surroundings. And to make him laugh, as he so often made others. The letter continued:

I have not seen a bookstore or a bar in almost 2 years—I have rarely used a toilet or a bathtub—I haven't hardly had a drop of alcohol or a cigarette (a few cigarettes). Richard hardly smokes dope (there is plenty of it up here—home grown marijuana). We lead an unexpectedly clean life [. . .]

I know people in their 40's–80's who have drawn all of their water all of their lives who still cook on a wood stove (all heat on a woodstove)—I know one woman who has raised 9 children without even a well. But things are changing around here—The question is will they change back with inflation—

[. . .] When I think of our living conditions and how they look to non-Arkies—I think of the farmer who was told it was unsanitary to have his chickens in the house—He replied, "Cain't see why. I ain't had one sick over 20 year."

After sealing the letter's envelope, she had another thought. She scribbled on the back an anecdote she had heard about women's liberation on the early frontier: "Tourist to Kentucky country woman: 'This sure is pretty country.' Woman: 'It's fine for a man and his dog, but it's hard on women + mules.'"

In mid-November, Momma hints to Granminnow that a trip to Colorado might actually happen before the end of 1974. "I hope you got the message that we bought a '62 (I think) Blue International Scout (like Dad's)," she wrote, "which will be perfect for all our farm needs and perfect for going to Colorado. We *had* to have a new vehicle + we wanted to drive to Colorado + we wanted a Scout-type vehicle, so all is perfect. I hope you approve."[45]

But we were still at home for Thanksgiving, on a warm November 28. We had a goat roast, and my parents invited all the people they knew, mostly newcomers like us with no family nearby.[46] There are a series of photographs from the following summer that give a glimpse of what this Thanksgiving described by Momma in the letter must have looked like. Daddy is in a white sleeveless T-shirt, the sun breaking through the trees. A pale, skinned goat carcass, splayed open by women holding a leg on either side, hangs from a tree while Daddy and his brother pull and cut the entrails out of its gut into a red wheelbarrow. Black instrument cases lie in the dirt, and men and women in cutoffs and bandannas and sandals and jeans are slouched in metal folding chairs.

My sister Katy and I helped Daddy pull bulbous sacs and twisted innards from goats during big musical get-togethers in later years. We hosed the carcass down after it was dressed and watched Daddy lay it on

*Daddy with Uncle Lewis and Mindy
butchering a goat in the summer of 1975.*

*Daddy barbecuing goat with me and
a guest in the summer of 1975.*

a cinder block and metal-grate grill rigged on the ground. As the meat sizzled and charred, the music began and continued into the night.

On a cassette tape Mammy and Pappy made during a visit, Daddy is playing guitar and singing outside the cabin, much as he must have that Thanksgiving Day in 1974. All but the smells of the day come to me from the tape. Amid the quiet hollow hum of outdoor sound rise children's voices and roosters crowing in the distance, false starts as Daddy tunes his guitar, a small burp, and then he sings the blues: "I saaaid noooooow, jelly, jelly, jelly momma, all that jelly roooooll is on myyy miiiind . . . jelly roooll killed my daddy, and my mammy stooone col' blind . . ."[47]

Seven

PICKIN' AND GRINNIN'

The glad clear sound of one's own voice,
the merry song, the natural life of the woods.
—Walt Whitman, "Song of the Broad-Axe"

Life in the woods was often isolated, exhausting, and shabby. Parties and music were the salve. Daddy had been seeking wild land and found it in the Ozarks, but we had also moved to hollows still echoing with the songs of a century ago, songs that had inspired the folk music Daddy had been performing for years. It was this music in fact that had first drawn back-to-the-landers into these stony hills. Most gatherings we had or went to in the woods included live music with the Jew's harp, mouth bow, dulcimer, mandolin, fiddle, Autoharp, washtub bass, guitar, or banjo. We children didn't usually join in, but wove in and out of the action, the music a background to our play. The whiny rake of fingers on acoustic guitar strings and notes vibrating out of a guitar's hollow body will forever seem to come from the hills carrying with them chickens and dirty feet and sweaty, play-drenched bodies. Along with the rooster's crow and the chirp and hum and croak of creatures, they are for me the very sound of Arkansas.

Mountain View, in fact, is the self-proclaimed Folk Music Capital of the World.

Years ago, in a used bookstore, I stumbled on a 1973 book published by the National Geographic Society called *American Mountain People*. I flipped to a chapter on the Ozarks and the word "Fox" jumped out at me. I bought it. The author had been taken to the house of a Fox local named Lonnie Lee for a Saturday night musical tradition. I knew the name well!

Daddy and Momma had both told Lonnie Lee stories over the years. As I read Momma's letters, I came across one she wrote Granminnow the month before Katy was born:

Daddy, Uncle Lewis, and an unknown woman
playing outside the cabin in the summer of 1975.

Tomorrow is Lonnie Lee day when we get our regular Sat. afternoon
bath (in a galvanized tub heated on the stove—very pleasant)—I'm dying
for it. Lonnie Lee is a neighbor here in Fox who has a musical every Sat.
night and has since the late fifties and invites young + old to come see
and listen and gossip—Richard goes every Sat. night come hell or high
water and plays his heart out (he's become something of a local
celebrity)—You *must* be here on a Saturday so that you can go and hear
some *real* country music—just hope that the hippies haven't taken over
by then as they along with the powers of money that be around here
threaten to destroy all the real culture that exists in Stone County—
but more about that when you arrive and can really see the Ozarks for
yourself.[1]

At the Lee house, women, children, and menfolk gathered round to
listen to six or so musicians sing and play at a microphone hooked up to
a PA system, the musical tones drifting out from the small house into
the yard where others mingled.[2] Cup after cup of coffee was consumed,
the locals' drug of choice, as a hodgepodge of performers played country, bluegrass, folk, and the old-timey mountain music it all came from.
Daddy was most impressed by two of the local legends who played the old
music: Seth Mize, a fiddle player, and Bookmiller Shannon, a five-string

banjo player. Alan Lomax had recorded Shannon in 1959, and both men had played at The Smithsonian Institution Festival of American Folklife in 1970 with Pete Seeger. But Daddy didn't know this at the time. He just knew they were "really good ol' country musicians." These musicians and the music Daddy had followed in high school and after would make up our musical world. The pop and rock bands that rose to fame in the 1970s missed us entirely.

Lonnie Lee usually sang his standard, Merle Haggard's "Swinging Doors," which Momma hummed around the house for years. But the flashing neon sign of the song and its swinging doors were nowhere to be seen in the Lee's humble home. There was a large central room, blankets hanging for doors, and beds all together in a big room with a heat stove. I don't remember their house, but I saw others like it, and Momma has kept the story alive for us, so that it's as though it's mine.

Lonnie was born and raised in the area, as were his parents Garther and Flossie and his wife Neda Merle, their names a sort of music too. For generations their people had farmed and worked the stony land. Neda Merle Lee was a big woman, and she had nine children. While the men played, she plied Momma with stories and went on about how people from outside the Ozarks—she had lived in Colorado for a time with Lonnie—thought their life was so crude with outhouses and such but that it really wasn't.

"I didn't let on that I was positively bug-eyed with surprise when I first moved to Fox, because everything seemed so old-fashioned and rough," Momma laughed. "Neda Merle told me that when she was young she'd been so poor she'd had to eat water gravy!" Water gravy, made with water instead of milk, is a thing, but Vance Randolph, famous and prolific chronicler of Ozark folk tradition and culture, noted in his time with native Ozarkers that they liked to tell tall tales of their lives to tourists. The explanation one gave him as to why became the title of his 1951 book *We Always Lie to Strangers: Tall Tales from the Ozarks*. Momma and Daddy both had an ear for this kind of thing, and the Lee stories were added to their family stories and became in a sense our own. Unlike Momma, who came in with bug-eyed wonder, I was being raised in this world of Neda Merles and water gravy and felt a kinship with the stories. I would share them with friends as I grew older, now my own tall tales.

Despite how poor and backwards they initially looked to Momma, the locals were mostly bent on modernization. They had not been raised in the confident air of generational prosperity, a subconscious privilege that allowed my parents to consider the whimsy of building cabins and milking cows. We would be living more primitively than many of the local families in the coming years, our homestead harkening back to an Ozark past that had been slowly dying since at least the 1950s. But by mainstream standards, theirs was still a quaint and rustic life. According to the US Census Bureau, in 1970, 44 percent of homes in Stone County—probably the vast majority of which were in the most remote areas around us—still had incomplete plumbing.[3] (When a local friend of Daddy's finally set up a trailer on his land so he could move out of the wood shack he lived in with his family—a hole cut in its floor for spitting tobacco juice into—he didn't move out. He found the trailer too stuffy compared to his drafty, woodstove-heated cabin.)

The Saturday musicals at Lonnie Lee's attracted a mix of locals and newcomers, and Daddy fit in particularly well; he was Southern and used this to his advantage. On some nights, more country and western came out of the mic, and Daddy was singing mostly folk, but they liked it. Daddy had inherited a good voice from his father and had taken piano and violin lessons as a young child, but he learned to play guitar in high school, spending hours lifting a record player's needle and pulling it back to learn the chords by ear, listening over and over. In army basic training, he gave the army psychiatrist guitar lessons. Later in Germany, he played guitar and sang at a folk club and in USO shows back on base opening for bigger bands, like the British duo of Colin Wilkie and Shirley Hart, and he played small shows in Colorado.

The Earl Scruggs and Lester Flatt version of the Carter family song "You are My Flower," sung just like Scruggs and Flatt, with a plaintive country whine at the end of words, was Daddy's most requested song at the Lee musicals. It's still my favorite song to hear him sing.

Two famous musicians actually lived in Stone County. One was the Elvis-faced, Louisiana musician Tony Joe White of "Polk Salad Annie" and "Rainy Night in Georgia" fame. His son went to our school. Larry, the leatherworker who took us to Arkansas in 1972, made leather outfits for him to perform in. The family had moved near Fox the year before us.

"I had bought some land there [. . .] and I just put the kids in school there in this little rural town—wasn't even a town. God, it was far so out [*sic*] you couldn't even imagine," White told an interviewer years later.[4]

White was always touring, and Daddy never met him. But Katy ran onstage and climbed boldly onto his lap while he performed in our small school auditorium that smelled of gravy and canned fruit. She strummed his guitar while he fingered the chords on the fretboard and pressed a wah-wah pedal with his foot.

The other musician lived down the ridge from us. When I was not quite three years old, Daddy took me out looking for our hound dog, Old Belle, who had wandered off. Dogs tended to wander far, so we drove down Fox Mountain searching other farms. We stopped at Morrison's Gas Station at the bottom of the hill, and Daddy asked Luther Morrison if he'd seen Belle. We drove on to Timbo Market to ask the owner Hollis Treat if he'd seen him. Hollis thought he had and sent us on to Jimmy Driftwood's ranch between Timbo and Onia (pronounced "Onee"). We pulled up to Jimmy and his wife Cleda's stone house, parked, and walked to the door. Jimmy came out and immediately welcomed us in like old friends. He was wearing a nondescript shirt and a pair of jeans rather than his customary uniform of red shirt, blue jacket, and black hat.[5] He brought Daddy a cup of coffee and paid special attention to me, asking about my day, delighting in my childish chatter, or so I'm told. Driftwood's Ozark accent was strong, and he was still living in the county where'd he'd been born and raised, but he was internationally famous and college educated and had traveled the world. He had been instrumental in bringing folk culture tourism to Stone County.

That day in his cabin, as Daddy talked of hound dogs, Driftwood pulled out his guitar and began to sing "Tennessee Stud" to me: "I never would have made it through the Arkansas mud/If I hadn't been a-ridin' on the Tennessee Stud." Driftwood's music is pure nostalgia to me now, perfectly capturing the spirit of that place and time.

Daddy knew of Driftwood before we moved to Arkansas, particularly from his song "The Battle of New Orleans." We had also seen him play at the Stone County Courthouse in Mountain View, where musicians performed music on the courthouse lawn and in a building filled with wooden benches, the audience rising from their seats as the music pulled their feet into the Ozark jig.

Driftwood asked where we lived, and Daddy told him about the cabin and our land.

"We sure need a log cabin builder for the Folk Center," said Driftwood.

The Ozark Folk Center State Park had opened in May 1973—after ten years of state and national lobbying by Driftwood and many others to find the money and the will—as a demonstration for tourists of the old ways. Daddy would go on to build the cabin for them sometime in 1975. By the time the park opened, most Stone County natives no longer knew the traditional music and crafts to be preserved, so the center became in some ways a precious recreation of Ozark heritage, providing jobs in large part for outsider artisans, Daddy's building of the cabin a prime example. Its early years were also plagued with problems, inexperienced staff and controversy around Driftwood among them. Opposing factions within the organization warred over how purely authentic they should be, Driftwood demanding that only music conforming to a narrow definition of traditional be allowed (ironically, considering he brought in my newcomer father to build the cabin). As Daddy had experienced at the Lonnie Lee musicals, many locals preferred more modern country music. But Driftwood was attuned to how much outside audiences craved the traditional sound and had a small number of local traditionalists on his side. In a strange twist, this made many other locals no longer authentic enough to play music at the center. Although Daddy saw that Driftwood was domineering, as an outsider, he felt ambivalent about the controversy and wanted nothing to do with it. He would have worked on a second cabin they brought in for restoration, but the tension became overwhelming, and he left. In 1975, the battle between the opposing groups grew so heated that a fight broke out between jig dancers backstage at a show.[6] Governor David Pryor finally got involved and fired Jimmy Driftwood. Driftwood went on to build his own performance venue nearby in 1979, the Jimmy Driftwood Barn.[7] The Barn and the Ozark Folk Center State Park are still popular tourist destinations.

But Daddy knew none of this yet as he told Driftwood about our cabin that afternoon we spent with him. Knowing Driftwood's traditional bent, I can imagine how his ears must have pricked up as Daddy divulged the rustic details of our homestead. What Daddy had not mentioned to Driftwood was something he knew about *him*: that less than a decade before, his wife Cleda had come home from work—while Jimmy was playing in Brussels—to find their two sons, two young men in their twenties, their only children, shot dead. A murder-suicide Driftwood speculated. They were both lying face down in the kitchen with a shotgun and a rifle nearby. "This is my cross to bear, and I can bear it," Driftwood—his poetry seemingly always near the tip of his tongue—told a reporter in the days after their deaths, "We have got to lay the dead away, and think about taking care of the living. Here were two boys who wouldn't even kill a bird. They loved people and never had any fights. They were crazy about each other, but I suppose Cain and Abel were too."[8]

My musical world was mostly the regular soundtrack of Daddy: the Beatles, fifties bands, Dave Van Ronk and other folk regulars, Delta blues, and the children's rhymes of his youth. The songs came to me through Daddy's voice and his guitar, rather than the hundreds of records he had stacked up (we had no record player). I danced the Ozark jig while he or friends played, hopping around tapping and shuffling my feet. Daddy sang:

> Up Fox Mountain on a Wednesday,
> There's a big to-do,
> Everyone's invited, bring your own kazoo,
> Long John's on the banjo, pickin' and a frailin' and cryin',
> David's on the fiddle, sounds like he's a dyin',
> Sarah's dancin' a jig, see her feet a flyin'!

A handful of songs and rhymes entered my consciousness more deeply than the others, songs I still sing to my own son or when we get together as a family, lyrics that are as much a part of the cabin as the white oak that made it. Just like his fellow musicians at the Lee Saturday night musicals, my sisters and I loved when Daddy sang "You are My Flower," but there were many more.

We giggled and danced when Daddy sat up tall, opened his eyes wide, and belted out the Kingston Trio's satirically British-accented "The Tattooed Lady" from 1960. She was a fair freak tattooed from head to knee with a union jack, queens in guarding line, a fleet of a battleships, and a little home in Waikiki upon her chest. The tattooed lady stood with The Lovin' Spoonful's 1966 "Baldheaded Lena" in my imagination; the women's portraits were absurd and tough and coarse. And they were part of Daddy's overall drollery and added to an endless stream of old camp songs he also sang—"Once upon a time, the goose drank wine, the monkey chewed tobacco on the streetcar line!" he rapped out as we played.

Sadness and misery were at least as beguiling as silliness. Country Joe and the Fish's 1967 "I-Feel-Like-I'm-Fixin'-to-Die Rag" sounded happy coming from Daddy's lips, but the chorus was enough to tell me differently: "And it's five, six, seven, open up the pearly gates, Well there ain't no time to wonder why, Whoopie! We're all gonna die!" Darling Clementine drowned in her song and was "lost and gone forever." Pete Seeger's "Where Have All the Flowers Gone?" had a poetry I clung to, the repetition, the poignant demise of each thing, the mournfulness of the "long time passing," and the full circle of the flowers. The young girls going to young men in the song was nearly as gripping a thought to me as the soldiers going to graveyards. (Daddy actually sang the Kingston Trio version. Seeger's lyrics have the young girls going to husbands, and I remember that Daddy's girls always went to young men, a romantic distinction.)

The songs sometimes merged with the stories in our books. I loved magical illustrator Gyo Fujikawa's 1976 book *Oh, What a Busy Day!*, particularly the "very, very sad story" of two babes lost in a wood, covered in leaves by robin redbreast as they died:

> My dear, do you know
> How a long time ago,
> Two little children,
> Whose names I don't know,
> Were stolen away,
> On a fine summer's day,
> And left in a wood,
> as I've heard people say.

My sister and I could have been those babes in a wood, two little girls running wild among the trees. But I wasn't frightened by the story, I was enthralled. The sadness of the words was eclipsed by Fujikawa's light-dappled drawing of an inviting forest and its soft, grassy floor upon which the babes appeared to sleep. And the story was bound up in the song that may have captivated us most, the hypnotic English murder ballad "Greenwood Side," sad and dark with those same two babes again.

Daddy sang us the Ian & Sylvia version of the song from their 1963 album *Four Strong Winds*, a sorrowful, folksy, wailing interpretation. Two illegitimate babes were killed by their mother with a wee penknife ("weeping" I thought) "down by the green woodsideee o." She rubbed and rubbed the bloody blade against her shoe and returned to her father's hall to find the ghosts of those babes wailing out that "scarlet was their own heart's blood." In the end it's hell for Mother O Mother, heaven for Babes O Babes.

The haunting songs and storybooks weren't so far from the real and commonplace tragedies on the farms around us—like the murder-suicide of Driftwood's sons—which were not always hidden from us. Daily life for our neighbors was akin to our own—work, play, family—but there were darker elements too, of domestic abuse and deprivation and alcoholism, Lord-infused folk songs of poverty and tragedy I couldn't ignore.

Eight

NEIGHBORS

We'uns is all hidden out here in the woods, y'know.
It do git kinder lonesome, times.
—Donald Harington, *Architecture of the Arkansas Ozarks*[1]

There was an old adage in the hills and valleys of Stone County that my parents have never forgotten: After five minutes you're no longer a stranger, but after twenty years, you're still a newcomer.

We were living in yellow-dog Democrat country (as in, they'd vote for a yellow dog before they'd vote for a Republican), but it was because the locals held tight to the days and party of the Confederacy.[2] It was just as conservative as it is now, which is solid red, or Trump country. Momma and Daddy were "furriners," or "from off." "Are you a Yankee?" kids asked Momma. But my parents had preconceived ideas about the locals too. The movie *Deliverance* was one of the biggest movies of 1972 and newly part of the popular imagination in the months before we left for Arkansas. A few months after arriving in the woods, Momma wrote home to her aunt and uncle, "Did however run into some types à la *Deliverance* the other day—very spooky—Otherwise, people here are nicer + friendlier than any I have met anywhere."[3] Stone County locals were a mix of families in modern trailers and brick houses and those still living in their old cabins. Except in the county seat Mountain View, there were no neighborhoods, but people spread out over miles of hollows and ridges and valley. They had their churches where we rarely ventured, but we all met at school events, Ticer's Market, the gas station, the feed store, the laundromat, or at the courthouse musicals in Mountain View.

Most of the locals were happy to chat and share small farm tips, their sentences a stream of vivid backwoods colloquialisms that fed Daddy's already rich South Carolina repertoire. Daddy fell subconsciously into a slight rural accent—it wasn't quite the locals' vowel-bending, clipped twang, but it wasn't the Yankee he had adopted nor the r-dropping Carolina dialect of his childhood. Daddy had shed the south for New York City, and now he donned it again, albeit in a more hill-country form. It was his personality to throw himself into each new adventure full bore.

My parents were not inclined to offend people with their more secular and urban mores, particularly not these locals they admired. Already the locals were becoming to Momma and Daddy like gods, so full of practical knowledge. They were the masters of that world, the professors, and my parents felt dependent on them. The mountain people, mostly isolated from mainstream society by the rough terrain of steep ridges and deep valleys, were charming.

We were careful. I made sure to never let a "God damn" or a "Jesus H. Christ" escape my lips at school. (Or, worse yet, "Jesus Fucking Christ.") We were told or had sensed to keep quiet about politics and money and religion. Momma and Daddy had learned this growing up, in that reserved Protestant way, but it was a practical necessity in the woods. These were topics for the private spaces of home. Katy and I were also warned to never speak of marijuana at school. This was a dry county and teetotaler Baptist country. Some older boys on the school bus asked Katy what our dad smoked.

"I'm not supposed to tell," she said.

The marijuana plants contributed to my fervent need to be a good girl out in the world. I was a high-strung child, aware as I grew older that our life was often precarious. I dreamed up catastrophe—venomous creatures in crevices, roiling black storms that ripped houses apart, cataclysmic bombs falling from the sky. And we knew Daddy's plants were illegal. Katy and I slunk down in the backseat when the state trooper drove by as if by being invisible our father's sins were too. But Daddy felt no misgivings about the plants. They were well hidden from the ground and sky, situated as they were among the constant sprouts of young trees. Momma, who didn't smoke marijuana, was more apprehensive. She felt nervous when a neighbor saw a roach clip and wondered what it was; Momma mumbled something and changed the subject. She feared we would be ostracized if the plants were discovered.

My parents also learned to ignore what they found distasteful, something they hadn't always done in the past. Momma wrote Uncle Chuck in 1974, in a list of things that were different about their new life, that in the woods "most of our friends are Baptists + some are [n-word]-haters."[4] She was borrowing the local language intentionally to emphasize how far they'd travelled. It was in the woods that I first heard men refer to something being "[n-word]-rigged" or to the black fiberboard used on houses as "[n-word] board," the only word ever used to name it at the local lumberyard. I didn't yet fully understand what it all meant, but I sensed something amiss. Momma and Daddy knew, of course, and had witnessed more, casual derogatory comments and off-color jokes. My parents didn't like it, but they knew it came with the territory. Eight years earlier, Momma had resigned from her sorority when they refused entry to a Black student, writing to them "I am opposed to racial prejudice, whether latent or expressed, and especially in any organization of which I am a member. [. . .] There are some beliefs which I would compromise for the sake of harmony within a group, but this is not one of them."[5] Before leaving South Carolina in 1964, Daddy had joined the Student Nonviolent Coordinating Committee to protest segregation. He teamed up with Black students attempting to integrate local restaurants and dated a Black girl who went with him. They were often threatened with violence. But it was now harder to make such a stand as a lone outsider in the country, and, there being no Black people, there seemed less at stake.

Daddy had also grown accustomed to these racist words in childhood. They were an inseparable part of his Carolina past, the social structure that ordered so much of his early universe. So ingrained was racism in the world of my father's upbringing—and so complete the segregation of the races—that it wasn't until high school that he even became conscious of the issue. The only Black people he'd known to that point were Emma, his family's maid, and Lurleen, the next-door neighbor's maid. Emma worked for his family from the time he was a small child, and she stayed with them until well after my father left home at twenty. My father took a baby me out to visit her at her home in December 1972, to show me off to the woman he'd known his entire life. She had fussed at my dad and his siblings, cleaned their house, done the laundry, and worked at their parties.

But one day, when my father was in his teens, he stayed home from school feigning an illness. "Emma was there," he told me. "I made lunch for both of us and set our places at the breakfast room table. Emma was scandalized and said she couldn't eat at the table with me. She took her plate into the kitchen and sat on a stool at the counter." Daddy sat there, stung by her reproach and shocked that she felt they would be violating propriety by sitting together. She was like a second mother or a beloved aunt. But Emma knew more than my father did about the way of things.

When I was a kid, Daddy did not shy away from racial stories or jokes—he told them to us without censor or lecture, but with sarcasm making it clear that they were the work of fools and worse. Momma and Daddy wryly threw out phrases like "Free, white, and twenty-one" and "that's mighty white of you," subtly highlighting our unearned racial privilege. Daddy spoke of KKK attempts to recruit him and later intimidate him, of segregated water fountains and schools and music halls, of the so-called genteel racism of his mother (even she didn't allow the N-word). Daddy spoke Gullah phrases to us that Emma had used, and I liked to leaf through his book *Ain't You Got a Right to the Tree of Life* about the Gullah, looking at the pictures—their homes not so unlike our own—and taking in the poetry and meaning of the title that seemed obvious to me even then.

A few years after leaving the woods, I would become radicalized in a mild, young-girl-in-rural-Arkansas way (mostly inside my head), recognizing the real power of the N-word. In seventh grade, in Little Rock, I wrote in an embarrassingly earnest essay about my present and future self, "I have a very, very strong feeling about Negro people. I think there is nothing different about them toward us except their color. My anger boils over when anybody says anything against Negroes. If I had lived during slavery time, I definitely would have spoken up against slavery."[6]

I wince as I look back on the fact that Daddy didn't take a stand at the lumberyard, that he didn't force the word Celotex rather than succumb to the derogatory "[n-word] board." How could he have used it if even his own mother didn't allow that word? I suspect he used it in part to show that he wasn't too good for them—it was a low-class word in his upbringing, and he wanted to diminish the class divide that separated him from the Fox locals. But perhaps there's no way to fully explain the banality of white supremacy—how it can invade daily life and infect even those who would normally fight against it.

We went to church for Easter 1974 at a "Pentecostal Evangelist!" church, Momma wrote Granminnow, obviously amazed herself at the novelty of such a cultural excursion.[7] (My grandmother had offered, absurdly, to send Momma an Easter dress; Momma declined.)

We went with Joyce Whitcomb, the wife of Johnny, for whom Daddy had built a chicken house the previous summer and with whom he and I had stayed when Momma was in the hospital after giving birth to Katy. Joyce had felt sorry for Momma, alone with two babies, and invited her to stay one day while the men worked. She made eggs and biscuits and gravy in the morning for all the men and us, and at lunch, a big farm meal of fried chicken, beans, cornbread, and greens. She stood at the kitchen sink washing the dishes in bleach water and talked a mile a minute telling Momma how to do things. She went to a little Pentecostal church in Fox and pestered Momma to go, and so we finally went that Easter.

"It was quite an experience," Daddy told me. "Talking in tongues and the like, generally 'holy rolling' as my mother would say. Johnny never went himself—he was a hard drinking, carousing sort."

Daddy worked with local men like Johnny on chicken houses and in sawmills and livestock sale barns, went out haying with them and cutting wood to earn extra cash. He hired them from time to time on the farm and in his later construction business, developing relationships with various families. He played music at Lonnie Lee's, fished with Hollis Treat, bought vehicles from Everil Farris at his garage/junkyard in Timbo, and talked pigs and dogs and land with many others.

Our family delved into local life in other ways too. My sister and I went to the local public school, Rural Special, and were sent at least one summer to Vacation Bible School to fill our hours with crafts and singing, Momma somehow confident there was no risk of our falling under the spell of fundamentalist religion. I sat in a plastic chair at a big folding table in a side room of the church and carefully glued pieces of macaroni to cardboard in the shape of a cornucopia and spray-painted it gold. It's amazing, I thought, and I breathed in its sweet, chemical smell of glue and paint while singing along to "Jesus Loves the Little Children."

When we ate dinner with a local family, Momma followed the custom of letting men eat first and respected the separation of men and women at gatherings. Momma let Daddy fill his own plate, but the other women brought their husbands their dinner and then sat around the kitchen table drinking coffee and griping about how angry they were.

"I know he's the boss, I just think he should be more considerate of me!"

a woman lamented. As the woman said it, Momma recalled something her grandmother had once said, "The man is the head of the family, but the woman is the neck." Perhaps this was a fact of life she would have to accept, Momma thought. Although she was taken aback that a woman could accept her husband as the inherent boss, she knew to keep quiet among the local women. Burying her true nature under a smile and conformity felt instinctive, but it was exhausting.

This cultural fatigue, more of a cultural dissonance, was in a sense a legacy of our move to the woods. I too would suddenly feel its weight in my twenties, after years of living in rural and suburban towns where our family had a private life always different from our friends' and neighbors'. But at some point, I realized others were no less different—it was a question of perspective. It was like a story Momma told me. A Fox local once asked her for her name.

"Wendy," she said.

"That's a strange name!" he replied.

"What's your name?" she asked.

"Ruminer," he said.

Scattered along the three-mile-long dirt road out to our land, were locals and newcomers, although we were the only farming back-to-the-landers. George and Mollie Bersch were a retired couple who moved onto our road in the late seventies and lived with their developmentally disabled adult son, Tom, and George's mother, Mary. George and Mollie both appear almost the same in my memory, their bodies thick, robust, solid as though nothing could topple them, both grey-haired and scrubbed clean with homemade lye soap, George in black horn-rimmed glasses.

George was a retired Episcopal minister from Wisconsin, and he held small services in their living room. It was remarkable enough that my parents were both Episcopal—considering they came from opposing worlds in many ways—and for an Episcopal couple to be living on our remote dirt road in the wilds of Baptist Arkansas, almost impossible.[8] But the Ozarks were an attractive retirement location for midwesterners. Four of our fellow congregants were another retired Episcopal minister and his wife who lived in Mountain View and an ex-Roman Catholic priest and his ex-nun wife who lived in what had been the center of Mozart (when it had had a post office and existed). The Bersches even hosted an annual seder in the spirit of fellowship.

In early 1978, Momma would write,

> We've been going to George + Mollie's church services quite a bit lately and have met a whole bunch of new people, which is just wonderful for me. They are more, in some cases, my type than others around here and I really enjoy the socializing—I foresee even the beginnings of a community theater next year but I don't know how much time I'll have to devote to it [. . .] Anyway, it's a spot of light in a somewhat gloomy winter.[9]

George was a woodworker and had built their house from timbers and lumber salvaged from a barn on his Wisconsin property. It was a beautiful home with walls covered in artwork—one of their daughters was a printmaker—and a large woodworking studio for making his intricate dollhouses and other woodcrafts. He handmade a fine carved pulpit from which he read the Bible in lieu of a sermon. He used a real silver chalice to serve "the Blood of Christ, the cup of salvation," and they baked flat, yeasty round loaves with a dusty crust that George broke into chunks carefully with his thick fingers for "the Body of Christ, the bread of heaven." I was entranced by this ritual and practiced the careful, intentioned breaking of the bread at home in our play. The services were intimate and inspiring for the adults, despite my parents' atheism. But I always felt restless, anxious for the potluck that followed. A long table in the room adjoining the living room was filled with food. The house was strong and modern, the antithesis of our own, and its smell has stayed with me: air laced with the aroma of bread and yeast, furniture oil, wood, and lye soap.

Neither of my parents was religious and both were wary of organized religion inasmuch as they gave any of it much thought, which they did not. Daddy was sick of it all after a childhood wading through the murky waters of convention, expectation, and sermon. But he accepted the new brand founded in Fox. Momma, in particular, found reading from the Bible at the Bersches to be inspiring and thoughtful, the passages poetic, the camaraderie afterwards and the sharing of food a blessing in that isolated environment.

Going to church at George and Mollie Bersch's and being baptized was also about a cultural tradition that at least Momma still felt close to. Granpa Will had been born to a large, influential Catholic family in Denver—one of his aunts was a nun—but he considered himself an atheist. Granminnow went to church regularly, as had Momma and her siblings. Granminnow was the granddaughter of the founding rector of an Episcopal church in Colorado Springs. And she was the great-granddaughter of one of America's most famous nineteenth-century ministers, Richard Salter Storrs of Brooklyn's Church of the Pilgrims (a Congregationalist), a contemporary and friend of Henry Ward Beecher. It was his daughter Miriam's saltcellars we had on our Thanksgiving table in the woods, and it was her 1883 wedding dress that both Momma and I wore when we married.

Momma's family had a strong ecclesiastical background, but Daddy's family was more religious. Daddy had spent part of his early childhood living with his maternal grandparents. His grandfather, the Reverend Lewis Nathaniel Taylor, was a slight, impish man, with playful eyes under eyebrows arched like a grasshopper's antennae. He was a beloved Episcopal rector, "the pastor to all Columbia."[10] Daddy's great-great-great-grandfather, also Lewis Taylor, had been a priest too, a "well known, and really intellectual Episcopal clergyman," according to an 1889 newspaper article.[11] I have on a bookshelf now a small three-by-six-inch sermon of his from 1806—"Lazarus and the Balm of Gilead"—written out in a cursive so small and dense it's barely legible.

Mammy had wanted my father to be a priest too. He dutifully fulfilled his role as an acolyte, but when he neared the end of high school, and she asked that he begin the first formal steps in the ordination process, he refused. But Daddy didn't forget the hymns, which he could sing as well as any blues song, sitting erect at the edge of a chair like a good choirboy.

Momma sent us at least one summer to Vacation Bible School at a local Baptist church. Mammy and Pappy brought us Daddy's Bible story collections that had been Mammy's as a child too, and we leafed through the old pages with brightly colored illustrations and took in nothing but danger and tragedy. I don't recall a moment of religious thought or of questioning God's existence or power—his was just another fantasy like the rest of our stories.

There is a residue of Jesus left in me from those years. I still feel a piercing moment of grief and jubilation when I hear a call to the Lord in a song. I always remembered "The Fox" song Momma and Daddy sang as, "The fox went out on a chilly night, He prayed for *the Lord* to give him light." The words are actually "he prayed for the moon," but I knew what followed prayer and had decided subconsciously that God, Jesus, and the Lord added weight to a line. We were living in the Bible Belt, our household was filled with the rhythm of folk and blues and their religious undertones, and we were going to the Bersches' services. I also preferred the classic religious Christmas songs we sang each year to more contemporary, secular ones, although the power was only in the words and not in my heart or mind. Just as Momma did at the Bersch services, I internalized the poetry of religion without the belief. Singing to the Lord was code for the beauty and crisis of each day. The songs' poetry was speaking to something Uncle Chuck had written to Momma about in the summer of 1975, "I remember you saying that the doubtfulness of life in Fox made a first hand experience of the Greek libations to the Gods . . . i.e. you could understand why a bull or two might be cut up and offered to the Gods if only in the hope that they wouldn't get too frisky with human life."[12]

I remember many of our other road mates too. Taft and Mary Sutterfield lived in a small, old house a few hundred yards from the Bersches. As I remember it, the floor sloped, a potbellied stove sat in the center of the room, and newspaper covered the walls. They were a kind, elderly couple who gave us mealy, too-fragrant apples at Halloween and sold us eggs before we got our own chickens. Taft was a soft-spoken farmer and banjo player and the one-time sheriff of Stone County.[13] There was Etta, a middle-aged woman with a big mound of black hair on her head, who lived alone. I only ever remember seeing her behind her trailer door, the air seeping out smelling of heat and cats. There was an old ne'er-do-well who lived across from Etta. And down a bit, three developmentally disabled teenagers lived with their grandparents in a small white house. They were kind enough to share their chewed gum with us on the bus (a forbidden delicacy in our own home).

Our closest neighbors lived about a mile from us, by the bus stop and our mailbox, in three homes hidden in the trees. Judy Klemmedson was the folksinger we'd stayed with in 1972 when we came to see and buy the land. She was perhaps the first back-to-the-lander to settle in Stone County, drawn to its hills from Wisconsin by the folk music.[14] She lived in an old farmhouse with a stone well out back and made dulcimers. Her well scared me—a dark, wet, stony maw in the ground where dogs fell to their death, and perhaps little children could too, and so her house felt slightly haunted (its wood floors were those on which Momma had groped for me in the pitch of night when we first visited Arkansas).

A childless couple from Memphis lived in a comfortable, modern cabin just east of Judy and across from our bus stop. Their names and faces have gone hazy, but the man was a heavy drinker. He shot his gun drunkenly in the direction of us kids one day as we got off the bus, aiming at a target he had nailed to a tree behind us. I don't remember if the bus driver got out. I don't really remember hearing a gun or seeing the man. Maybe I don't remember much on my own at all. But according to my father and a cousin, we walked like always with our cousins through the wide field to their house, and then Katy and I walked alone up the long narrow road to our cabin to tell our parents. Daddy stormed furiously down to the shooter's cabin that afternoon, threatened grave consequences if it happened again, and simply confiscated his gun for a few months until he was sober and contrite.

Dalton Moody, Daddy's mentor, lived in a double-wide trailer on his small farm behind the bus stop. When Daddy slipped into his hill sound and let some country aphorism fly, I suspect he was often channeling Moody. He left the property in the mid-seventies after divorcing and remarrying and moved closer into Fox, so I have only one memory of him: he and his balding head, leaning forward on the edge of the couch in our living room with a hand raised to show me and Katy a half finger. He told us he'd lost the other half somewhere in our house—in a glass jar, I think he said—and I believed it. Perhaps he repeated the story again and again, each time he visited, his storytelling skills such that it resonated for years. Moody sold his land to the LaJeunes, a working-class couple from Massachusetts, who came with their teenage daughter, Ruby, and also lived in a trailer on the land.* Ruby looked like a woman—she was big bosomed—and behaved like one too as far as I was concerned.

I was alone in the tall blackberry patch near the cabin one afternoon popping inky berries into my mouth when Ruby LaJeune came riding up the road. By herself. On her own horse. As she drew near, her horse was startled by something and stumbled on the loose rock. She leaped off just before it collided with the barbed-wire fence and tore a fist-sized chunk out of its breast trying to free itself and stand. I ran to get Daddy. The

* Pseudonyms (LaJeunes, Ruby)

horse spent weeks in a stall in our barn with its head tied so it couldn't gnaw the wound. Every day, Ruby and Daddy would hose out the cavity. In a month or so, the flesh regenerated and filled the hole, leaving nothing more than a little dimple where the deep tear had been. The name Ruby LaJeune feels like legend to me for no other reason than the melodious sound of it and the air of rugged womanhood it represented in my imagination.

John Weaver, one of our nearest neighbors, lived in a secluded cabin southwest of ours through the woods and was Daddy's closest friend. He was independently wealthy, but he lived in a tiny, rustic log cabin he built himself. It was a single room with a loft space overhead where he slept, accessible only by ladder. He was a tall, lanky man who had retired from society and lived in solitude, except for a succession of girlfriends Momma befriended. I remember very little of his nature—it seems he saved himself for the men and the woods—but I recognized his voice immediately when I heard it on the cassette tapes we had recorded over the years for our grandparents.

Our next closest neighbor was Daddy's sister, my aunt Rhett (short for Henrietta), who would run away from suburban South Carolina and a bitter divorce in 1978 and come to Fox. She had visited us only once, with her kids and Mammy and Pappy the summer before she moved. This visit, much like many things surrounding Rhett and her motives, is missing from any of our memories or the letters. A consistent family rumor is that, after this visit, she was starry-eyed from a brief tryst with a man who made brass belt buckles for a living out of a school bus near us. Hoping for a romance—that would never materialize—she brought her three boys, aged fifteen, twelve, and eight to a three-room, red board-and-batten house down the road from our property.

Aunt Rhett—with her wide hips and round face and tight dark curls like Momma's—is an enigma to this day, but she was a warm, big part of my life at that time. She was loving with us girls, singing "Old Aunt Mariah" to us over and over. The chanting cadence was seductive, and I sang it to my own son and niece and nephews, invoking Aunt Rhett each time: "Old Aunt Mariah jumped in the fire / Fire was so hot / She jumped in the pot / Pot was so black / She jumped in a crack / Crack was so high / She jumped in the sky . . ."

Aunt Rhett had an art degree; to make ends meet she taught art and piano and hand-painted commercial signs, which impressed me greatly.

She also made ornate Ukrainian Easter eggs known as pysanka. The verb *pysaty* means to write, and the intricate designs of the eggs were essentially written on with beeswax. My strongest memory of Aunt Rhett is watching one of her smooth, neat hands hold a half-painted jewel of an egg while she slowly moved a small wax drawing tool in the other, the heavy sweet smell of beeswax all around her. She had a piano pushed up against one wall of her very small living room. In an old photo, sheet music for Saint-Saën's *Danse Macabre* and Bach's "Two-Part Inventions" lean on the stand. I listened to recordings of each in my room on a Friday morning as I wrote this, hoping to recapture the notes I'd heard fill that miniature house in the woods, wishing I could really remember the moments we sat listening to her play. She had a soft, distinct South Carolina curl to her words that I rarely hear in people anymore, only in a few places on the cassettes and where it still swims in my head.

Aunt Rhett and Momma were sometimes comrades, other times at odds. Momma had encouraged her move, desperate herself for the female companionship, and she was a friend. But Aunt Rhett had a southern belle attitude that sometimes clashed with Momma's more independent ways. Rhett had been the perfect southern daughter until she divorced her husband and later moved to the Ozarks (no small feat of metamorphosis). Daddy had once felt that he disgusted her in his early rebellion from the family. In retrospect, any anger or loathing she displayed during that time may have been envy. Perhaps she already felt trapped in her suburban married life and wished she could be more like her wild brothers.

There were problems between us children too. In their first September with us, Momma referred to my cousins in a letter as "a *big* help" and "good kids."[15] A year after they arrived, she wrote Granminnow that the twelve-year-old had turned to Katy one afternoon and snapped, "Get out of my way, you dumb shit!"[16] Momma, uncharacteristically, grabbed his arm and disciplined him sternly, leading to weeks of silent treatment from Aunt Rhett, who could be as unforgiving as she was loving.

The older boys focused on me in particular, calling me a runt, stuffing me in the Bersches' giant mailbox, pushing my face down to tracked-in mud like a dog; I was whiny, and it fed their teasing.

"On the way home from school the *15 yr. old* told Sarah 'You sure are ugly,'" Momma wrote, "Many times—Can you imagine?"[17]

But David, the youngest, was often a playmate, and we enjoyed treasured moments watching TV with them after school on a tiny set at their

*The Neidhardt/Roberts families in 1979 on our land,
from left, back row: Aunt Mindy, Uncle Lewis, baby Jason, Daddy,
Sarah, Edward, Katy, Momma, Miriam. From left, front row:
Little Richard, Aunt Rhett, and David.*

house. Their bedroom had three twin beds in a row, and the walls were covered with their expertly drawn pictures of barely clad, muscular Conan-like men and women, and a Millennium Falcon model hung from the ceiling. I had no idea what any of it meant.

Aunt Rhett stayed in Fox long after we left—even after her boys had all graduated from the local school—until 1993 when she moved to North Carolina. We rarely saw her and our cousins after we left the woods—probably due to her reclusive nature and lack of closeness with my parents—but I maintained an email relationship with her for years. I saw her in the early aughts at Daddy's house in the Bay Area. Despite gray hair and the lines of age, she was much the same—and as in my childhood, it was her charm that stayed with me. She died in 2014 of a smoking-related illness. Whatever so deeply troubled her, whatever led her to isolate herself, has mostly died with her. But her love of art and music and children lives on through her Ukrainian eggs and her songs. And all three cousins have grown into kind, thoughtful adults.

Though our neighbor Dalton Moody once told Daddy, about getting boys to work that, "One boy is worth a boy. Two boys is worth half a boy. Three boys ain't worth shit."

More and more back-to-the-landers and other outsiders came to Stone County as the years passed: candlemakers, leatherworkers, woodworkers, bakers, cavers, and Vietnam vets—even actor Robin Williams' half-brother had a patch of land for weekend camping down the road and through the woods from us. There were a few small communes, with which we socialized a little; I vaguely remember a skinny-dipping episode—and red pubic hair—that left me perplexed if not exactly scandalized. There was a couple making heavily scented chunk candles by the hundreds. There was a family with two adolescent girls we visited regularly. Their house lives on in my memory as a ramble of spaces and loft rooms, unfinished floors and walls, resting on a gentle slope amid roughshod animal pens and rocky dirt and forest. It wasn't a home so much as a large, makeshift playhouse. There was also a couple my parents enjoyed who built their first house out of hickory poles dug into the ground, bent over in a dome, and tied together. They covered the structure with burlap, then chicken wire, and finally plastered it all with cement; it cracked and leaked like a sieve, so it was abandoned, and they built a proper house. But I remember the brown hump. And a nearby scrap of barbed wire that I stepped on accidently one afternoon with a bare foot. The man worked with Daddy for a time, eating oranges and bunches of raw garlic each morning, the smell overwhelming the small cab of Daddy's truck.

There was a basket maker named Woody who dropped by from time to time, always at mealtimes. "One time he came over unexpectedly just as we had finished eating, stood by the sink and said 'Mind if I clean up?'" Daddy told me. Upon being given permission, he promptly sat down and scraped all our leftover food onto a single plate and devoured it.

Two others who used to drop in at mealtimes were the Pickle brothers. "*Voracious* doesn't quite do them justice," Daddy remembered. They were English and had met John Weaver in Mexico when he rescued them from a broken-down vehicle. They wore out their welcome with everyone in the community—eating their way from house to house—before they finally left as suddenly as they had come. I have no memory of the brothers themselves, but of the yellow school bus they parked in a large clearing of huckleberries down the road from us and of a fateful jar of peanut butter they left on our side porch. Daddy heard a racket outside one late night and went to the living room where the hulking body of a black bear pressed against the window. Daddy grabbed his rifle and opened the side door to see the bear on two legs with a paw in the peanut butter jar. He shot the gun into the air, and the bear slipped back into the dark, ripping up John Weaver's truck before he was done. And thus Pickles and peanut butter and bears were forever linked.

Outsiders were spread out on farms and in campers and tents across the hills, so it was not a particularly tight community, considering it could take an hour or two to drive a relatively short distance. We did get together for holiday feasts, however. As a subculture within the Ozarks, there was an immediate bond, and we often shared common interests. Daddy and Momma shared building and farm tasks with another couple over the years. I remember watching with curiosity as the adults pushed the framed walls up and into place and the eating and music that followed in the yard, one weekend at their house, another at ours.

But just as with any expatriate community, there were some who chose to embrace local culture and others that shunned it. Momma and Daddy had no patience for the latter. Like the expat who both misses her homeland and wants to be seen as belonging to the new world, Momma told me, "On occasion I would be offended if some local immediately thought we were friends with all the hippies." And hippies by Momma's definition were the couple homesteading for a short time at the far end of the dirt road through the woods east of our cabin. They made pulpy, weak watermelon juice from the whole fruit and had wheatgrass growing everywhere, their fey earnestness "more than she could take."

I still see a slow, terrifying drive along a vertiginous mountainside road, the other edge an unprotected drop, to a small wood hovel far under the cover of the forest, where another family of hippies made their home and a small child sat eating a piece of his own feces in the leaves. This is such an enduring memory that I asked my parents who I could be remembering. Momma had no idea. Daddy said it was most likely the watermelon juice couple as the description of the drive and land fit. Neither were shocked nor doubted the details.

Within weeks of our leaving Fox when I was in third grade, we got news that the parents of two good friends of ours from school, Amy and Patty,[†] had been killed. Their prosperous parents came from elsewhere—the father was older and had been a military officer, so they weren't like us, but we were all outsiders. I listened to the adults talk and recorded the details that then fell like a pall over thoughts of Fox. The girls had looked out from a window as a local man gunned down their parents in the front yard with a gun with a silencer. Their parents slumped quietly to the ground by open car doors as the girls watched. We had been to that house. I had driven down that gravel driveway and parked in front of those windows. These images would haunt me. The next day the killer wandered through the woods to the Key Place (or so my father remembers it)—*our* old home—where a young outsider we didn't know was now living and shot him in the stomach. This man's young child ran for help, and he survived. The killer was a cousin of one of our teachers. It was the violent outburst of a crazy person, but it was hard to ignore that the victims were all "from off."

Within months of arriving in Arkansas, Daddy had made a drastic change to his physical appearance for the sake of blending in. Even if mostly for reasons of respect rather than fear, there had to have been some sense that it was safer too. In the spring of 1973, Momma wrote her mother:

> Almost forgot to tell you—Richard has cut his hair *short*—no beard, no hair, jeans + a cowboy hat. He has turned into Arkansas Slim—He looks terribly handsome this way, but also terribly young. Ray just recently followed suit—I think it's partly because the work + the heat dictate short hair—But also they want to distinguish themselves from the average run-of-the-mill hippy who occasionally turns up around here—I suppose it's the fashion among people our age—no one wants to appear too pretentious in front of the people around here who are so simple and god-fearing—and they are so friendly, the idea of shocking them is frightening—so off with the symbol of rebellion—amazing!![18]

It was a story repeated around the country and abroad by back-to-the-landers coming up against often rural and opposing cultures and wanting

† Pseudonyms

to be taken seriously in their new ventures. In April of 1975, Momma's brother, Jock, would write her with a similar story from the Greek village of Anidrous, "The hippies abroad, indeed, have become a bourgeois sub-culture as bad as the middle class ever was. I wear my hair short (still a beard) and try to look presentable when I can these days 'cause I don't in any way wish to be mistaken as one of that crowd . . . oh, yes, indeed, I am a hippie, but not of the sort filling up the cafes in this area these days . . . not by a long shot."[19]

Nine

IN THE KITCHEN

When from a long-distant past nothing subsists, after the people
are dead, after the things are broken and scattered, taste and smell
alone, more fragile but more enduring, more unsubstantial, more
persistent, more faithful, remain poised a long time, like souls,
remembering, waiting, hoping, amid the ruins of all the rest; and
bear unflinchingly, in the tiny and almost impalpable drop of
their essence, the vast structure of recollection.
—Marcel Proust, *Remembrance of Things Past*[1]

 "All my clothes have a line of stove black right where my stomach hits the stove as I cook," Momma wrote in our first autumn in the cabin, "After a year and a half of cursing, I've grown quite used to the old thing and on a cool September morning there's nothing more pleasant than the smell of wood fire."[2]

Whether it was 20°F or 100°F outside, Momma heated water and cooked all of our meals on the hot woodstove that had to be constantly fed and tended. She woke early like pioneer women of yore to build the fire and cook Daddy's bacon and eggs or grits with pats of butter and salt and pepper. The stove's fuel was plentiful on the farm but required work—you didn't want to be caught on a cold, early morning with no wood for the fire. "Wood cookery takes organization, planning, + patience," she had written Aunt Ruth in our first months in Arkansas.[3]

Momma got a propane stove in the summer of 1977 but kept the woodstove, which came in handy when gas went up 50 percent in 1980.[4] The woodstove and its heavy iron lids under which the fire burned is the only appliance I remember inside the cabin.

The cupboards and counters of the kitchen were cluttered with dishes, kitchen implements (from a KitchenAid mixer to a hand-cranked,

*Uncle Jock with Momma in the cabin
feeding me and Katy in June 1974.*

*Uncle Jock with Katy on the porch with the blue
propane fridge and Momma in the background in
the kitchen/main room of the cabin in June 1974.*

wood-paddle butter churn), and washed plastic bags and jars for reuse. (Much as our front yard was the outdoor version, crowded with the various tools, scrap lumber, and machines in use or waiting to be.) There was a propane refrigerator and then an electric one in later years, "a frost-free which automatically defrosts on the kitchen floor."[5] All were bought used or given to us.

More of the book staples of our childhood were in the kitchen too: the *Tassajara Bread Book*, covered in flour dust, grease spots, hardened and dimpled over the years, a recipe for Momma's Thanksgiving crescent rolls taped inside the front cover; *La cuisine et un jeu d'enfants* by Michel Oliver with recipes in English and French for children and bright whimsical illustrations of measuring spoons and ingredients (I have this one now, its soiled paper spine hanging off in chunks, scales of glue crumbling off the threads); the indispensable *Joy of Cooking*; and, least useful, but most memorable, the *Gourmet [Magazine] Cookbook* two-volume set my parents got for their wedding. Katy and I opened the maroon covers adorned with gold filigree designs over and over to admire mouthwatering, full-color images of creamy pastry desserts and exotic lovelies like œufs à la neige that looked like a sweet dream to eat. I sat on the rough kitchen floor in tears of longing as I gazed on the glossy pictures.

To satisfy the sugar cravings they aroused, Momma occasionally mixed butter, sugar, and raw oatmeal into balls for us to devour. On special occasions, she made dense but satisfying whole wheat cakes or lemon quick bread with a sugar, butter, lemon icing drizzled down the furrow split open across the golden crust. Occasionally, one of Granminnow's foil-wrapped carrot breads would arrive in the mail. But desserts and sugar were rare and, with whole wheat flour and molasses having a firm hold on Momma's recipes, often a bust.

I wrote a letter to Santa when I was five with one simple request: "Please send me some chocolate cherris. Thank you & Merry Christmas, Sarah."[6]

The first year in the cabin, Momma hauled water back from the well a distance of nearly two city blocks with us in tow. We grew our own vegetables and raised our own animals for meat and milk. Although we would always supplement our food supply at the grocery store, it was very much a farm-to-table diet. The learning curve was steep. Momma was a college girl, and dinner had been a perfunctory act in her home growing up that didn't involve children: roast beef and potatoes on Sundays; lamb with mint jelly and peas; quivering tomato aspic with avocados and shrimp that her great aunt Minnie made, set out on fine china with a sterling spoon to serve. Daddy grew up with pork roast and pickles, spaghetti, fried fish, shad roe and grits for Saturday brunch, canned butter beans, candied yams, and Brunswick stew. Our food came from the land and was a time-consuming endeavor and sometimes in short supply. Momma had to learn to cook standard fare over wood heat but also foods unusual to her: hearts, tongues, kidneys, and liver, since we were butchering whole animals; wild game; and foraged foods.

What wasn't produced on the farm, Momma got at the local WIC office (of the Women, Infants, and Children federal low-income nutrition program) or bought during a weekly trip to the Nu-Way Foods in Mountain View: dried beans, flour, sugar, grains, cheese, Pace picante sauce, Tabasco, pickles, fruits, fruit juice, coffee, tea, spices, vegetables when there were deficiencies in our own supply, Ivory dish soap, Bon Ami, Ajax, Windex, and vitamins. I have a memory of leaving the parking lot of a grocery store and unwrapping liverwurst in the car, Katy peeling off the thin white strip of fat to eat. And of playing with the S&H Green Stamps the stores gave us; Momma bought ceramic plates for a cousin's wedding from the S&H catalog with saved stamps, one of the few things we shared with the rest of America. We also occasionally bought large chunks of cheese cut from a wheel at Hollis Treat's Market in nearby Timbo, and Momma ordered some specialty health foods from the Walnut Acres catalog out of Pennsylvania.

A few things were also purchased at Ticer's Market in "central" Fox—a feeble scattering of businesses and homes—but the store was small with out-of-date canned goods and limited fresh food. I remember the screen door, the low ceiling, the standard convenient store shelves, but mostly the name, Ticer's, Ticer's, Ticer's. Like ice, like trike, like tick. And that it was at Ticer's Market that Uncle Lewis taught us to pour Planters salted peanuts in the tube-shaped bag down the neck of a bottle of cold Coke, a sweet, salty delicacy that would normally have been forbidden.

In the summer of 1975, Momma wrote of torrential rains and a garden not up to the locals' standards but "good enough for us beginners—corn, squash, melons, potatoes (huge), green beans, peppers—yeah!"[7]

Daddy pulled tomato plants out in the fall with green tomatoes still clinging to the branches and hung the plants—root and all—upside down inside above the doorway between the original cabin and the kitchen addition. The fruit ripened in the warmth of the woodstove and provided us with fresh tomatoes as late as Christmas, imperfect red tomatoes that were at least better than the watery flesh at the grocery store, which Daddy refused. I relished thick slices of tomato covered with homemade mayonnaise and salt and pepper. Or the green ones, dipped in cornmeal and fried, sweet and sour and warm.

In warm weather, Momma and Daddy would process as much chicken meat as they could for the freezer that was kept outside hooked up to the propane tank. Daddy lopped their heads off with an axe on a big stump by the side porch. Katy and I played in the dirt nearby, unimpressed by the black-red stain soaking the wood but amused by the chickens' last headless leaps.

The local country people spun chickens around and snapped their necks, as they did to snakes. Pappy claimed to know how to hypnotize a chicken, something he'd spoken of since Daddy was a child, perhaps picked up in the small-town Ohio of his youth. When he visited us on the land, he flipped a chicken over on its back and moved his pointer finger around and around the bird's beak. The chicken lay still and silent, mesmerized by the turning digit or perhaps entering a state of frightened semi-paralysis to feign death. (A quick Google search revealed this as the Oscillating Finger Method with how-tos on everywhere from Wikipedia to the Smithsonian to HGTV.)

Momma and Daddy would dip the headless chicken carcass in boiling water to loosen the feathers, pluck it, light a stick of tightly rolled newspaper or paper bag and wave it quickly over the bald skin to singe off tiny white splinters of pinfeather pushing through the pale flesh, dip it in cold water, cut it up, and freeze it—dip, pluck, singe, dip, cut, freeze—dip, pluck, singe, dip, cut, freeze. That smell of burnt feather is still in my nose. A table was set up outside to process the chicken, and flies were everywhere dropping quickly onto the meat leaving their tiny white eggs behind. But Momma refused to throw the labored-over meat away, instead rinsing it and hoping for the best.

Daddy only ever butchered one cow, an eight-hundred-pound steer for a friend, who was called away suddenly by news of a farrowing sow just after the steer was killed. He took our cows and hogs to be slaughtered in Mountain View. Our home freezer was not equipped to freeze that quantity of fresh meat. The butcher cut, wrapped, and froze the meat for a cheap price. In our first September on the land, Momma wrote, "We now have a freezer with a pig and ½ a beef in it. We raised 2 pigs + traded 1 for some beef."[8] Daddy wrote a year later, in a rare letter, that we'd had a calf butchered and had three hundred pounds of beef in the freezer and two hogs ready for the butcher.[9] In the early summer of 1977, Momma wrote Granminnow that they'd just filled the freezer "with 510 lbs. of meat, a calf and hog that we had butchered. It gives me a nice feeling of security as you can imagine."[10]

Scrapple was a delicious breakfast, crispy and rich from hot fat in a well-used iron pan. Momma most likely got her recipe from the first *Foxfire* book. In the chapter titled "Recipes for Hog," is:

> SCRAPPLE—As told by Mrs. Mann Norton, "Take th' head, an' take th' eyeballs out, an' th' ears, an' cut down in there. Then y'got all th' hairs off of it. Y'put it in a big pot an' cooked it til th' meat just turned loose of th' main big bone.
>
> "Y'lifted them bones out, an' laid your meat over in there an' felt of it with your hands t'see if they wadn't no bones in it. Then y'strain yer liquid through a strainer so th' little bones'd come out. Put'cher liquid back in a pot, and put that mashed meat back in that liquid. Put'cher sage an' pepper in there. Then y'stir it 'til it got t'boilin'. Then y'stick plain corn meal in there til it's just plumb thick. Then y'pour it up in a mold, an' cut it off'n fry it, an' brown it. Tastes just like fish."[11]

Our large top-opening freezer outside in the yard was filled with neat, odd-shaped white bundles of beef and pork; or the occasional wild animal: snake, snapping turtle, deer, possum; and sitting on top, a large, black trash bag or two hiding a hog's head.

"I boiled about two of those pigs' heads and then I had to put a stop to it," Momma told me. Daddy was telling everyone who didn't know what to do with their pigs' heads to give them to us. "But it's a lot of work messing with a big pig's head," she said. I watched her in the kitchen peeling back the black plastic and hoisting the enormous, fleshy pink head, gone cold and rubbery, onto the counter, breaking it up into smaller bits that would fit in the big black stockpot. Those two heads created enough scrapple to last in my memory over thirty years.

But Momma's crispy, thin, panfried pork chops were my favorite. She served them with collard greens, cooked the hippie way by boiling them lightly with no pork fat, and topped them with apple cider vinegar—tangy pools of caramelized pork fat and pot likker and vinegar melting into mashed potatoes and iceberg lettuce. (I loved vinegar, often sipping slowly from glasses of vinegar and water Momma gave us.)

More memorable than meat are bowls of pinto beans with cornbread or the just-firm, dry curds of homemade cottage cheese with a generous sprinkling of black pepper on top. I loved cold pinto bean sandwiches with mayonnaise; grits with butter and Pace picante sauce; and "tortillas," as we called burritos, a make-your-own smorgasbord of beans, ground beef, cheese, tomatoes, onions, and lettuce. Momma ground corn once or twice for tortillas, but found it too time consuming, so she stuck to making whole wheat ones. She included a recipe for her tortillas in the Head Start newsletter she put together after we started school in 1977:

Tortillas De Harina Del Norte
(Wheat Tortillas from the North)

2 C. all-purpose flour (I use 1 c. white and 1 c. whole wheat)
1 t. salt
1 t. baking powder
1 T. lard
¾ c. cold water, about

Thoroughly mix the ingredients. Cut in the lard and add enough water to make a stiff dough. Divide into egg-size balls and roll out on to a lightly floured board, making them as thin as possible. Bake about 2 minutes on each side on an ungreased frying pan. Makes about 1 dozen.

May then be fried for crisp tostadas, or, if not fried, they should be immediately placed between paper towels to keep them soft for tortillas. Fill with meat, beans, onions, cheese, etc., or put honey in them for a dessert snack.[12]

Biscuits and gravy were also on regular rotation, the gravy just a salt and pepper béchamel with no sausage ("milk gravy"), the biscuits mixed with whole wheat flour but moist and toothsome under the cream. And chiles rellenos with bites of sweet, sharp pepper covered in egg and cheese were on the table enough for me to remember them.

Occasionally we had Shit on a Shingle—memorable only for its name—creamed chipped beef on toast, an army food Momma had eaten at a friend's house as a child. There was brewer's yeast on our popcorn and Tiger's Milk from Adelle Davis's book—milk, banana, brewer's yeast, and wheat germ. (A store-bought commercial version was also available that we occasionally drank.) Celestial Seasonings Red Zinger and Sleepytime teas were in the house when we could afford them, both introduced by the hippie company in Colorado the year I was born. There was buttery cornmeal mush; thick cream from the Jersey cow in Momma's morning coffee; and homemade butter from the churn slathered on thick, warm slices of freshly baked brown bread. Momma didn't make butter often—too much work—but I do recall unctuous swirls of creamy, yellow butter stuck to the wooden paddles in the big glass jar. ("I'm not called a fussy man, just give me a little piece of butter for my bread!" Katy and I declare on the tapes we made for Granminnow at the time, quoting loosely from the A. A. Milne poem Momma had been reading us.[13])

Around 1980, Momma gave up smoking. This "has put an extra 9 lbs. on me—which is awful," she wrote Granminnow, "I really don't want to smoke anymore, but it is a substitute for putting food in the mouth."[14] I remember Momma standing in the kitchen around this time, on a high-fat fad diet, putting thick slices of butter on cheese in her mouth.

After one of my grandmother's visits, Momma wrote to her with two recipes for dinners she had cooked during the visit, recipes she told me she cooked at least once a week throughout those years, cream and rice making leftovers stretch for days. I remember the curry well and now have it in my pile of clipped recipes to cook. It hasn't happened yet, but I know from memory that it will be filling and good when it does:

1—Sauté onions
   add + cook hamburger

cook rice, add 1 or 2 eggs, stir.

mix all together + season heavily with curry powder

2—In top of double boiler put:

    3 T. cream cheese

    1 clove garlic

    3 T. oil

    3 T. parmesan cheese

    salt (1 tsp. I think)

    chopped parsley

mix together

add: ½ c. cream (or milk, or powd. milk, or canned milk). At this pt. beat until thick then add mushrooms/or canned shrimp/or anything you want

This is enough for about 1 person, so increase amts. accordingly. Serve over spaghetti.[15]

It was exciting to find these recipes in the letters since Momma never taught us much in the kitchen. My maternal grandmother had made clear that play was the realm of children, and Momma followed her example, another remnant of privilege that stayed with us. Preparing food was the drudgery of womanhood, even if at times also its triumph. And Momma was too harried to stand by while young children spilled the flour and slowed dinner down.

We had our animals and our garden, government staples, and grocery food, but we also had foraged fare. On a late July afternoon in 1977, it was 100°F outside and Momma was spending the day "freezing tomatoes and picking elderberries."[16] She made elderberry juice and jam, but it is the distinct earthy taste of a fresh elderberry I hold on to.

Sumac (*Rhus*) was a shrub or small tree that flourished like a weed all around our land with upright panicles of fuzzy, flat sour berries covered in acidic red hairs. (The locals called it "shoe-make" or "shoe-mak."[17]) Momma made sumac juice in the washing machine on the front porch. She had read in Euell Gibbon's book *Stalking the Wild Asparagus* about what he called *Rhus*-ade:

When we go out for elderberries we also gather a bushel or two of
sumac. Formerly, we only used it to make a cooling drink very like pink
lemonade to ease us through the August "dog days." [. . .] Try to gather
your sumac before hard rains wash out most of the acid. The American
Indians liked this cool, sour drink so well they used to gather large quantities of the heads when they were in their prime and dry them indoors,
so they could make this beverage all winter.

Once, our method of preparing it was to put the heads in a large
container, cover them with water, and pound and stir it for ten minutes
with a wooden pestle or potato masher. My son, disliking hard work in
hot weather, invented a new process. He just dumped a basket of sumac
heads into the washing machine, covered them with water and set the
washer to run ten minutes, then caught the *Rhus*-ade in our big canning
kettle as the washer pumped it out.

Always strain this juice through several thicknesses of cloth to
remove all the fine hairs. Sweetened to taste, it is quite as palatable as
lemonade.[18]

I gulped down faint pink glasses of the mildly sweet juice.

Daddy picked morel mushrooms when he could find them. When out
on walks in the woods with us, he remembers pointing out the pale orange
and yellow frillery of coral mushrooms that we plucked from the ground
to take home, being careful to eat only a little to avoid diarrhea.

Katy sprinkled cat-shit sand from our sandbox on crackers and sucked
dirt off earthworms she pulled from the ground. I stuck to eating the
wood sorrel that grew everywhere. I coveted the seedpods with their
concentrated burst of sour oxalic acid. And I popped cherry tomatoes
in my mouth in the garden and ran through the rows, peeked under the
cold frames made from old windows hinged to frames, and poked at the
compost pile. When I was four, Momma transcribed my thoughts for
Granminnow:

> Dear Granminnow,
> I found some okra in the garden.
> Thanks for sending books to me.
> Sarah[19]

Even grasshoppers entered our palate a few times. Daddy would pop
them in his mouth on occasion to thrill us and did get us to try them. He

explained how to hold the large hind jumping legs back between our two fingers to experience the nutty body without getting kicked. He had been taught to eat them as a child by the assistant minister at his church who was interested in the outdoors and survival skills. Daddy had kept the practice up throughout high school to gross people out and get attention. Most of the oddities introduced to us in the woods were quotidian. I didn't flinch at butchering blood or eating game, but grasshoppers I knew were just weird and Daddy was a little savage, but I loved that.

We drank rose hip tea and ate lamb's-quarter, dandelion greens, watercress, and boiled pokeweed leaves in the spring (poke salat). Pokeweed grew prolifically wherever Daddy would burn a brush pile, and we only ate the tender young shoots to avoid too-high concentrations of toxic alkaloids. After years of thinking of it as an Ozark plant, I saw it suddenly in Portland a few years ago, and this year it's become an aggressive weed in my yard. I snapped off a leaf and broke it in half to smell. It was without a doubt the deep green, slightly astringent smell of the poke plant I remembered growing in our Ozark garden. My neighbors have let one grow unfettered in their front yard—the red-fuchsia stalk, big green leaves, glossy falls of poison purple-black berries. An ugly plant. Too red, too purple. Too gangly. The singer Tony Joe White, who lived in Stone County too, wrote his famous song "Polk Salad Annie" about eating pokeweed:

> Used to know a girl lived down there
> And she'd go out in the evenings and pick her a mess of it
> Carry it home and cook it for supper
> 'Cause that's about all they had to eat

We picked blackberries in the overgrown, perilous bramble down the road, full of thorns, snakes, and who knows what. We also had a wild native persimmon tree in our front yard, but I hated persimmons. They left a chalky tackiness in the mouth when not quite ripe and were too fleshy and rich otherwise. I have a clear memory of standing next to Momma in the kitchen while she mashed persimmons with a wooden pestle and conical strainer, maybe making a recipe she refers to in a 1975 letter to Granminnow: "I've been using the [nursery] school cookbook quite a bit lately. Ask Bish E—— (if you see her) if her persimmon cookies are supposed to have flour in them and, if so, how much?"[20]

Dogs loved to eat ripe persimmons rotting on the ground, but the seeds were large and flat with sharp edges that came back out tearing at flesh.

In Stone County, when a man had a fright, he shook "like a dog shittin' persimmon seeds."

George Bersch wrote Momma a letter in the early nineties right after Granminnow died. He reminisced about a musical and potluck we had had at their house in the cabin years for which Momma "had cooked a 'coon'" and Daddy "had killed a rattler which he skinned, cut up, and cooked [. . .] for our supper."[21] We were hardly possum-farmers—living off what we hunted and trapped—but Daddy experimented with wild animals. Possum and snapping turtle were creatures that made it into our freezer if not our stomachs, but we definitely ate squirrel.

"Welp, today we moved the freezer [. . .] we got six squirrel in the freezer. Wooo . . . that's a lot of *squiirrrels*!" my cousin David says on the audio recording I have from Christmas 1978, "Edward got, uh, lemme see, four of 'em, and Dingo [the dog] killed one, and Richard got one, *Little* Richard."[22]

The tape breaks off and starts up on another day.

"We cut a lot of wood today," says Edward, the oldest brother.

"It's almost five o'clock in the evening and boy, we got a lot," says twelve-year-old Little Richard, in his thick accent.

"Kilt my back," says Edward.

"Yeah, it was hard. But we did it. [. . .] We've got six squirrels and Mom's cookin' 'em all up tonight and Wendy and them are comin' down, everybody up thar. We got seven really, because this morning we went out huntin' and got another squirrel. Well, it's gonna be a pretty big supper and it's gonna be good," says Richard.[23]

I remember the squirrel. Or how it looked, not how it tasted. It was an emaciated little body, clearly discernible as a rodent, spread out naked and pawless under a thick brown blanket of gravy and dumplings. The boys cut the paws off with an ax, made slits up the legs and belly and around the head before pulling the fur from their bodies like latex gloves from a hand, leaving gleaming pink skin.

Daddy ate fried squirrel and squirrel and dumplings over mashed potatoes for lunch when he built chicken houses for locals. For the midday meal, even on the hottest days, the wife of the house would set out huge lunches with the squirrel or fried chicken, two or three different kinds of beans, corn bread, biscuits, boiled potatoes, sliced tomatoes, green beans, and collards.

Momma couldn't bring herself to cook squirrel at our house. She got it as far as the cutting board, but it looked too much like a rat. She did occasionally cook the rabbits we raised. We avoided wild rabbits for fear of "rabbit fever"—also known as tularemia or, more repulsively, meat-cutter's disease—at that time more prevalent in Arkansas than any other state.[24] (I've since learned that my parents were fooled by the local nomenclature rabbit fever, as we could have gotten the disease from any number of wild creatures, including ticks, deer, and squirrels. "Mad squirrel disease" comes from eating their brains, which Daddy did.)

In the late seventies, on his way home from Mountain View, Daddy rounded a curve to see a man standing next to his car on the side of the road with the radiator steaming. Daddy pulled over to help and saw that the man had hit a deer, still alive and flopping around in the ditch. A regular mountain man by that point, Daddy took out his gun and walked around the truck. He planned to put the deer out of its misery, but it died before he had to pull the trigger. (Before they moved to Arkansas, Momma had said there would be no guns in the house. But Daddy had at least four—a pistol my paternal great-grandfather had used during WWI, a shotgun for bird hunting, a .22 rifle, and a deer rifle. In a photo taken after we left the woods, two of the guns lie ominously in a rack resting on a box of *World Books* from Pappy in our living room while Katy dances in the foreground.)

According to state law, you were required to report such an incident to the Fish & Game Department, but the man who'd hit the deer was from out of state and confused. Daddy saw an opportunity.

"I'll take care of that—just help me put him in back of my pickup."

He brought the deer home, dressed the carcass, and put it in the freezer.

Our first Thanksgiving table on the land in 1974 had not included the sterling silver and turkey and creamed onions and crescent rolls we would enjoy later. Instead, Momma had written, "We are to have a goat roast for Thanksgiving—One of our goats will be butchered + barbecued outside—many are invited, but I don't know how many will come."[25] Although we had numerous goat roasts through the years, Momma told me, "I have only one memory of Richard killing the goat before he butchered it. He had a pistol and shot it in the head." She and Katy and I held each other in the cabin as the human cry of the goat rang out and then stopped. It was a good lesson for us, she felt, that meat involves killing, and it did not dampen our appetites.

Our youngest cousin, David, was eight, new to the country, and wearing white when he first experienced a goat roast. He walked around a corner just as Daddy ripped the knife down the goat's gut, and some of the butchering blood got on his clothes. He threw up on his shoes. A few hours later we were all sitting in front of the cabin gnawing on the dead animal.[26]

Only Daddy developed a lasting taste for goat. He still appreciates a meal where all parts of the beast are on offer—he wants to taste the animal's musk in his bite—but this is partly a trait of nature rather than nurture, and years of goat and wild animal meat did not inure me to the flavor. The goat's musky fat gives its meat and milk a flavor that to me tastes like a goat smells, or worse, like the rank stink of a rattlesnake.

Ten

BACK ON THE FARM

Cool weather + flowers + dogwood + redbud.
—April 23, 1975, postcard from Momma to Granminnow

 "Thank you again for giving us such a wonderful vacation," I read with great relief in Momma's first letter of 1975, to Aunt Ruth, "Home was in satisfactory condition when we came back and all the livestock seemed healthy and happy."[1]

We had spent Christmas in Colorado at last.

We stayed with Granminnow and visited with great uncles and aunts. And we visited my grandfather, Granpa Will, in the high-altitude meadow town of Allenspark surrounded by mountain peaks and thin, piney air. He eventually fell into drinking while we were there, setting into what Momma called in a letter, "harangues + bad morning mood," but not before he had time to show us a little warmth.[2] He leaned his tall, heavy body down to Katy one afternoon and said, with genuine and not often expressed feeling that moved Momma, "I love you Kate." He was a brilliant, once-successful sociology professor, a tall block of a man, charming, angry, and manic-depressive. On the handful of occasions that we spent any time with him in the years to come, he was alternately warm and gruff, snapping at his son, Uncle Jock, or bringing Momma to tears. He was overweight and slightly disheveled, pushing stray, long gray-blond locks back flatly with his giant hands. We stayed quiet and watched him, not daring to speak, but somehow liking him all the same, a great sweet soul seeping silently from him.

The trip to Colorado was restorative in the luxury of Granminnow's home, and Momma wrote to her that she "suffered a bit of culture shock readjusting to housekeeping in the woods" but that she was "fired with new energies."[3] On the outside of the envelope, she apologized for a bounced check, complaining, "We are completely broke—We will get a

Daddy holding me on the porch and Katy
crawling up to it in about January 1975.

check the 1st—and Richard has work which should start bringing in a little money by the weekend (also we have food stamps to eat on) so all is not lost." It was such an economical life with so much salvaged, bought old and cheap, grown and raised, and there were bits of money coming in regularly and even occasional chunks. But it all dissolved as quickly as it came, in large part to the creation of a farm infrastructure that would in theory pay for itself in the long run—housing, electricity, plumbing, barn, fences, animals, and feed—and a construction business that required a vehicle and tools. And for many weeks of the year, Daddy was without paid work, lost to weather and illness and injury.

Within days of Momma's letters home to family, sickness gripped our household, and this time the life-threatening fragility of our arrangement was even clearer.

On a cold morning that January, when people around the country were turning on TVs to watch the news of Watergate and a new show called

Wheel of Fortune, I woke from a fitful night of coughing.[4] I lay huddled with my parents and baby sister on a mattress in the tiny loft of our cabin. The forest closed tightly around us and all around stood bare, its once green finery lying in a crumpled brown carpet for miles. I was almost three and my sister was one. A green plug of mucous still hung from her nose from the intractable colds we had had that winter. I labored next to her, weak and hot with a deep, hacking cough.

Momma and Daddy, with uncharacteristic alarm, dressed quickly under the low roof and descended the ladder staircase. My wheezing chest was now an emergency, and the nearest doctor was in Clinton, twenty-five miles away down Fox Mountain through the craggy undulations of the Ozarks. Momma poured cold water from a plastic jug she'd filled at the well into a metal basin on the woodstove and splashed her face. Chill air blew through the cabin's cracks, but there was no time for a fire. Momma buried us in her lap under a down sleeping bag.

Daddy carried me to our old Chevy sedan still bundled in the downy nylon, a vivid orange parcel against that gray-brown morning like one of the wild persimmons in our autumn yard. Our hound dog, Old Belle, loped out from under the porch and lingered by the warm spot the car left as Daddy pulled onto the dirt road. We drove slowly down the heavily wooded hill, bouncing and jolting along the deep ruts, to the main highway three miles away.

After nearly an hour's drive on winding country roads, we pulled up and parked in front of an old brick building. As Momma held me in the small, crowded waiting room, she suspected even before the doctor gave his diagnosis that I had pneumonia. She wrapped me in the itchy down again, and we drove home with a bottle of penicillin. Within a few days, I was well.

The episode frightened Momma. She felt more insecure than ever in this neo-pioneer life she had reluctantly entered. What if she had waited a day or two longer to take me in? What if the car hadn't started? Illness and danger lay in constant wait: venomous snakes or spiders in brush piles; poisonous mushrooms breaking through the leaf mold; invisible bacteria and parasites swimming in our cold glasses of raw milk. We could get lost in the woods, fall down a cliff, or drown in our pond. Momma's letters speak very little to this fact, but since my sisters and I have had children, she has spoken openly of how anxious she was about our well-being. But her nature was to take anxiety and mull it over maybe late in the night or in a sudden flash by the well, but to just as quickly tamp it down as deep as she could, a Pandora's box in reverse, her demons being sucked back under a closed lid.

That winter began sunny and warm but was followed by cold, a week of rain and sleet, and then "a foot of beautiful powdery snow" in mid-March.[5] The construction business was in its usual weather-induced winter slump, and Daddy was unemployed again, looking hard for a job. "He even has little cards printed: 'Richard Neidhardt—Carpenter'—but all quite futile in these hard times," Momma wrote Granminnow.

The worrisome ebb and flow of money was aggravated by "tensions around the house [with] monsieur home all the time with nothing to do."[6] Momma hints at his irritability throughout her letters but resists open complaint. She had remarked in a fall letter that when he was a child he "had to have something like 100 little shots to find out what he was allergic to and *then* a shot every week for *years*—No wonder he's a little testy sometimes!"[7]

Her casual tone disguises the fact that his temper and biting, impatient words left her chronically furious and hurt. Neither of them had the language to communicate their real feelings to one another effectively, both raised to endure or explode, but not to ameliorate with apology or explanation. Nor did they ever show any physical affection towards one another—other than a healthy marital sex life, which Momma has alluded to. They never held hands or cuddled or hugged, nothing more than a quick kiss each morning as Daddy walked out the door. This was a cultural norm for both of them, and one which I in particular, as the eldest child, absorbed fully. To this day, I cannot utter the words "I love you" to my parents or sisters without feeling immense discomfort, although we have a warm, close bond. (On a cassette tape for Granminnow when I was *five*, I said earnestly, "I love Aunt Sarah. Give her a kiss." Momma responded with a laugh, "You're so *saccharine*, Sarah."[8]) Casual, regular physical affection with fellow adults is not in my body's vernacular. My warmth comes through laughter and conversation and a relaxed acceptance of others, as it did for Momma and Daddy.

As March turned into April, my health and the weather improved, as did building activity. The deciduous world surrounding us was erupting in a glorious pointillist fuzz of lime, pink, red, and yellow leaf buds. Katy and I ran around under the spring colors in hot pink and yellow, our new coats from Granminnow. To thank her, we drew chicken scratch pictures on some of Mammy's old South Carolina Eye Bank letterhead (she was the executive director of the bank), "A wild squirrel that would hurt you," and "Another squirrel with little scraper things on it that would hurt you."[9] (Annotated by Momma, of course.)

May brought another setback. Daddy fell from a scaffolding at work onto his leg and dislocated his knee. Momma wrote:

> Richard [. . .] must sit or lie down all day. He was injured a week ago and is still a long way from recovery (the doctor had to take fluid off his knee today which put him in the worst pain since the accident). He was about to finish one job and start another—the 1st work he's found since winter—He had just started his own contracting business—and now he's really slowed down—It is maddening. Thank God we had some alcohol + books on hand or he wouldn't have made it through the week—How he will face another week like this and possibly 3 or 4, I don't know—But he remains marginally cheerful.[10]

Daddy was out of work for four weeks. The morning after his accident, Momma taught herself to milk the cow, and from then on, they shared the milking chore. "Which, for me, was not really a chore, but more like meditation," Daddy told me, remembering fondly how in the early mornings before work, he would sit on an upturned bucket and lean his head into the cow's warm flank and milk away. Momma wrote Granminnow that she felt she was "working like a dog trying to do both [of their] chores."[11] After a month, Daddy was still walking with a limp but back at work building houses.

April's daffodils and dogwood and redbud gave way to the blooms of iris and clover in May, and the wild azaleas and black locusts were "perfuming the forest."[12] It was our third spring in the Ozarks, and Momma marveled at how "It's harder to cut the trees down here than to grow them!"[13] Daddy fenced the garden with the same black locust poles he had used elsewhere, and Momma looked forward to a rich harvest to fill her new propane freezer set up in the yard and melons for relief in the August heat.

Mammy and Pappy visited at the end of June in cool, damp weather with, Momma wrote, "a nauseatingly rich lemon meringue pie" in hand, symbolic of the excesses my parents had left behind.[14] "They are *so* nice to me," Momma wrote my grandmother, "but I find their visits an increasing ideological strain."

How they arrived is a mystery. They drove in from South Carolina, or they flew in to Little Rock, then drove in. They arrived one June day in their tidy suburban clothes with suitcases in hand and slept in a tent, tiny Adelaide and tall Dick. They were musical and light-hearted, but believed in spare the rod, spoil the child. Mammy's voice was thick with the south, her *r*'s disappearing into *h*'s as she spoke, and her stories were interesting to Momma but dripping in genteel racism and classism. Their politics were Strom Thurmond and Richard Nixon (Pappy knew Thurmond— Mammy called him, "Dick's friend, Strummy"; she hated him). Momma and Daddy took pains to avoid all talk of politics; when they visited us the summer before, Nixon had just resigned, but no one dared broach the subject.

One afternoon, Pappy chatted with Katy and me outside the cabin, and he captured the moment on a tape recorder. Nowhere on the recording do I hear the stern father or the conservative businessman, just a grand-father delighting in his grandchildren.

"Sarah, can you sing for me?" Pappy asks me in his radio-star voice, "What kind of song do you know?"

"The song what Katy talks about," I say, my three-year-old syntax a bit confused.

"Is that right?" says Pappy.

"What is going over my bloon [balloon]?" I say.

"There's that old bee, back again," Pappy replies, "Bee, get out of here. Get out of here, Bee. It's on Mammy's suitcase. Don't swat at 'im!"

"Why?" I say.

"Cuz he might get mad and bite you!" Pappy says.

"Why?" I say.

"Cuz ol' bees get mad quick."

"Why they get mad?"

Pappy doesn't reply and a bee-shooing scuffle ensues. Katy babbles in two-year incoherence about honey. I giggle. A cock crows.

"It's nice when bees make honey for us, but it isn't nice when they sting us," says Pappy.

"K-k-katy, you're the only girl I ever saw," I begin to sing, finally getting

back to the song I know, "K-k-k, pig . . . The moon is over the pig sheeed
. . ." A bird sings and the cock crows again.[15]

Earl Morris's son drove up to the land in July 1975 on his tractor with a
trencher and ripped a ditch for a water line from the pump house to the
cabin. Three days into August, Momma could write, "we *finally* have running water. [. . .] What a weight that is off my mind (+ body)—Life seems
much happier."[16] The water did not run inside, but to a spigot right outside
with a hose attached. Momma no longer had to make the long trek to the
pump house for containers of water to be carried haltingly back while
prodding two children along or, return to find us awake after napping,
screaming hysterically at the window. (A traumatic memory for a mother,
not remembered by us.) A month later, Daddy plumbed cold water to the
kitchen sink.[17]

Torrential rains in August renewed a parched garden, and we enjoyed
our first watermelons and cantaloupes. Corn, squash, "huge" potatoes,
green beans, and peppers also filled the rows. Momma worked hard to
freeze and can it all.[18]

Daddy's job situation, which changed as rapidly as the weather, was
finally stable in that relatively cool summer. He had started his own construction company with two official employees and was working on a
small retirement development twenty-five miles away in Fairfield Bay. "So
we have great hopes that this will provide a future for us here," Momma
wrote.[19]

And indeed it did seem that way for at least a short time. I was completely surprised when I read a letter from mid-August in which Momma
discussed a "pleasure trip" she and Daddy took to Little Rock, with a bit
of pocket money from Granminnow. I had never known them to do such
a thing in all their years of marriage, but especially not in those years of
poverty and farm demands. Although Little Rock was only a few hours
away, we rarely went. The farm couldn't be left for long, gas was expensive, our cars were unreliable, the roads were windy and slow, and what
could we afford once we got there? Even Momma was sure this couldn't
have happened, but there it was in the letter. They left me and Katy in
Fox with some friends (no one remembers who), and, Momma wrote,

"3 children, a billion baby kitties, and a baby pig rushed out to greet the kids when we left them—they did *not* shed a tear the whole weekend over our departure." My parents spent the night at Uncle Lewis's house in Little Rock, where he had settled. They heard disco for the first time, and hated it, but Momma wrote, "I bought new clothes and we went out to dinner at a wonderful seafood restaurant ($6.95 a plate but worth it)—an elegant evening and a really wonderful short vacation."[20]

Their needs were still too great for Momma to wish for any more frivolity. She asked her mother for forty dollars for her twenty-ninth birthday in September, to pay for a new pair of eyeglasses. "I desperately need them," she wrote, "My old ones are held together by masking tape."[21]

Momma had enrolled me that August in the local public school, Rural Special. I was only three and a half, but Momma wrote Granminnow, "They have a kindergarten here (Head Start*) but not enough 5 yr. olds, so they let in 4 yr. olds—but they don't have enough 4 yr. olds, so they let in 3½ yr. olds."[22] It meant a mile drive to the bus stop and then an hour ride to school each way, five days a week. Momma worried I was too little, but the teachers talked her into it, and she knew there were other kids on our road to watch over me on the bus. I left each morning at 7:30 a.m. and arrived home at 4:00 p.m. It was stimulation for me, a break for Momma, a free hot lunch and snack, and a nap.

Momma spent an early September Friday at school with me. It was muggy and hot even as we left in the morning, and the temperature rose to almost 100°F by the end of the day. Momma knew it was a bad day to pass final judgment on the school, but she wasn't happy with what she saw: "Richard is going to build them some playground equipment—they have *none*, except a very rickety and quite broken down swing set."[23] I was the youngest of sixteen children with two teachers, who were kind and relaxed, but who provided little direction other than a twice a day "carpet time" of talking, singing, and listening to stories. "The kids seem to wander everywhere, outside, inside + unattended for the most part, while the teachers discussed Sears' clothes, what to make for the bake sale, etc.," Momma wrote. A few weeks into the year, I refused to go back unless Momma came too, so she could take me to the bathroom. It was in

* Head Start is a national program that was started in 1965 to address systemic poverty.

another building, and even the very youngest students had to walk to it on their own, just as they were left to play outside unsupervised.

It was a failed experiment. She didn't send me back and lamented to Granminnow, "I just blew up at her for the 99th time for whining, fighting with her sister, etc. But, while she was at school, her personality seemed to be improving—she had an excellent appetite and generally everything seemed wonderful—she loved being with the other kids. Her worst enemy up here is loneliness, which is true of all kids here."[24]

The letter implies she was disappointed it hadn't worked out, but she still remembers actually feeling great relief. On my first day after two long bus rides, I had come home exhausted and frightened, a tiny figure Momma watched emerge alone from the bus.

Daddy left for a hospital in Little Rock in October to have surgery on the knee he had injured in the spring. Momma wrote to Granminnow that he had been "a bundle of nerves about his operation."[25] He was worried about keeping his business running smoothly while he was away and afraid of being permanently disabled, a rare clue to the sort of anxiety he was hiding behind his snapping and barking. Mammy flew in to Little Rock to help him in the hospital, while Momma stayed home with us. He spent ten days in the hospital and another four to five weeks of recovery at home.

Daddy devised his own physical therapy system for his recuperation. He stuffed cast-iron sash weights from salvaged double hung windows inside a leather shoulder bag of Momma's and hung them from his leg. I must have been astonished by this clever arrangement, because the weights have a fixed place in my memory. I don't remember my traumatic first attempt at school earlier that season, but I do remember hanging on his chair while Daddy's legs lifted the iron bars and leather.

Confined to the cabin, Daddy wrote the only letter I have of his from our years in the woods:

Dear Minnow,

   Just a short note to wish you happy birthday and let you know that my knee seems to be knitting nicely. With a little luck I'll be back on my feet in 4 or 5 more weeks. (I'm hoping for less).

I guess Wendy told you that we finally made the plunge and bought
a brand new vehicle. Actually, I guess bought is the wrong word to use
since it will be 3 years before we'll actually own the thing. Ah well, we
may be hopelessly in debt, but at least we can get in, turn the key and go
with a certain amount of confidence that the thing will get us where we
need to go. Knock on wood.

We're really looking forward to the arrival of Jock & company. I hope
that Wendy will let him relax a little this time. We're fairly well ready for
winter now, so I know she won't have too much for him to do. Actually I'm
hoping that he'll be able to sit around a great deal & keep me company.

Had our calf butchered recently, so we have 300 lbs. of beef in the
freezer and 2 hogs soon to be ready for the butcher.

> Well, enough for now.
> Love to all,
> Richard[26]

Uncle Jock and his then-girlfriend (now my aunt) Liza arrived in
early November, sleeping in a tent in the pasture.[27] They came in a car
loaded down with furniture and boxes of old housewares and food items
Granminnow had cleaned out of Aunt Ruth's condo—she had died that
summer. Jock pulled out an antique wooden rocking chair with lion heads
carved into the headrest, a gift from family friend Helen Jackson, the
great niece of the writer and Indian activist of the same name, that would
grace all the homes of my childhood.

Uncle Jock was so tall and jolly and fun. Aunt Liza was small with long,
wild blond curls, and silver and gold bracelets lacing her arms. They called
each other "Ho" and "Ha," after the Mexican terms of endearment *mi hijo*
and *mi hija* (Liza was Mexican and Dutch, raised between Los Angeles
and Mexico). They indulged us with little gifts and lots of attention.

Thanksgiving wasn't mentioned in the 1975 letters, but we spent
Christmas Day in Little Rock with Uncle Lewis and his future wife
Mindy, missing a deep snow in Fox.[28] We returned to the cabin before it
all melted, to see the farm tidied under its cotton drifts.

Momma had tried to get Granminnow to fly into Little Rock too, and
though something kept her from coming, it did not keep her from sending
gifts. (Ever the crusader for health food, Momma sent Granminnow a
mysterious "healthy substitute for Instant Breakfast."[29]) Under the tree for

On my swing in the yard about 1976.

us there were tree decorations; books; underwear, a bra, and a nightgown
for Momma; shirts and socks for Daddy; and pajamas, tricycles, a truck,
and an easel for us girls. With money Nana gave her, Momma filled stock-
ings at the end of our beds with paints, puzzles, play money, play combs,
play jewelry, paper, and crayons from the Ben Franklin in Mountain View.
An old pickup came soon after as a present from Daddy to Momma. "So I
could get away from home once in awhile," she wrote.[30] (The Chevy sedan
she'd used at the Key Place now sat broken in the driveway.)

In the early months of 1976, Daddy built the barn at last with lumber he
had helped mill from pine trees logged off the Morrises' land. It was a partially enclosed loafing shed with two stalls and a small corral in front; an
open, roofed section for hay storage off the back; another enclosed section
for feed (with a defunct freezer to keep feed in and mice out); and a small
loading chute to load pigs and cows. I hung close by and helped while
Daddy built the feed room, holding one end of a board while he nailed the
other in. (The memory is his. I was only three and a half, an age when so
few memories stuck. But I am disappointed I can remember nothing of it.
In later years, we would never spend so much time together.)

Winter came and went quietly, its usual mercurial temperatures jumping, literally, from 0°F to 60°F in two days, and the skeletal, brown landscape of naked trees and frozen mud gave way to the slow greening of spring.[31] In February's early warmth, Momma wrote that she had a "bad case" of spring fever, by which she meant she did "less and less each day."[32] The freezing mornings had passed, and Daddy no longer had to carry a metal bucket of embers from the heat stove out to the pump house to keep our water from freezing. Letters were a mix of health chatter, the needs of children, and unending thank yous—one for a Curious George book: "Unfortunately, Katy fell asleep on it and peed on it, but it survived quite well."[33]

Momma's lethargy soon broke, and spring called her to the labors of the garden and the farm, so much so that she didn't write again until June 2. By that time, she was already preparing to harvest cabbage, broccoli, cauliflower, lettuce, and new potatoes.[34]

Momma's uncle John and aunt Jean, with two of Momma's teenage cousins and a Sara Lee frozen cake, drove up onto the land unexpectedly one evening in June on their way back to Colorado from her cousin Charles's graduation from Andover. John and Jean, determined to see the life their niece had carved out for herself in Arkansas and undeterred in their rental car by a lack of directions or the falling darkness, stopped along the way to ask where they could find our cabin. After a series of "over yonder"s and "around that bend"s that Charles still remembers, they found us.[35]

"They arrived to a totally messy house (*totally* means *totally*)," Momma wrote Granminnow, "and just as they arrived a man came to help Richard install a light in our pump house (this all occurred at about 8:30 at night), so it was all totally mad, but we enjoyed their visit."[36] We had no room to put them up, and they came unprepared for camping, so they left around midnight for another hour's drive to a motel.

Uncle John and Aunt Jean—with her patrician accent, a onetime classmate of Jackie Kennedy's at Vassar—must have seemed alien in that setting. This ever-present dichotomy in my parents' lives was writ large in Momma's early June letter to my grandmother. In one paragraph, Momma discusses inheritance taxes (Granminnow was dealing with Aunt Ruth's estate), and then in another, "Well—spent the morning trying to load a pig into a truck to go to the butcher, so I am covered with mud + hog shit—Now I must go to a local furniture factory to load up some firewood for my cookstove (scrap wood which is all beautifully seasoned + cut up)—then defrost the freezer, freeze some greens, etc., etc."[37] I suspect she herself was aware of this contrast even as she wrote it, both pleased with and sorry for herself at the same time.

"Richard and I went from the depths to the heights in a few days," Momma wrote in late September.[38] Granminnow had written that she was sending $1,000—probably related to an inheritance from Aunt Ruth—and the insurance company had also written agreeing at last to pay Daddy's medical bills and back wages. They planned to use the money to pay bills and build a bathroom and screen a porch Daddy had already started. Over the next few months, Daddy scrapped the screened porch plans and instead began the addition of a small living and dining area, a bathroom space, and another bedroom.

Momma was also busy outside the home that fall. "My 'Children's Workshop' went beautifully," she wrote Granminnow, "We'll probably be having one every month [. . .] I think teaching + acting to me are one— and I enjoy both."[39] She was teaching French to us and a few other children. She had been lent a classroom space somewhere in the county and another woman helped her. We sang "Sur le pont d'Avignon," "Au claire de la lune," and "Ainsi font les petites marionnettes," which I would conjure up again in high school French class and, many years later, as I held my nursing son.

Again, it was a book that inspired her. She was reading *Teacher* by Sylvia Ashton-Warner that summer and fall: "I have only read bits and pieces, but I have already stumbled on her 'organic' teaching of reading method—a brilliant idea."[40] Ashton-Warner had developed a method for teaching English to Maori children in New Zealand that allowed them to develop language through culturally appropriate means, using their own words and ideas and terms, rather than a traditional foreign text.

Teaching was an estimable profession in the family (Momma's father, her mother, and her uncle Chuck were all teachers), and she was increasingly drawn to it. With Granminnow's help, she did her best to enrich our lives beyond what the farm could offer. But the French classes quickly fizzled out, and we simply sang the same handful of songs again and again at home. Momma was struggling with the pressing requirements of a farm and motherhood, and there was little local interest in French classes.

Aunt Ruth had now been dead a year, so Momma could not write her a letter about her teaching experiments. It was Aunt Ruth who had funded our 1975 winter trip to Colorado, Aunt Ruth who sent us magazines and checks, including $200 just three months before her death.[41] She was in many ways the matriarch of the family, although childless herself. She spent her life with a woman, a "friend." She was also a forward-thinking child psychologist. Dorothy Canfield Fisher—social activist, writer, education reformer, and one of the early twentieth century's most influential women—wrote in an introduction to a parenting book Aunt Ruth wrote in 1942 that one of the book's greatest values was its "acceptance of reverence and poetry and fun as food for growth as essential as bread and meat."[42] I have no memory of her, but I still speak of her regularly: Aunt Ruth made it, Aunt Ruth used to say. Her ideas about child-rearing had influenced Granminnow, and now they influenced Momma in the woods.

Being a mother and working with children would be a lifelong passion for Momma, and a struggle. I have always had a vision of her from childhood that painted her a saint, nothing but self-sacrifice, warmth, and love. When I really think back, I realize that, although warm, she was not a touchy-feely kind of mother but matter-of-fact and often exasperated and irritable. The year before, while telling Granminnow how Katy and I had blossomed, Momma also wrote:

> When I get overtired as I have been helping Richard, I have *so* little patience with them and I do scream too much—not unlike Dad—but they seem to sail through it relatively untouched. I try to make up for it in loving later on. Wish I had your ability to be patient with children even when I have little time for patience—*Can't* imagine how you did it when we were young since Dad was so difficult and you had so much on your shoulders. I'm afraid Sarah is developing a little temper more of imitation than anything else. Richard and I both blow up like steam engines when we are mad—so if she is angry, she can really put on a show à la Mommy + Daddy—She is not often very angry though—few temper tantrums (Katy has the temper) but too much whining still.[43]

I once told Granminnow that Momma was like a big bear. But she was deeply respectful of a child's humanity and right to be, never trying to mold us into any particular kind of woman or person, always open, always encouraging and proud of our accomplishments. Daddy was a more complex figure, worshipped by us from a bit of a distance, his temper more frightening but also more rare. I sensed that he could be judgmental even if I never really experienced it, for he too let us be who we would be. Momma was dissolved into daily mothering and chores, the reader of our stories, the soother of our wounds, the maker of our pork chops. She cuddled us and told us we were amazing. But Daddy with his emotional distance and strong arms and irreverent, humorous songs was our hero when we were very young. (Already I see my young son reserving his highest praise for his father, not for me.)

Humor was always a part of both of their interactions with us. There were certain behaviors expected outside the home—never discuss money or religion, always be polite—but otherwise we were given total freedom. We were allowed to be dirty and naked, to curse and cry, to soak and disfigure Barbie and other dolls, to listen to the adults talk of gossip and politics, and to play unaware of allowances and chore charts.

"If you have time, could you call the airport for me and find out the cost from Little Rock to C. Spgs.—and if Sarah + Katy could ride free?" Momma wrote Granminnow in September 1976, "I hate to ask you, but if I call Little Rock to find out it will be a long distance call and you know how hard it is for me to get to a phone."[44]

In late October, Momma, Katy, and I flew to Colorado for Granminnow's marriage to Irving Howbert and to pick up a white Volkswagen hatchback she was giving us to replace a "clunky old truck."[45] Katy and I were flower girls in the wedding in floor-length, diaphanous dresses printed with pale flowers and trimmed with lace, single gardenia and red rose bouquets for each of us. Granminnow wore a long, simple bright pink wrap dress, her signature pearls at the neck and a gardenia at the V of her neckline. I remember only the reception, at Irving's mother's house, a wall of gold-embossed antique books in blue and maroon and brown in a well-furnished room. Katy and I hovered around the wedding "cake" of cream cheese and caviar the whole night and loaded cracker after cracker.

I have hazier memories of the trip home. We drove the nine hundred miles back to Arkansas in the hatchback with Aunt Sarah. She, with her youth and scarves and city clothes, was the most glamorous thing I could imagine. We drove down into New Mexico, across Texas and Oklahoma, and into Arkansas, and she and Momma sang and talked to us all the way. Aunt Sarah was impatient and overwhelmed by us. "I made us stop and we ran in cornfields on the side of the highway," she told me, "because I couldn't take all the talking going on in the back!"[46]

Aunt Sarah still recalls her first impression of our lives that trip, "I remember the house as adorable and with a sweet feeling about it and so cozy. The kitchen just seemed so homey, you were a family to me." She was too young to absorb the hardship it represented. When we drove up to the cabin, after a terrifying last hour of driving for Momma in a dense fog, a litter of scraggly puppies crawled out from under the house. Aunt Sarah loved animals and was shocked that Momma could let these dogs be alone outside. It was only on reflection years later that she realized each puppy was one more hungry, fertile animal, and that this was the country way.

Eleven

FAUNA

Dead armadillo, dead by the side of road!
—Sung by Daddy, loudly, whenever he saw roadkill[1]

"That's when we had about seven too many dogs," Momma wrote me in an e-mail.[2] She was commenting on a photograph of her and my sister Katy standing on a winter-rutted dirt road, our dog Abbie with two of her puppies in the corner of the shot. Over the eight years on the farm, we had Old Belle, Abbie, Chigger, Junior, Tiny, and Kitty Hanya—our dogs and one cat, respectively (not counting their offspring).

I was fascinated by the wild creatures around us, the skinks and fence lizards, dog ticks and tadpoles, and the uncatchable moles, but I mostly ignored our pets and farm animals. I did not play with them or cuddle them or even help care for them. They were just an ever-present part of the fabric of our days, clucking and mooing and barking alongside our giggles and screams, exposing me to the cruelty of country life—to the cycle of life and death as they coupled and birthed and met their often violent ends.

Old Belle was a brown brindled Plott hound from Dalton Moody's dog's litter—her mother a "very, very fine dog," according to Daddy, but Old Belle "stupid and useless." Years later Belle tried to eat through the anus of a dead cow—"not uncommon," Daddy told me recently, "it was the path of least resistance." The sight of the opportunistic hound enraged Daddy, because the cow had given us so much, and Belle so little, so he shot her. Belle's demise left not a ripple in my memory.

Abbie and Junior were both strays. Abbie, a border collie, had turned up one day at our Mountain View rental in 1973. She eventually drowned in our neighbor Judy's well. Junior—another great dog in Daddy's estimation—was a mutt that showed up at the Dew Drop Inn in Mountain

Daddy with Old Belle on the front porch.

View where Daddy was doing some work. We kept him until he died of a rattlesnake bite. Chigger, named after a prevalent and nasty little mite, was the only puppy (Old Belle's) that we ever kept, her demise long forgotten.

In her letter to Aunt Ruth on our return from Christmas in Colorado, Momma wrote that we had lost one puppy (out of eight) the night after we arrived. "I'm afraid," she wrote, "as awful as it was, that's not much of a loss—considering how hard it is to find homes for dogs around here."[3] A regular topic in the letters is the coming, and—in my parents' ever-practical and unsentimental view—fortunate going of domestic creatures. A postcard to Granminnow read, "Tell [Aunt] Sarah we got 4 kittens on her birthday this year—so maybe we'll save 1 for her. (1 was killed by Belle—unfortunately—or rather, fortunately, since they're hard to get rid of.)"[4]

I have a strange memory of a dead kitten I long ago discounted as not real. Katy and I were rolling around in a pile of pillows in the narrow addition along the back of the cabin. A kitten had crawled beneath a pillow and was crushed to death. Did I dream this? No, Katy remembers something similar—that it was Daddy who came along and stepped on the pillow and accidently killed the kitten. My parents remember nothing. Animals were born and then they died.

Farm life was often less like lines from Daddy's dear Walt Whitman and more like those from Shirley Jackson with country people and their many tortures for chicken-killing dogs.[5] Momma proved how far she'd acclimated to the country when she was faced with a kitten shitting in her clean laundry repeatedly, a cat she'd already caught with a long, flat worm dangling from its butt at the threshold to the house. She snapped its body against a tree, filled with purpose to solve an untenable problem. And it was her turn, she thought, since my father usually handled the culling of dogs and cats. She in some ways was born to work on a farm, being almost anti-sentimentality. Even now, I find myself feeling slightly shy to let her read my more emotional thoughts about the land, fearing they might veer too far into treacle for her taste.

There was no SPCA (Society for the Prevention of Cruelty to Animals) in the area and neutering was too expensive and logistically difficult. Many locals abandoned animals on the side of the road. During deer season in particular, people who'd been raised in the area would come from the city and buy a couple of hounds for the hunt, leaving the dogs behind so they didn't have to feed them all year.

Knowing all this made me question why, according to the letters, we got a *new* dog as late as April 1980, a Great Dane named Tiny, who birthed an inevitable litter of puppies.[6] My parents rarely knew how the dogs got pregnant—they wandered freely across bluffs and hollows and other farms. But Tiny was a mangy stray (another one) who had wandered up onto our land two separate times, the owner in the valley town of Timbo finally refusing to come get her. The only animals we consciously acquired—besides the cows, chickens, pigs, and mules—were Kitty Hanya, Daddy's cat in Colorado, and Old Belle. Tiny grew so sickly from the parasitic mites of mange, however, that Daddy eventually shot her and the puppies.

I never witnessed the killing of these pets, and I was unperturbed by their deaths. They were half wild, living independent lives outdoors. My most disturbing animal memory was the act that led to at least one litter of puppies. Our bus driver Scotty's dog came up onto our land one day and mounted Abbie by the side of the cabin. They were locked together by their swollen genitals, yelping out in pain for what seemed like forever. I stood by horrified and frozen watching with a vile, sinking feeling that there might be some correlation with human sex.

On a cassette we recorded for Mammy and Pappy in December of 1978

with our cousins, who had just moved down the road from us that summer, a perverse conversation unfolded between my twelve-year-old cousin
Little Richard—so named to differentiate him from Daddy—and me.[7]

"In case you don't know, Chigger is one of Belle's brand new puppies,"
Little Richard says into the tape recorder with bravado and a deep southern twang.

"Little Richard, it's my turn!" I whine as I draw near. (I was eight
years old.)

"We killed the rest of 'em."

"Oh, shut up!" I scream.

"We just took an iron bar and, *Bam!*" he says with exaggerated violence.

"You, shut up, we did not!" I yell again.

"Uncle Richard did," he says.

"Uh, uh!"

"How did he kill 'em?" Little Richard responds.

"He ki—he got a *shotgun* and killed 'em," I growl.

The crowbar was Little Richard's invention to shock me, the killing
itself being commonplace.

"How did he *shoot* 'em? Did the blood go everywhere?" Little Richard
says, as the room explodes into shrieking and fighting.

Killing animals didn't preclude loving them, or at least not for Daddy—
Momma had a more ambiguous relationship with them. Daddy sent me
an e-mail several years ago about Abbie's puppies, that he later shot when
they'd grown big enough for him to stomach it:

> She was due around Thanksgiving. On Thanksgiving morning we woke
> up to about a foot of snow that had fallen overnight. I went out to feed &
> milk, & Abbie came up from the woods below the cabin. She would come
> up to me, yip at me & run a short distance back the way she had come,
> stopping & looking over her shoulder to see if I was following. I followed
> her down to Fossil Rock Bluff, & she crawled into a little cave formed
> by a flat slab leaning on a larger rock. She turned around & pushed her
> puppies toward the entrance for me to see. Really cute! She was one dog
> in a million.[8]

A little later on our cassette, Edward, the oldest of the three cousins, speaks softly into the recorder, "Chigger caught a big red squirrel
yesterday."[9]

"Junior did too. It was *frozen!*" I add.

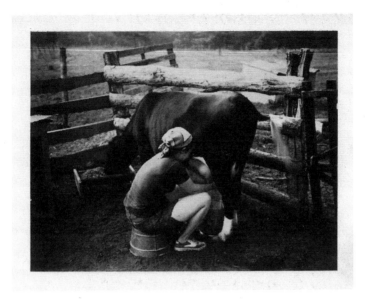

Momma milking the cow.

In the first week of November 1978, we had recorded another cassette for Mammy and Pappy. With the crackle of the recording come the sounds of commotion and greetings as Aunt Rhett and her three boys arrive at the cabin, Momma and Katy and I offer the boys popcorn, and they wonder why we didn't go to school (we were sick).

"Are you gonna be here for awhile, Rhett?" Momma asks, in her new hint of a drawl, "I'm gonna go milk the cow in a few minutes . . . did you notice that the pigs aren't eating the corn?"[10] And then begins a discussion about needing to buy feed that the pigs will like; Rhett points out that it's her turn to buy it; and Momma tells fifteen-year-old Edward to soak the corn, they like it better.

Little Richard speaks slowly into the recorder, "Well, we're having a lot of fun up here. The first week we got here . . ."[11]

"My pigs are doing good!" Edward interjects.

"Yeah, Edward got two pigs, they're doing good, they're . . ."

"Pappy knows about that," Edward softly scolds Little Richard.

Little Richard continues, slow and proud, "Well, anyway, we killed dead a rattlesnake first week we got here and I cleaned it. David, [. . .] he saved Uncle Richard's life and he saved Katy's life while Uncle Richard was killing the rattlesnakes 'cause Katy was about to walk into one and he leaped over there and grabbed Katy and pushed her out of the way. [. . .] It was a real rush."

We came to the top of the hill where the rocky road had grown warm in the September sun. Down below, we saw Daddy standing outside of his truck beating a long rattlesnake as thick as a flagpole that lay in the road in front of him. As we all walked down the hill, another large timber rattler slithered out of an upturned tree stump and brush pile headed towards Katy's bare foot as she moved along the road's edge. This was when my cousin David jumped in and pushed Katy out of the way. Daddy now knew a den was nearby. He hooked a winch to the back of the truck and to the large stump and dragged it loose exposing, to my horror, a writhing nest of rattlers (called, strangely, I've learned, a rhumba). The many lethal little snakes slipped off into the bush. We referred to that stretch of road thereafter as Rattlesnake Hill.

After the incident, Momma wrote to Granminnow:

> This is also good snake weather but I think we've seen the worst of the snakes. I wasn't going to tell you about the rattlesnakes until several years hence—but since Vic [a visitor from Colorado Springs] let the cat out of the bag, I'll tell you—it was a very exciting day—They were living in a brush pile down the road a ways—Momma Snake, Daddy Snake, and umpteen babies. Glad Richard killed them—We are all very careful now believe me.[12]

When we first moved to Arkansas with the Connors, Susan had wanted a gun in case a strange man should come to the house while the husbands were on the land. Momma was appalled. Snakes are the only thing we need a gun for, she thought. Every day we ran the risk of being bitten by one of a handful of venomous reptiles—copperheads, rattlesnakes, and cottonmouths.

Momma lay awake in the pitch dark of night worrying about how to protect us, although the snakes never harmed us. But their lives and ours were often entwined, an encounter between us lurking in every crack, every hidden corner. I hated them and feared they were coiled in the dark of the outhouse hole. A copperhead wound itself into a Fisher Price parking garage we'd left up against the foundation of the cabin. Black rat snakes occasionally sought warmth in feedbags stored in the barn, the quiet hiss of their scales as they slid through the grain alerting us to their presence. I saw my cousins pull thick black coils of rat snakes from the pink insulation lining the walls of our pump house and drop them rustling into a bucket with a lid. Snakes were caught in mousetraps in the house too, one falling from an interior loft window into the kitchen while Momma was cooking. A thin coil of green snake fell from a tree by the porch onto a friend's head as she walked next to me. As we floated down rivers, cottonmouths sunned themselves in black strips like bacon on the rocks; I can still see the open white mouth of a riled one charging our flat bottom boat. There were also the harmless, but unnerving, hog-nosed snakes, called puff adders locally, that hissed and flattened out like cobras with false eyespots on the neck. If that didn't scare you off, they played dead. I encountered the fat, dirt-colored body of one in the wispy tall grass in the fields between the bus stop and Aunt Rhett's house after school and gave it a wide berth.

Another large rattlesnake stretched itself across the road near the cabin as Daddy drove up onto our property. He stopped the car and killed it with a board he had on the seat beside him, cutting off and smashing the head, still deadly as the jaw nerves worked for a time after decapitation. Daddy loved snakes and hated to kill them, but they were too dangerous to leave alive where we lived and played. Katy came running up to the house mirthfully dragging the rattlesnake's body that was longer than she was. She threw its headless body on the floor in front of Momma and watched it jerk and twitch. We kept its large rattle to play with but passed its skin on to a friend for tanning. Mottled snakeskins staked to boards leaned against trees and houses throughout the area. Daddy told me that this one was fifty-four inches long, the largest he'd ever seen. It is not hard to see why the locals often said of someone who did things in a tizzy that "he does everything like he's killin' snakes."

Momma had written Nana in 1974 that we could come to Colorado only "if we [could] find someone to care for our animals—6 goats, 2 rabbits, 3 cats, 2 dogs, 42 chickens."[13] Animals were a vital part of a sustainable farm plan as they provided food and labor, but they were a lot of work,

work from which there were no days off: every morning and every evening, water and food from fifty-pound feed sacks had to be distributed.
A friend of Daddy's wrote him in 1977, when we had even more animals,
complimenting our farm, "Except I wouldn't have any animals. Too much
like prison or the army."[14]

Over the years, we had a succession of mules, hardy, heat-tolerant draft
animals. The first was Liza, a scruffy russet mule bought from a local
named C. W. Tapp to plow the garden and carry logs out of the woods
for building the cabin. Daddy sold her once those jobs were complete. It
wasn't practical to care for and feed mules that weren't needed for work.
Later, another local gave us Mike, a gigantic, one-eyed mule that helped
Daddy log free pine timber from Earl Morris's land (he "could pull hell
off a mountain" Daddy says). And we had Katy, a friend's old mule that
retired to our place in the mid-seventies, breaking Daddy's as-needed pol-
icy. Katy the mule was a known fence jumper that regularly had to be cor-
ralled back in, and Momma was incensed that Daddy took her in. It was
she, Momma remembers, who ran around after Katy one afternoon, trying to get her back in the pasture, while John Weaver and Daddy watched
laughing from the yard. (Daddy has no memory of this, but Momma is
adamant that it happened.)

Daddy purchased some milk goats in the first year in Arkansas and
other goats through the years from the sale barn, mostly Nubians and
Alpine mixes. Goats were smaller and cheaper to buy and feed than cows,
easier to butcher, and their milk was healthier. The kids were as rambunc-
tious as any human child, escaping from their pen across the yard and
jumping gleefully onto the back of the inoperable Chevy sedan, running
up and over the top and down the front and around to start all over again,
stomping and bucking and leaping. The stinky, spitting billy goat was so
aggressive with the females in heat, and with us, that Momma, Katy, and
I were trapped in the house one afternoon when he broke free, Momma
frightened of what he might do with his sharp horns.

"In my experience, the goat was a tell-tale sign of farmers 'from off'—
and probably back to the landers," the Ozark historian Brooks Blevins,
who grew up in the small Arkansas community of Violet Hill, wrote me,
"The native Ozarkers I grew up with almost always scoffed at the notion
of raising goats, the implication being that it was 'low-class' farming or
perhaps even unmanly."[15]

Momma made cheese with the milk of the goats, but we only drank
it the first year or so in Arkansas, my parents perhaps not taking to the

Daddy with Liza the mule.

*Momma feeding the goats and Liza with me
in late 1973, early 1974.*

flavor. After they went into debt to buy their first cow, an Angus-Holstein cross, and her calf in 1974, we drank cow's milk.[16] The frothy warm milk was pressed from the udders into metal buckets that Daddy carried to the kitchen to be strained through a cheesecloth to rid it of cow hair and other debris and poured into glass bottles for the refrigerator. We also briefly had a brown Jersey cow that gave a creamy, high butterfat milk before she died of an unknown cause.

The first cow, Mama Cow, was bred each fall with Dalton Moody's bull, and later the LaJeune's when they bought his land. As soon as she went bellowing and restless into heat, Daddy would open our pasture gate and drive as fast as he could the mile or so down to Moody's pasture and open the gate to his bull. Mama Cow ran in her frenzy of estrus from our pasture to his and made directly for the bull. She gave birth to one calf in the spring.

We also had eggs with firm whites and apricot yolks from our laying chickens, Buff Orpingtons and Barred Plymouth Rocks, that lived in a chicken coop with a small, fenced yard. When Katy and I tried to catch the chicks, the momma hen would often attack, pecking at us mercilessly. We had a flock of smaller game chickens—and the occasional free Baby Huey–sized white chicken from a chicken house—that roosted in the persimmon tree. They were mostly for eating and roamed wild on the land devouring bugs in the garden, shitting on our paths—for years, my parents told the story of how I, at a very young age, turned to my conservative grandmother and warned her, "Don't step in the chicken shit, Mammy"—and occasionally laying their eggs in random nooks for us to happen upon. Once found, it was unknown how old the eggs were. I watched Momma place them in a bowl of water and wait for any rotten ones to float to the top.

Someone also gave Daddy a couple of guinea fowl that pecked around the yard for a few years looking like Yayoi Kusama creations in their black and white spotted finery, until we ate them. Two sisters from Louisiana were staying at the Dew Drop Inn in Mountain View where Daddy was doing more renovations. As he worked, he overheard them talking to the owner, also from Louisiana, about the delights of guinea gumbo. Daddy chimed in that he had a couple of guinea fowl, and so they were cooked into a guinea gumbo, their peregrinations from persimmon tree to back hillside cut short.

In the yard, between the cabin and the chicken coop, was a small wire rabbit hutch on high wooden legs. We had at least two rabbits in it over the years, if not a few more. They lived on a bed of straw, wilted lettuce and carrots thrown in, the ground beneath them littered with their black pellet feces.

And last, but not least, were our pigs. There were three pink Yorkshire sows and a boar. They lived in a muddy pen next to the barn with a low wood shelter attached and a simple electric fence once we got electricity. The low-amp pulsing current of the lines was safe. I closed my eyes and touched a line just once, long enough to be startled and avoid doing it again. When Momma read *Charlotte's Web* to us, the pigs did suddenly take on special import—the piglets were so cute—but I never seemed to develop much sorrow over their conversion to meat. Daddy kept the four main pigs for breeding and raised any piglets for meat and to sell to other farmers as feeder pigs. At one point, he even considered making an operation of this, but realized he didn't have the time or wherewithal to be a pig baron.

Perhaps he could have been a fish baron. Daddy hired a local, Webb Berry, who lived across the hollow from us, to build a pond with his Caterpillar bulldozer in the mid- to late seventies (there's no mention of it in the letters, except a drawing indicating that a stock pond had been part of Daddy's plans since at least August 1973).[17] The government paid half the cost of the project through an incentive program for rural landowners, so the whole project cost less than $200. Daddy bought catfish fry through the government program to stock the pond. I watched him spill the barrels of tiny fish into the water, as though filling a giant fishbowl.

Little sunfish invaded the pond. Daddy had strung sunfish from Dalton Moody's pond on a trotline across our pond as bait for catfish. A few of the sunfish—"the rabbits of the piscine world," Daddy told me recently—pulled free and multiplied rapidly. Eventually, the pond became overcrowded with sunfish, and the catfish couldn't thrive. Daddy tried to kill all the fish with rotenone for a fresh start, but the rotenone at the feed store wasn't water-soluble. So Daddy and John Weaver engineered a pipe bomb with black powder in plumbing pipe, with wires run to a car battery. They started the car, and the bomb detonated silently, nothing but a glossy, fat bubble rising in the middle of the pond while we stared on in awe. All the fish floated to the top, stunned to death. My sister and I hopped in a flat-bottom metal boat and scooped into nets as many fish as we could from the brown water. That night friends, packed into cars with guitars and banjos and kids, arrived for a fish fry and big bowls of fish soup.

In late November 1976—not long after Aunt Sarah's visit after which she flew off to Brazil—the weather was nice enough for us to have Thanksgiving

Daddy, Katy, and me at the pond about 1978.

dinner outside, with dogs and cats and chickens puttering around the table and between our legs. "We had a wonderful Thanksgiving with some friends," Momma wrote two days after Thanksgiving. "Richard and the other men built a rough plank table so that I could set out all my silver— and we had a real feast. The first turkey I ever cooked at home—Tell Janey I tried to recreate as much as possible the good old days up at their house—I even had creamed onions—but I couldn't manage the poetry."[18] Momma refused to let living in the woods force her to forsake her roots or throw out the past. Perhaps our life, or her internal struggles against it, even heightened her sense of these matters as she longed for home on her low days. Family silver set out properly on the unpolished table—fork to the left of the plate, knife on the right with its blade protecting the spoon to its right as Momma made sure to teach us—meant Thanksgiving to me. As did the slightly dented silver candlesticks, the bone-handled knives that couldn't really cut anything, and the small nineteenth-century silver saltcellars with Lilliputian spoons. Along with the turkey, creamed onions, and crescent rolls, these were the most iconic thing of the day.

On Christmas Eve that year, we piled into one of our old cars and made the short, bumpy drive to George and Mollie Bersch's house. They held a Christmas mass followed by a potluck dinner. Momma wrote of "a wonderful group of people" who drank, sang, ate, and talked while a handful of kids bounced around in anticipation of the next morning.[19]

While mild skies outside drizzled, we had an "old-fashioned" Christmas Day in the cabin. Daddy woke Christmas morning violently ill from imbibing too much at the Bersches' the night before and vomited throughout the day. But Katy and I opened our eyes to the ecstasy of Daddy's old wool ski socks tied to our bedposts, bulging with tape and pencils and toy cars and small pads of paper and oranges and nuts. We also got Madame Alexander Sweet Tears baby dolls from Granminnow that we loved and promptly bathed. Daddy received a pair of dry wick socks, and Momma a sweater and a new shirt that made her feel like she was in a "*New Yorker* ad."[20]

I was struck, as I read the letters, by a simple line. Momma had found the Christmas weekend so relaxing, she wrote, that "when Mon. morning arrived, I nearly forgot to make Richard's lunch."

She made his lunch? That she should have made his breakfast and lunch each morning seems strange—her days were as full as his. And she considered herself an equal. "And he didn't expect it," Momma says now. Even Granminnow had told her she should stop. But it was Momma's attempt to control something in their life, in his day, a way to make herself invaluable.

"I have a million chores to do—gardening time again and dishes piled to the ceiling," wrote Momma in March, in one of her few letters in the first months of 1977.[21] She greeted the spring gardening "with a groan," but Mama Cow had given birth and freshened—begun her milk production again after giving birth—and we were getting two or three gallons of milk a day and raising a calf. "A baby calf has to be the most beautiful newborn," she wrote.[22]

By the first of March, the floor was down on our new addition, and Daddy had all the windows and some lumber for the rest of it piled under tarps. The new space was about thirty feet wide at the back and eighteen feet deep, slipping onto the existing kitchen space like a U—an additional 460 square feet of living space to add to the previous 240.

But heavy April rains forced us all indoors, and the addition was temporarily neglected.[23] Between downpours, Katy and I finally learned to ride the tricycles Granminnow had sent two Christmases before along the finished plywood floors of the addition; they had been too difficult to maneuver on rocky dirt. "I'm afraid we are quite broke—a *tiresome condition*!" Momma wrote, but she let herself dream of the past and wrote that she would like for us to have new Easter hats: "I would love for them to have straw 'boaters' with ribbons and fake cherries."[24] We were going to George and Mollie's for an Easter breakfast and egg hunt, and Momma wanted to see us in the hats she'd worn as a child. Granminnow sent two Easter dresses with white gloves and two white hats with ribbons and silk flowers.

On Easter morning, there was a lumpy biscuit rabbit for each of us, a stuffed rabbit in a basket from Granminnow, and dried fruit to find nestled in exposed stud walls. We dressed in all our new finery and rode with pride and excitement to the Bersches' where the short service was followed by a finely attired hunt for eggs in the leaf-littered woods.

In the weeks that followed, the walls of the addition were framed and in place, and most of the roof was on by mid-May.[25] There was now a new main entrance to the cabin on a side porch that faced east into the woods. This opened into a dining area next to the kitchen on the left and a living area that led to a small future bathroom space framed in studs and a bedroom for my parents on the other side of the kitchen.

By the last week of June, the work was finished enough that Katy's birthday could be celebrated in the new space. "We all went to the zoo and then came home for cupcakes and ice cream," Momma wrote.[26] I faintly recall a scrappy little petting zoo with domestic animals on the side of the road somewhere nearby, but the closest real zoo was in Little Rock, which Momma does not mention. No one remembers what this could have been. She might as well have said we went to the moon.

Twelve

ARCADIA

Do you not see how everything conspires together
to make this place a heavenly dwelling?
—Sir Philip Sidney, *The Countess of Pembroke's Arcadia*[1]

In June 1977, we were "in the grips of a terrible heat wave," the constant refrain of summer.[2] The temperature was in the nineties and unusually dry and hot for a typically damp time of year, though we continued to have plenty of water in our well. But Daddy was suffering in the heat at work, taking salt tablets to compensate for the rivers of sweat he lost each day, small white pills I would sneak and hold in my mouth as long as I could.

Momma mentioned nonchalantly in a June letter to Granminnow that she and Daddy were "considering" a third and final child. ("After #3, assuming there is one, one or both of us will be sterilized and end this madness!"[3]) She worried that the pill was unhealthy. (Where did she get the pill? She doesn't remember.) She also really wanted another baby. We children were her greatest comfort, and children were a great comfort to each other. And a baby needed her unconditionally.

The heat worsened in July with a day or two of warm rain, and all labors came to the usual slow crawl. "We have been relaxing and partying a little and not getting much done," Momma wrote.[4]

This line was a revelation to me. I hadn't considered that all the interruptions from weather and injuries were anything but stressful. They were, in fact, what made the woods work in part. Nothing got done and the bank account was bare, but my parents could recover a bit, play music, read, socialize, and listen to the crickets. I imagine Momma and Daddy lying in their old bed feeling relaxed after a hot July party, reading from the bedside stacks, Momma mentioning the idea of a baby in the house again.

After the lazy days of July, Daddy was working again in August with "a steady $200 a week until the end of October." (The equivalent of about $900 today.) He was building a house alongside his business partner of almost a year, Dean May, a Baptist preacher, "who is as straight as Richard is 'crooked,'" Momma wrote. His demanding client said Daddy was "the fastest and the best carpenter" he had ever watched at work, Momma bragged in the letter.[5]

In early September, after work, Daddy drove to a neighboring town to pick up a load of furniture Granminnow had shipped (in May Momma had told her, "There is a truck line going through *Marshall* which is near us, and *Leslie* which is even closer"[6]). Under late summer skies, he drove home with Momma's childhood mahogany bureau, three mahogany beds with pineapple finials, and vintage white chenille blankets to cover even older blue-ticking mattresses from Nana's house—stained with generations of human activity. Nana had died that February. A delicate mahogany vanity with a trifold mirror that had belonged to Nana's sister came too, and Momma placed it against the bare studs in the bathroom.[7] Momma had sat in front of it as a little girl, handling her great aunt's silver brushes and her jewelry, and she loved it, a vestige of femininity she must have clung to in the woods. I too sat in front of it, opening the delicate drawers and moving the side mirrors to catch myself from all angles, ignoring the less glamorous stacks of paper and pens and old household bits.

The furniture inspired stories of Nana and Aunt Ruth and Aunt Minnie and the family as Momma grasped for her roots out of homesickness and filled our heads with storybook visions, so antithetical to the life we lived each day. I absorbed these women's stories, viewing them as mythical figures in my own. Even at that young age, I must have caught the pride in Momma's voice that told me poverty wasn't our only narrative.

Momma filled us with tales of another world, read us our books, and sang nursery rhymes in English and French. But Daddy kept us grounded in Arkansas. "Richard took the girls caving (!!) Sunday night," Momma also wrote in early September.[8]

Stone County sat over a maze of caves. Katy and I had been in three wild caves with Daddy already by the time Momma wrote the above:

Blowing Spring Cave, Salt Peter Cave, and Arnold Cave.[9] With brass carbide lanterns on our heads, we walked into partially obscured openings in
the forest. I still smell the sour, dusty lit carbide, see the rock rooms and
the trickles and pools of clear water, feel the cold subterranean air. I was
scared of tornadoes and nuclear war and snakes, but not caves.

As we moved through a constricted passageway in deep, cold water in
one, a swarm of bats flew at us, brushing our cheeks as they passed. In
another, we climbed ropes up a vertical cliff and crawled on our bellies
like salamanders through a flat, narrow crevice into a magnificent room
of stalactite and stalagmite floors and ceilings, every surface a crystal.

"I went in a wet cave, and I got very cold," I told Granminnow on a cassette tape after being prompted by Momma and Daddy to tell her what
we'd been doing.[10] I had nothing more to say on the matter.

We started this cassette for Granminnow on a cold, hoary November
morning that year, just as the sun was peeking above the horizon.[11] As I
play the recording at my desk now, I marvel at how easily I am carried back
through time to my five-year-old self and my young parents, then younger
than I am now. I hear Momma clanging pots around in the kitchen while
Daddy tries to rouse Katy from her bed in the adjacent room.

Katy is groggy and slow, and whines, "Weeendy, will somebody help me
put my clothes on?"[12]

Daddy is soft and patient with her. She grumbles and moans when he
tries to put her shirt on that his way is wrong, she does it differently.

"Oh, okay," he says gently with an edge of impatience, "you do it a different way. Put your underpants on."

"Saary is all dressed and looks beautiful!" Daddy exclaims when he sees
me fully dressed.

Daddy had probably already milked the cow that morning, but Momma
must have waited with anticipation for us to leave, to finish washing the
dishes from breakfast, feed the animals, chop some wood, hang the laundry on the line, and drive to school to help before taking us home at noon,
which she did for a few weeks after we grumbled about the long day.[13]

Or she just waited to sit and wait out the waves of nausea and fatigue
overtaking her. She was three months pregnant. Her letters never
announce the pregnancy, but in early December she wrote Granminnow,
"I loved my maternity outfits," so they had presumably spoken by phone
from a neighbor's house, an occasional luxury for important news.[14] A
third child was a joy but hardly the central focus of her days.

I was almost six that December, and it's the first Christmas I remember well. We made pencil holders—painted toilet paper rolls glued to pieces of wood—and helped Momma stuff fragrant cedar shavings into cockeyed heart pillows for family gifts. It was almost, but not quite, as Uncle Chuck imagined it facetiously in a letter to Momma: "a wind howling, cold raindrops spattering on a thatched roof, soap boiling in a large vat in the corner, a small new-born goat sleeping nearbye and all the family busily making things . . . a little like Santa's workshop."[15]

The weeks leading up to Christmas in our cabin were filled with electric excitement. We pricked our fingers stringing popcorn and cranberries onto needle and thread to make garlands. It was tedious work to push the needle through the fragile-edged popcorn. The cranberries lay heavy and Christmas red against the bright white corn. The room smelled of smoky popcorn. The tree was put up just days before Christmas, a small pine Daddy cut on our land. We decorated it with the garlands we'd made; salt-dough ornaments; a little bird's nest made from an acorn cap that clipped to the branches; and painted, worn glass balls and German wooden pieces from Momma's childhood. Momma set out a brightly painted clay crèche from Mexico on a wooden desk and read stories to us from the *Tall Book of Christmas* of sugarplums dancing and edible mittens and limburger cheese and fairy lights in the woods.

We woke on Christmas morning to Daddy's ski socks bulging with small gifts at the foot of our beds and went through the kitchen and into the living room where the tree stood suddenly surrounded by presents. Momma wrote that we had been "wild" before Christmas, but that Barbie dolls from both our grandmothers under the tree "soothed [our] madness."[16] "Sarah said it was the best present she ever received," Momma wrote. We balked at tights and skirts that were sent, refusing to wear them. "They prefer old rags," Momma wrote or, "*frilly* dresses." We loved our frilly dresses from Granminnow's wedding. "They wore their wedding dresses [. . .] twice this week, and would wear them more if I allowed it—I want those dresses to last," Momma wrote. We also threw them off and sat in mud-filled ruts in front of the house, filling our hand-me-down underpants with goopy scoops of rain and earth.

That winter also brought various visitors who went nameless in the letters—acquaintances or friends of friends coming to get a peek at the land—and a very last-minute New Year's Eve wedding for Uncle Lewis and Aunt Mindy.

*Katy and me in our frilly wedding dresses
at our baptism in 1978.*

Enjoying the muddy front yard in about 1975.

"They told us Friday that they planned to be married here Saturday!!" Momma wrote, "It was great fun; I planned a wedding supper: homemade French bread, wedding cake, homemade mayonnaise, homegrown roast beef and various other goodies—I was very proud of it. The wedding was fun (just us, Lewis + Mindy, and the Berschs—George officiating)."[17] A photo was taken of Daddy pointing his shotgun at Lewis and newly pregnant Mindy. I have the vaguest memory of the night, of wearing our flower girl dresses from Granminnow's wedding and being in the cramped living room watching Mindy and Lewis stand up together.

Uncle Lewis brought cloth rolls of pocketknives he was selling. He unfurled the thick bundle of soft silversmith's cloth on the living room floor and let Katy and me each choose one. There were whorls of mother of pearl and slivers of metal bordering chunks of stone. My knife was wonderful, and quickly lost.

Three days into 1978, Momma announced to Granminnow that we finally had an outhouse and an indoor toilet of sorts from Sears—there was a small distribution center in Mountain View where catalog purchases were delivered—which wasn't "much more than a chamber pot," for inclement weather and late nights.[18] Granminnow had been complaining about our lack of proper bathroom facilities since we moved to Arkansas. In our first year in the cabin, Momma wrote her, "Your need for an outhouse surprises me since you have pooped in the woods without mishap off + on since I have known you—however, I see the possibility of improvising a very comfortable toilet for you and all visitors."[19]

But that winter Granminnow had said she would not come back unless we had at least an outhouse. She may have been grappling with the same thought I had as I read all this—my mother was pregnant, almost four months along and growing big enough to wonder if she was having twins. Pregnant again with no indoor bathroom, much less a weather-protected outdoor one.

There was no bathtub or shower—just metal tubs and hoses outside. During the year we lived at the Key Place, a few months of which Momma had been pregnant with Katy, we'd gone to the bathroom behind trees and bushes and used a chamber pot. For the past three and a half years in the cabin, we had been using a metal kitchen chair with the vinyl seat

Katy and me in front of the outhouse.

replaced with a toilet seat. This chair-toilet was kept in the woods behind the house and moved from place to place. Daddy thought it a cleaner way to go and hated outhouses. But he built one that winter, an eight-foot-high plywood box with a shed roof facing into the forest with a bucket of lime to sprinkle after each use.

The New Year also brought heavy snow. We were snowed in for a month and a half, and Daddy was only able to work a little building cabinets. Granminnow sent twenty-five dollars to buy me new shoes that "went to keep us eating." Momma wrote that the children at school had been teasing me about my clunky boots, and I had begged for new shoes, but "Sarah has been very understanding and I'll be able to get her some shoes when spring comes." (I remember no teasing.)[20]

Again, the vagaries of the weather dictated so much of our financial and emotional health. Daddy was finding some success as a housebuilder, but it was never enough. He had seven possible houses lined up to build that year. "But houses always start with foundations and foundations cannot be poured in this freezing weather—would that he could start with cabinets," Momma wrote.[21]

Meanwhile, Katy and I were stuck inside the small cabin, with no school, so we made houses under chairs and blankets like most children, pulling the chenille blankets off our beds and piling in pillows and books. We played with whatever we could find around the house. Momma had written in a prior year that our favorite toys were "masking tape, plastic bags, cans, bottles, orange juice cans, pens, paper, dress-up things, baby kittys (we have 3), dirt, rocks, flour, water + books."[22] Granminnow also periodically sent what Momma called in one letter, a "box of surprises." We were overjoyed as we pulled out the sundry items she pulled together from her cocktail closet, discarded medicine cups, and reams of paper left from my great-grandfather's Denver business in the 1930s and 1940s— "a definite windfall for these drawing children."[23] We busied ourselves on the floor drawing or dancing and listening to stories on *The Spider's Web* series on NPR, or, after Granminnow sent a tape recorder the year before, to countless books on tape—mostly from Disney movies, which only existed for us on the tapes and in the flimsy books they came with; we never saw the movies. "Robin Hood and Little John walking through the forest, laughing back and forth at what the other one has to say," we bellowed around the cabin.

Most memorably, we read, each title now as sentimental to me as a childhood garment or quilt saved in a box (the physical books are long gone): *In the Night Kitchen*; *Sylvester and the Magic Pebble*; *Blueberries for Sal*; *Madeline*; *Ant and Bee*; *Richard Scarry's Cars and Trucks and Things That Go* (the Gold Bug!); *Harvey's Hideout*; *Dooly and the Snortsnoot*; *Eloise*; Tasha Tudor's *A Time to Keep*; *Mrs. Piggle-Wiggle*; *Fish is Fish*; *Animals Should Definitely Not Wear Clothing*; *Where the Wild Things Are*; and a book of Andersen's fairy tales with lush, sinister Arthur Szyk illustrations. We found Mother Goose and other children's verse riotously funny in illustrator Wallace Tripp's inspired collections *Granfa' Grig Had a Pig and Other Rhymes Without Reason* and *A Great Big Ugly Man Came up and Tied His Horse to Me*—there were the Slithergadee and peas with honey and barley butts and dirty sows with sweethearts enow.

On Saturday, May 27, 1978, labor pains woke Momma in the early morning. Daddy drove to the Bersches' and called the doctor. He didn't answer. Daddy began to mentally prepare himself for a home birth. But he made one last call, and the doctor answered. Daddy and Momma dropped me and Katy off with someone—perhaps the Bersches, perhaps a family we knew that had two older girls to keep us preoccupied—and drove down the mountain. Momma was admitted to the tiny Mountain View hospital. This time, unlike with Katy's and my birth, Daddy was allowed in the room, they didn't shave her, they didn't give her an enema, and they didn't give her narcotics. Her nurse was a woman they knew. Miriam was delivered in the early evening after a painful but uneventful birth.

One of Daddy's caver friends arrived at the hospital the next morning to see the baby and tell Daddy and Momma they had discovered a new route in a local cave, the Janus Pit, which they had descended the day before. They named it the Miriam Bypass. I remember a foggy morning and Momma and Daddy walking across the front yard towards me with Miriam wrapped in blankets.

Granminnow came to help Momma after the birth and to be there when George Bersch baptized all three of us girls in front of the cabin. Katy and I wore the long fanciful flower girl dresses we'd worn at Granminnow's wedding with white tights and saltwater sandals. In the photographs, Momma looks matronly in a large, collared shift dress, a design of red roses and greenery on white, her curly hair brushed out, frizzy, and disheveled by a gust of wind; Daddy conventional in khakis and a navy, short-sleeve polo shirt. In another photo, Granminnow sits at a card table set up in the grass and covered in a white tablecloth. She's in a green print shirtdress belted at the waist, drawing deeply from a cigarette, surrounded by trees and green growth. The cabin's rough logs, by then weathered gray, peek out from behind the trees—it looks quaint and absolutely ancient.

Daddy, in theory, got his dream job that summer. He was hired to take tourists around the area by a self-made millionaire from Louisiana,

*Baby Miriam and me at
the Bersches' house.*

*Clockwise from left: Granminnow (with cigarette),
Tricia Hearn (wife of Episcopal priest and Blanchard
Springs Caverns guide, Arnold Hearn), Mary Bersch,
Mollie Bersch, and an unknown guest in front of
the cabin on our baptism day, June 1978.*

a "heritage hustler," who owned the Dew Drop Inn, the 1886 bed and breakfast in Mountain View, and a new tourism business called the Ozark Outdoor Center.[24] He printed business cards with Daddy's name and "Program Developer" on them. Momma wrote a letter on Ozark Outdoor Center, Inc. letterhead to her aunt Cooie on Fifth Avenue in New York that July. A brochure inside for the Dew Drop Inn advertised: "If you are asking yourself how to make the best use of your time in Mountain View call the Ozark Outdoor Center [. . .] If you want to do some of the things that most folks miss, like going on a coon hunt, or finding a bee tree, visiting an undeveloped cave, going to a baptizing or a quilting bee we can help with transportation, equipment, guides and advice. Tours and activities include wilderness camping, trail rides, Indian Archeology, homesteading seminars, folk medicine and musical get-togethers and fellowship."[25] Daddy never met with a single tourist, and eventually fell out with the owner when he later refused to pay Rhett for a sign she'd painted for the Dew Drop Inn, but he spent that summer focusing on the splendors of our area.[26]

Mammy and Pappy and Daddy's divorced sister, Rhett, arrived in early July to see baby Miriam. Rhett came with her three boys and planned to stay, for good, in a small house down the hill from us. Meanwhile, Momma was now juggling three children and her housework. "My dishes are stacked to the ceiling, my wash is stacked to the ceiling and I have diapers to hang out," she wrote in August 1978, and the following month, "I am on the go from 5 a.m. to 11 p.m. and still the laundry mildews in huge piles."[27] She was using an old, white, electric wringer washer set up in the yard and a more modern machine that sat on the front porch, depending on which was working at the moment. When winter came, the cold would freeze the water or chap and crack her hands, so she would have to resort to the laundromat down the mountain. (And to think that she had written to her mother as a single, childless young woman from Boston nine years before: "if I ever have to walk to another laundromat in the middle of the night with sweat streaming from every pore I shall commit some terrible atrocity I'm sure."[28])

But Momma found time for leisure, as did Daddy. She wrote in the wake of her birthday in September, "All my free time I spend reading novels which is a great way to get away from it all (Richard + I loved the *Poldark Saga*)—but as a result I don't keep up with housework or letter-writing."[29] Our house was so filled with books, and they must have been therapy on that lonely mountain. How rejuvenating, if not entirely relaxing, to let the laundry mildew while you lose yourself in a novel. On a windowsill in a photo from the time, presumably in mid-read, are a handful of *National Geographics*, a Samuel Johnson, a collection of Edith Wharton, the *New American Review*, and a selection of other paperbacks too blurry to make out.

Aunt Rhett brought Daddy's antique secretary desk from childhood with her that summer, and Daddy placed it next to the long, reclaimed bookshelf in the living area. The bookshelf was bursting with all the books my parents had brought with them from Colorado, spines that, like the art on our walls, were a constant through all my years at home, etched into my memory from a thousand passing glances: deckle-edged, ivory-papered French classics with hand-sewn spines, half the pages still uncut (although we had fun remedying that); Daddy's Henry Millers and Anaïs Nin and Walt Whitman; Momma's Françoise Sagan and Colette, both of whom I would turn to in my teens; a warped Aubrey Beardsley full of art nouveau farting madams and gigantic penises that I gaped through countless times; a hardback of thrilling Charles Addams cartoons; *Ain't You Got a Right to the Tree of Life*, the book of South Carolina Gullah stories and songs; *Black Elk Speaks* by John G. Neihardt—I always thought he was a relative and puzzled over the missing *d*; *Trout Fishing in America* by Richard Brautigan; *The Milagro Beanfield War* by John Nichols; C. S. Lewis's *Space Trilogy* and its surreal covers; Lawrence Durrell's *Alexandria Quartet*; *The Dollmaker* by Harriette Arnow (Cassie's legs severed by a train!); and countless other novels.

I took note of the books and paintings and mahogany antiques that were not in the homes around us. The antiques, Momma once wrote, "fit *perfectly* in our imperfect house," even if their tops were soon water stained and drawn on, their drawers broken and warped.[30] A steady supply of books came from the Chinook Bookshop in Colorado Springs too, to keep us all entertained through impenetrable roads and illness. I nearly wept when Momma sold most of them off at a yard sale in the early nineties, lugged through so much, then finally too much of a burden.

"There are no books or bookstores anywhere nearby, except 2 rather grim public libraries in Mtn. View + Clinton," Momma wrote to Uncle Chuck in 1974.[31] In addition to the books that were regularly sent, Granminnow and Aunt Ruth gave us annual subscriptions to *National Geographic*, the *New Yorker*, *Country Living*, *Ranger Rick*, *World*, *Highlights*, *Organic Gardening*, and *Fine Woodworking*. In the early days on the land, Aunt Ruth sent my parents her old copies of the *Saturday Review* and *The Guardian*. The latter "was very handy because it was printed on thin paper—almost like tissue paper—so it did double duty as TP," Daddy told me. Momma wrote at the time:

> Tell Ruth that we are *really* enjoying the magazines—Richard + I manage to sneak time every day to read one article or another, and they are our major touch (really our sole touch) with the outside world intellectually—In Fox, most people watch T.V.—We do not, so we have a hard time finding out the news (the radio stations are inadequate)— What a pleasure to have something to talk about besides garden + *gossip* (thick in Arkansas).[32]

Although she mentioned inadequate radio stations in this 1974 letter (from the Key Place), Momma told me that our land was near a radio tower that gave us excellent reception, and she often spent her days listening to National Public Radio and music—Willie Nelson and the Pointer Sisters were her favorites—on a small black transistor radio that sat in the window or on top of the refrigerator. I remember quiet days when all had been scrubbed clean and dust particles floated twinkling in the sun through the windows to the comforting drone of NPR. (Although sometimes the peace of the moment would be shattered by talk of nuclear war, the root of some of my earliest anxieties, or the sound of conservative radio host Paul Harvey's voice—something he once said, or my parents said about him, filled me with dread when I heard it.)

Katy and I escaped the farm for hours, with sheets of butcher paper and pencils, creating tall, slim houses with many detailed floors and rooms: reading nooks concealed under staircases, dining rooms, bedrooms, attic hideaways, balconies covered with potted plants, table lamps, and bookshelves everywhere. None of these drawings have survived—considering how often memory fails, maybe we never made more than one—but I've never forgotten them, never forgotten the silent joy of designing them. These houses were nothing like the world we inhabited then and could only have been informed by our reading and listening. Momma talked of Aunt Ruth's homes—legendary in the family for their beauty and taste— her historic Beacon Hill townhouse in Boston and the red farmhouse in Vermont.

Or perhaps we were also inspired by *New Yorker* cartoons. Removed as we were from the worlds my parents had come from, it wasn't until I was in my late twenties that I fully understood the scope of the *New Yorker*'s readership, that it wasn't just our extended family's obscure find. I discovered in my thirties, first in an old autograph book I have of Nana's, my maternal great-grandmother, that she had been a close friend and college roommate of Katherine Sergeant White, the one-time *New Yorker* fiction editor and wife of E. B. White. Her son, the *New Yorker* writer Roger Angell, was married to his first wife in Nana's living room in Denver with my great uncles in attendance. The *New Yorker* wasn't just a magazine, it was in many ways a portal into the world Momma left behind.

National Geographic was another dependable monthly window on the world outside of our farm, and I was enthralled. Like the prince I had read about in Hans Christian Andersen's "The Garden of Paradise," I "could read about everything which had ever happened in the world, and see it all represented in the most beautiful pictures."

Equally enthralling were the regular missives from Momma's siblings: Uncle Jock was in Mexico, Belize, Nicaragua, El Salvador, and Samoa; Aunt Sarah went from France to England to Brazil to Palo Alto, then off to Colombia with, "I'll be sending P-cards from Bogotá."[33] In 1977, she wrote to us from Brazil that "the children here live on black beans and rice and watermelon and you guys look upper-class compared to most," and in 1980 from Mozambique: "And you could have a farm just like the one you have in Moz. but you would go crazy (and probably starve) because you would find it impossible to buy tools or fertilizers or sugar or flour or anything else."[34] She wrote to us from an archipelagic island in Sweden and from Stockholm, where she would make her lifelong home. Katy and I started to collect our postcards in albums. I absorbed all those images and plotted my adult life of foreign adventure, not realizing my parents were on their own similar adventure. I was determined to be a world-traveling archaeologist—the confines of the woods inspired my daily play but not necessarily my dreams. I wrote a fictional piece about my future self years later, in sixth grade, that had its origins in this time in the woods:

> We land in Africa and drive in a jeep to a tribe of Aborigines. [. . .] Night comes on and we eat a dinner of fresh caught rabbit. We work here for two months washing babies, hunting, talking to older tribe members and I am keeping a journal of my days here. Now we are to leave Africa [. . .] and fly to go to Egypt for an archeological dig. [. . .] Now after living in a grass hut and eating Egyptian food for three months, I must

leave Egypt to go to France and be *married* to Philip in the gardens of Notre Dame. It was the most joyous wedding I had ever even dreamed of having. [. . .] We are now living in Austria in a small town in a nice cottage. I have started writing a book called *Peace Corp and Archeaology: The Two I Like Best*. I spend night and day writing this book. I have become quite cranky and restless sitting at a desk so much.[35]

Daddy completed more renovations to the cabin that summer. He installed a washing machine indoors (that soon broke), with hot water, a bathtub and a sink, and a medicine cabinet—but still no flushing toilet.[36] Daddy got the water heater from a man at work who had kept it stored in his barn. Daddy turned it on for the first time, and a putrid stench filled the room. The cavity was filled with dead mice. He got it working after removing the decaying remains and cleaning it thoroughly, running gallon after gallon of Clorox through it.

In September came welcome changes in the kitchen. Momma was happy with "a new [used] cookstove (smaller to fit in my kitchen)," and, with birthday money from Granminnow, new linoleum over the rough planks, insulation in the ceiling, sheetrock on the walls, simple shelves in place of the salvaged cabinets she hated, and fresh paint everywhere.[37] "It is beautiful," she wrote.

We made a cassette tape for Pappy's birthday the following month. It is mostly Katy and I telling stories, singing, reading, fighting, but there is one short segment about seventeen minutes in that gives Daddy a small voice amid all the letters from Momma. Daddy was a man of few words for the most part. Unless sharing a colorful story or joke, he was quiet, reading in his chair, swiping a black tube of ChapStick now and again across his lips (his signature scent until he upgraded to Burt's Bees Honey Lip Balm in recent years), and interjecting with snippets of songs that flowed like a tic from the words spoken around him.

"Richard is here but he won't tell you what he's been doing, but he's building a house and doing really well," Momma says, and then laughing, "Maybe he will tell you something."[38]

"Tell 'em sumpin', Daddy," I say.

"Richard, tell 'em sumpin'!" Katy barks in the background.

Katy on the counter in the newly remodeled kitchen.

"Tell 'em something. I'm building a house," he says with a reflective pause, and then begins slowly, "that is . . . thirty feet by thirty-six feet, three stories . . . post and beam construction, four-by-ten, sixteen-foot-long four-by-ten red oak ceiling joists . . . the walls are framed out of oak and pine six-by-sixes." He mutters something else and goes on softly, "And . . . uhhh . . . it's a dandy, it's a dandy, that's about all I can say for it." And then the tape clicks off. My memories of Daddy in those years are cluttered with his thick, rectangular, hand-sharpened carpenter pencils; his pocketknife; his chalk box with the powdery straight red lines he snapped when building. He was so caught up in carpentry details and plans, slightly removed from us and our world of play and cooking and school.

Daddy was also his beard. He cut his long hair off before I could remember it, but I've only seen him without a beard two times in my life. The first time, we drove as a family to Mountain View and dropped Daddy off at the barbershop. He was waiting for us when we returned, his face smooth and hairless and pale.

"We want our black daddy back!" we cried in the car. I didn't trust this new man. Katy and I refused to touch him for days.

A month later, we made another recording, this time for Mammy and Pappy while celebrating an early Christmas at Rhett's tiny red house nestled in the trees. The tape gives a rare glimpse into our lives with Rhett and the boys, but, more importantly for me, it illustrates the loose, playful nature of our family time in general—lots of laughing, Daddy filled with tales of youthful devilment and intrigue, bawdy asides we couldn't understand, Momma full of theatricality. My parents never censored themselves much around us children nor do they around their grandchildren today, to our occasional chagrin.

The tape begins with an obnoxious group screaming session of "Deck the Halls" in the days before Christmas, followed by my eldest cousin Edward saying in his soft southern accent: "Pappy and Mammy, tonight I went huntin' and got me another squirrel and I bin cuttin' wood with the chainsaw and, let's see, my pigs are gettin' fat, pretty soon we'll have to go get 'em butchered."[39] It was a hard time for the boys, away from their father and the middle-class suburban life they had left behind in South Carolina, but all you hear in his voice is the adventure of it.

On the next side of the tape, Little Richard, the twelve-year-old, has just shown off his stack of newly chopped wood to my father and John Weaver with pride. "I chopped it all day," he says.[40]

"Didn't even cut his leg off," says Daddy. "That's more than your Uncle Lewis could cut in that amount of time, I believe," he adds, jokingly.

"Course your Uncle Lewis wouldn't get right after it," Momma says, in that surprising slight accent she had at the time (picked up she said, not from locals, but a Tennessee girlfriend of John's).

The conversation wanders around and lands on pouring drinks from a bottle of cheap wine they had been given that they found hilarious. I notice the tape recorder in the room and wonder why they have it, Momma says she leant it to them, Edward teases me that they stole it, and Rhett tells everyone it's recording.

"You're going to edit this I presume," Daddy chuckles, and the laughter and talking resume with no further comment on the recorder.

"That shit is damn near poison," Daddy then says and laughs, "I don't think the kids should be drinking it at all. It should be reserved for me and John."

Momma bursts into giggles and says something loud but inaudible, and then mumbles, laughing again, "Now I know the real truth behind the happily married life of Richard and Wendy."

Between waves of laughter and other conversation, Momma adds, "I may not be able to drink my whole one."

Little Richard pipes in addressing Daddy, clearly trying on the adult ribbing for size, "I'm sure Richard'll drink it."

"It looks divine," Momma drawls.

Daddy, in a comic and enunciated southern accent, says merrily, "Grinnin' like unto a possum."

Momma takes a sip of the low-grade alcohol. "Oh, my God. Oh, it's not bad," and then dropping into a British accent with a chuckle, "Really not bad at tall."

"When you're desperate," Aunt Rhett interjects, laughing.

"Reminds me of the army," says John sending Little Richard into squeaking giggles.

"When you'd drink anything," Daddy adds.

Momma, in her British accent again, orders jokingly, "Wine steward, this is fine, bring the extra bottle."

"Y'all just drunk up all my wine," says Little Richard. The room erupts into peals of mischievous laughing and under-breath joking, and the older boys try the wine.

"Wendy, everything's ready except the dumplings, do you want to go ahead and . . . ," Aunt Rhett pipes in and the two discuss timing of the meal in the background.

"I think it's rather good," says Little Richard.

"Dare I try a second sip?" Daddy giggles. "Okay, here goes. Anything for a buzz."

"Give these kids something to make them real sick, and they'll never drink again," Momma jokes.

"That's God-awful stuff," says Daddy. Little Richard thinks this is hilarious and laughs more as Daddy and John discuss all the rotgut liquors they've tried.

"A twelve-year-old'll drink anything. First thing I ever got drunk on was vermouth," says Daddy, "I stole a bottle of vermouth out of Dad's liquor cabinet. Went down in the basement, went down in the basement, and got drunk."

"If you swish it [Thunderbird] around in your mouth, you get the real taste of it," says Little Richard, followed by more laughter.

"Makes you want to *vomit*," adds Daddy, and the boys laugh hysterically again.

"Well, I probly never tasted good wine, then," says Little Richard. (How much wine could he have tasted at all—he was only twelve?)

"Back when I was in college," says Daddy, "we used to drink this cheap red wine. It was just a cheap red Burgundy type wine that, just, turned your mouth red. . . . We'd make Purple Jesus. Make a bathtub full of Purple Jesus."

"That Afghan looks beautiful on David's bed," Momma remarks to Rhett.

"Purple Jesus is, a, a, one of these, it's a grape-juiced based vodka [. . .] thing [. . .] You know you dump, variations . . . ," Daddy continues while Momma and Aunt Rhett continue to discuss meal timing inaudibly.

"You used to have parties when you were in college? Get the whole clan up and have a big ol' party?" asks Little Richard.

His brother Edward teasingly mimics him, *"The whole clan."*

"Once a week, at least?" Little Richard continues, ignoring his brother, so interested in my father's answer.

"Every night, every night," Daddy begins, amid pubescent, warbly giggles from Little Richard, "We had a party one time. Had gotten evicted from an apartment that a bunch of us were living in, had a big party one night and got just stone drunk and took every piece of glass in the house to include nipping around the neighborhood and stealing milk bottles off porches. We threw them at the walls—knocked great holes in the Sheetrock and broke all this glass on the floor. There was broken glass, *inches* deep throughout the house; we broke every single glass object we could find. Just wrecked the place."

Everyone laughs, and Daddy adds sarcastically, "Nice, yeah, real nice."

"Must have been a real riot," Little Richard says, truly impressed with the story.

"Used to make neat little round holes in windows with ball bearings and sling shots. Neat little round holes," Daddy brags, to more howls of laughter, and then John tells of similar young deviance, including shooting out a window.

"Wonderful," Daddy chuckles with delinquent delight.

"I only do things like that when I'm in a terrible rage," he adds, with an almost audible smile.

Momma wrote to Granminnow—after an unusual hiatus in the letters— that we spent Christmas Day 1978 with Aunt Rhett and David (the older boys were with their father) and some new friends, Michael and Susie Warshauer.[41] The Warshauers were another outsider couple who lived in Mountain View. Michael was a serious caver, which had brought them to the area, and a chef and baker, eventually opening the HearthStone Bakery in Mountain View. He would on occasion bring the result of a "Baking Mania"—his words—to the church services at the Bersches': cannoli and linzer torte and rugelach.[42]

Michael and Susie were outsiders too, not hippies but not straight either. I thought of them as city people, because they lived in town. Michael was quirky and obsessive about his interests and Jewish, a novel identity in backwoods Arkansas. They would seem unsuitable to the region—with the exception of Michael's spelunking—but he and Susie stayed there long after we left. (They later moved to rural Mexico.) Susie was all smiles and softness with us and doted on baby Miriam, much like Aunt Rhett did. She already had completely gray hair when we knew her, straight and shiny and short, and clean, smooth hands that were seldom far from her knitting needles. It was she who taught me how to crochet, an activity I enjoyed, in the form of endless small squares, well into junior high.

For Christmas that year, Susie brought us all sorts of knit articles, and a promise of an afghan for Momma.[43] Granminnow sent us suitcases, and Katy and David and I played airport all day in the incongruous confines of the cabin. Granminnow had spent a weekend on route to Key West in Little Rock earlier that month—a fact strangely missing in the letters but present in my memories and notes on envelopes of old photos. We piled into one of our old cars and made the long drive to the city where we visited her at a Sheraton Hotel. I used her lipstick, clipped her earrings on my ears, and pressed my face into soft white towels embossed with a big *S*. As I played airport in the cabin, I was picturing flying to the exotic locations in books and family postcards with clean towels and lined suitcases and pretty clothes. Years later Granminnow would reminisce in a letter to her sister, who was then in Florida, about her own time in Florida in our early Fox years. She had been most taken, she wrote, by the beautifully dressed children with parents in minks that she saw at a Christmas Eve mass in Palm Beach: "I guess I was more struck by the elegant families because Wendy was then living in her worse state and I was yearning to see my grandaughters dressed like the dolls around me!"[44]

We were not dressed as dolls, but we weren't suffering. Momma wrote that Daddy and Michael did the cooking on Christmas Day. In the small kitchen, they prepared "exquisite Jewish food—chopped chicken livers, sour cream and pickled herring, corned beef, pot roast, potato pancakes, fruit cake, pecan pie, breads galore, etc., etc.," laying it all out on the old farm table.

"Fat I still am," she wrote.[45]

Sir Philip Sidney, in his sixteenth-century pastoral romance of Arcadia, wrote, "Doth not the pleasantness of this place carry in itself sufficient reward for any time lost in it, or for any such danger that might ensue?"[46] In the midst of this period of relative bliss on the land—when my parents seemed finally able to just enjoy family, friends, and our farm—were the usual dark clouds.

One of the most memorable moments in my parents' marriage, for Momma, happened around this time. When Daddy came home one afternoon and saw that Momma hadn't fixed the freezer in the yard as he'd asked that morning, he blew up, slamming the freezer door and spitting curses. Momma yelled back, and he followed her as she went into the cabin. In a blur of screaming and movement, she found herself backed against the front window as he reached for her neck. "He'll kill me, that was my thought," she told me later. But just as his rage reached a crescendo, Daddy stopped himself. He didn't lay a hand on her. He dropped his hands and pulled back, his physical anger diffused by the shock of what he'd almost begun. It was the only time she ever felt afraid of him.

I don't remember this fight, but we often heard them yelling and slamming plates and other objects. There was an almost palpable violence in Daddy, but he controlled it, the rage staying pent up in a beet red face or a ruined object or a curse word. Daddy was a powerhouse of will and determination for his own vision, fast-thinking and faster moving and irritable in day-to-day tasks, Momma strong in her own right but cowed into seeming-submission under the demands of children and a pioneer home. The physical demands on them both were intense, and the fury between them could be powerful. They met at the end of long, grueling days—Daddy exhausted from hard labor, suffering from his chronic headaches or motion sickness or back pain; my mother isolated, frazzled by whining, needy children and the constant demands of wood and water and food. It's the story of the power struggle in many marriages turned on high by an unforgiving environment and poverty, or, as Momma wrote in a letter, "the huge gaping jaw of our indebtedness."[47]

My cousin Little Richard told a story of Daddy's temper on that jovial evening we taped around Christmas 1978. The actual event had taken place four years earlier, but the story had been elevated to legend status by that time, and Little Richard tells it descriptively even though he had not been present:

"Like when you couldn't fix your car and you just walked back and Wendy *grabbed the baby and ran*," Little Richard says, laughing, speaking the last words with a guttural tone for effect.[48] "And you picked up a rock, turned around, *CRRRR*, knocked a big ol' hole in the windshield. Then he saw the sledgehammer. *Ooooh, The Sledgehammer*," he tells his audience, relishing the last bit, all the boys giggling now. "He picked that thing up and he just mutilated that car."

Unlike Little Richard, I was there. I wasn't yet three years old, but I do remember something: the scattered square jewels of glass on the gravel, pieces and piles of little blue-green blocks, like nothing I had seen before. It happened in the winter of 1974 as we were preparing to drive our newly acquired 1962 International Scout to Colorado for the holidays. Three cars were parked in our front yard of mud, river gravel, and weeds: a pickup, the Scout, and a Chevy sedan—none of which would start that December morning. Rage overcame Daddy, standing in the cold front yard, disappointed yet again by a junky vehicle. He picked up the closest rock and flung it hard through the back window of the Chevy, but his anger still itched. He saw the sledgehammer leaning against a pile of wood and within reach. He picked it up and shattered the front windshield, finishing the demon creature off, now overcome with the opposing sensation of relief. "Great relief," he told me. Daddy was as pleased with the story in 2014 as Little Richard had been telling it in 1978. (That was the Colorado trip we did make, so somehow they rustled up another vehicle, borrowed one Daddy thinks.)

"I didn't care about the car. I hope from now on any rage requires it be done outside," Momma says on the cassette after Little Richard's story, alluding to the possibility of Daddy bringing such a tirade indoors.[49] The lighthearted telling and Momma's calm commentary speaks to how, as volatile as the tension was, it was often followed closely by humor. Although as I listened to the tape, I found myself surprised to hear her sound almost amused—her anger over his outbursts was a narrative running through my adolescence and adulthood. I am sometimes overwhelmed by the anger Momma still has. She is by turns full of pride when talking of these days and full of resentment at my father, still carrying petty frustrations over stupid mistakes or irritating habits. I grew up close to Daddy on one level but carrying this anger for her sake. Now I find myself wishing she could just let it go like she does on this cassette but knowing that's too much to ask. The story was a proxy for so many explosive moments, often over vehicles.

"I really think I loved every minute of [our life there]," Daddy told me recently, "except dealing with junk vehicles, plenty of which I owned through those years."

After a while, reading the letters, I gave up trying to keep track of all the different automobiles my parents purchased over the years. There'd been a Chevy sedan and a sixty-dollar truck at the Key Place, a brand new Dodge van in October of 1975 for Daddy's business, an old pickup for Momma at Christmas that year, a Ford Galaxy, and on and on.[50] In 1977, Momma had written, "*no* vehicle really stands up to this country very well," so they were near-disposable, cheap, mostly used cars.[51]

The new Dodge van was a lemon, and after trying unsuccessfully to return it, Daddy stopped the monthly payments so they'd take it back. It worked. Two men in suits from Little Rock drove up our dusty road and stepped out of their car in front of the cabin, a terrified look on their faces. My parents were struck by their fear, by the realization that Daddy was in their eyes just another backcountry, gun-toting yokel who might refuse to give up his vehicle. That's who my parents had theoretically become. But Daddy was happy to hand over the car and default on his loan. Momma talked him out of his stubborn anger and into a renegotiation to save their credit. They continued the payments and the van limped along.

My parents did buy one other new vehicle, a reliable one, and they purchased it that pleasant summer of Miriam's birth. Momma wrote that we got a new Datsun truck—"the cheapest available, but it still cost plenty."[52]

Daddy went to Clinton State Bank for a loan to buy the truck. The bank agent simply said, "Just go pick out what you need and write a check and come back and sign the papers when you get a chance." (There were also books of blank checks from the local bank sitting on store counters for people who forgot their own.)

The white Volkswagen we got from Granminnow in the fall of 1976 was the only car I really remember from the woods. It stood out with its short, rounded body next to the old trucks and sedans, and, despite periods of disuse, we had it longer than any other vehicle. Within five months of driving it onto the land, the Arkansas roads had rendered it unable to reverse with an exhausted starter and out of alignment, so it sat in the yard for months until money could be found for repairs.[53] The letters contain a litany of thrown rods, kaput engines, leaking oil, and broken starters and varied sums—$5, $120, $50—dropping into a money pit for repairs.

As the 1978 cassette recording with our cousins went on, Daddy seemed completely unfazed by the story of his sledgehammer debacle and simply says, "I wish I'd kept that car. I'd like to see what it'd look like by now."[54]

"How much did you sell it for after ya ruined it?" asks Little Richard.

"Five dollars," Daddy says.

"More than it was worth," says John.

"Did they actually pay us for that?" asks Momma.

"Yeah, well, they never paid it all. Kathy finally sent some money and said, Will you call it even for this?" Daddy answers.

"What'd they want it for?" asks Aunt Rhett.

"They wanted the engine out of it."

The adults continue to discuss various cars that had been in the Roberts and Neidhardt families, and then Little Richard, angling for his uncle's attention again, asks, "Hey, Richard, take me to a police auction sometime? I hear you can get some good deals."

"They don't have police auctions here. They don't have police here," our neighbor John laughs.

"I doubt they ever did have *real* good auctions around here, 'cause nobody around here ever *had* anything," Daddy adds.

Thirteen

RURAL SPECIAL

If you have children and genuinely love them, don't cripple
their minds by subjecting them to the low level of 'education' that
prevails in such parts. [. . .] Do you want your children to be decently
taught, and to come under the influence of other youngsters at least
no more ignorant and savage than they are themselves? Then spare
them the stunting effect of deep-country residence, with
its non-education and warping social contacts.
—1975 *Mother Earth News* editorial on Ozark life[1]

 My elementary school mascot in Fox, Arkansas, was a Rebel
soldier with a Confederate flag and a rifle. In Head Start I was
a Rebelette.[2] On the long walk home through fields and dirt
roads from the bus stop to our cabin, I chewed on wood sorrel
and merrily sang songs I had learned in class: "Jesus loves me,
this I know, for the Bible tells me so."

"Christ on a fucking crutch!" exploded regularly from Daddy's lips on
the confines of our farm, but at school I accepted the Baptist air.

Katy and I went to the local public school, Girl Special, or so I thought
it was called. It was actually called Rural Special. I was there from Head
Start to third grade. The school consisted of four buildings and a gym for
Head Start through twelfth grade and had 225 students serving all the
kids in the towns of Fox, Rushing, Turkey Creek, Meadowcreek, Parma,
and Mozart.[3] (The school still exists, they're still Rebels, and still very
small, although their mascot is no longer a soldier but Colonel Reb, the
retired University of Mississippi mascot—a Mark Twain–looking southern gentleman.)

In his book *Hill Folks*, Brooks Blevins describes the school:

Rural Special is an official appellation used by the state Department
of Education to identify rural consolidated school districts. [. . .] As

far as I know, Stone County's Rural Special school district [formed in 1942] is the only one of the state's districts to retain the name instead of adopting the name of the local village or community as its unofficial name. Rural Special remains an apt title for the district, one of the most rural and isolated in the state of Arkansas.[4]

I had first started at the school, alone, at three and a half years old—with long bus rides and days—until I fell apart a few weeks into the school year, and Momma pulled me out. That fall, the reality of her environment sinking in, Momma wrote Granminnow:

> The other experience that left me worried was that I applied for a job teaching at Rural Special—I got a polite but flat no since I had no teacher certification—which was fine, but what made me realize how far in the backwaters I am was when I asked if he (the principal) thought he would need a French teacher in the future if I had certification. His answer was that they *might* put in foreign languages in order to get a better rating, but that they'd probably put in music instead—No art No music No theatre No FOREIGN LANGUAGES—these are courses I took for granted in every school I ever went to—and then I remembered reading that a neighboring school had just put in the study *of LITERATURE! HELP!* I may be able to organize some kind of a summer school for these subjects, but I don't know. I know I want my children as well or better educated than I am and there can be no 2 ways about it![5]

In this early naiveté, Momma was shocked that the school principal didn't recognize French on a document she showed him. She was until then also unaware that some people didn't graduate from high school! (Her own children would at least never be so naïve.) She made attempts to augment our education with the French classes she taught in the late seventies and art lessons with Aunt Rhett, but for the most part I did few extracurricular activities growing up and attended poor to average public schools. But I would learn one very important lesson: that my poverty had been both real and an illusion. It was real that we had little, lived roughly, and went to the same poor schools as everyone around us, but it was also true that I went home to shelves of books and was nurtured by educated parents and relatives and backed by generational wealth that told me I could be more.

Once Katy and I both started at Rural Special—together, in 1977, when Katy was four and I was five—Momma's frustrations were more immediate. "Head Start is unbelievable—government red tape everywhere. [. . .] Still *no* painting except when Mollie [Bersch] comes, + *no* carpentry—which infuriates me, because they have all the materials and equipment. But the teachers are nice, and they are swamped with paper work."[6] Even Rural Special suffered the bureaucratic woes of the modern world. Momma volunteered to put together the Head Start newsletter, mandated by the federal law that supported the anti-poverty program. There were eight federally mandated components the newsletter had to cover, and she gathered information on birthdays, volunteering, the teachers, events for the season, home remedies, and recipes. A drawing of a purple cow by Katy adorned the cover of the October newsletter. ("According to the teachers, [Katy and Sarah] are so far advanced in drawing compared to the other kids that their pictures keep turning up on the newsletter, no matter how hard I try to suggest other children's pictures.") Momma was a poor typist, so the teacher typed up her handwritten information and mimeographed copies for the parents.[7] (What's not mentioned in any letter, is that Granminnow would have recognized some of this. In September 1965, the year Head Start began, her nursery school, The Ruth Washburn Cooperative Nursery School, had the first Head Start class in El Paso County, Colorado. She was also involved in implementing the program throughout Colorado.[8])

When I was in first grade, Momma wrote that she was struggling with the school's paddling for routine offenses (even the teenagers), a campus store serving Coke and candy, and "racial prejudice."[9] One of my classmates, Brother Ray,* was the only student of color I recall, and I remember nothing of the sort ever being expressed, but Momma had heard the harsher talk of adults. She was also disgusted by what she referred to as "this favorite business" and "queen and king nonsense," which "Rural Special seems to indulge in it to a ridiculous degree":

Sarah was elected favorite—but not elected queen of her class for Halloween carnival—which absolutely crushed her—She does not lack for ambition—she also had the mistaken idea that *I* wanted her to be queen which I finally unraveled and translated—I wanted Sarah + Katy

* Pseudonym

to *both* be queen of their respective classes the same year—so that I wouldn't have to hear the cries and screams—Now I can only hope and pray that Katy will *not* be elected queen of Head Start.[10]

I still have a slim, red, Rebel-soldier-embossed yearbook from 1981, the year Katy was voted the second grade's favorite girl. The year before, I had finally been made queen of my class for the Halloween carnival. We drove to the carnival in the back of a pickup with our cousins singing, "Lions and tigers and bears, Oh my!" It was held in the school gym (basketball was the only sport the school had) with the customary cakewalks and other games; my favorite was Go Fish. I cast a brown paper bag hanging from a stick over a sheet. The bag came back filled with used makeup donated by the townspeople—half worn lipsticks and deeply rutted rouge pots. Pure heaven.

Despite her other frustrations with the school, Momma doesn't complain that we get the day off school for the opening of deer season and mentions it almost proudly on a 1977 cassette tape to Granminnow.[11] Nor does she seem concerned by the lunches and snacks we were served. Her health food stance was complicated. Despite her rhetoric, she never made our lunches; she was practical—these were free. I happily rattled off the list for Granminnow on the same recording: "We eat salads and mashed potatuhs and fruit cocktail and hot dogs . . . and . . . drink chocolate milk."[12] For snack the first year of school we had pineapple on toothpicks dipped in red Jell-O.[13]

I loved Rural Special: its chocolate milk; the scent of pastepots and colored paper and mimeograph ink; and the milky, cheap-gravy, processed-food smell of the cafeteria. Katy and I also discovered there that dried gum pushed up under desktops could be picked off and reconstituted in our mouths, as could pieces found on the ground. Like kids in towns across America, we counted pennies and ladybugs in math workbooks, sprouted seeds between damp paper towels, placed hands over hearts and said the Pledge of Allegiance each day, played Farmer in the Dell and Bubble Gum, Bubble Gum, in a Dish under the trees at recess. We had a small playground and a wide sloping field behind the school to wander in, where I watched a girl drink from the teat of a pregnant basset hound that roamed campus.

But the threat of corporal punishment weighed heavily on me. I was too afraid to interrupt Mrs. Nixon to ask to go to the bathroom in third grade,

My graduation from Head Start in about spring 1978
with Principal Rodney Rushing.

so I peed in my molded plastic seat. I was given a pair of blue polyester bell-bottoms from a milk crate in the Head Start room to wear. I went doo doo—as I called it then—in the designated teacher's stall of our shared bathroom and, afraid of being found out and paddled, decided I had to remove the evidence. I reached into the toilet and grabbed the lumps of shit and carried them gingerly to a student toilet and flushed them down.

Our first-grade teacher, Mrs. Anderson, was tall and thin with horn-rimmed black glasses set on a fine-boned, elegant face, a bouffant of dark hair piled on top. Through a brown-paneled door in the wall and one step down was her grey-haired mother, Mrs. Nixon, our second- and third-grade teacher. The second and third grades were so small they were combined, so Katy and I were once again in the same classroom each day. Many subjects may have languished or been nonexistent, but reading was taken seriously; we had old Dick and Jane readers and others that must have been from the fifties or earlier when I think back on their plain, solid linen covers. Our peers were a mixed group of mostly locals and some outsiders like us. Momma wrote Granminnow, her snobbery too hard to hide, "I can see that the schools here will not be an intellectual experience for Sarah and Katy, but a good social experience nonetheless."[14]

Socializing, Momma wrote, was a "heady + frightening game" for me.[15]

I made friends with other girls my own age for the first time and experienced my first crushes—on towheaded Jimmy and dark-eyed Danny. I was scared of a few rowdy boys from a big local family. For years, a shaggy-haired fourth grader would chase me through my nightmares. There was at least one child who came to school barefoot, and there were young children with Skoal rings already worn into their back pockets. There was a boy named Toby with Down syndrome beloved by all. Lisa, the prettiest girl in my class, had smooth, shiny strawberry blond hair that kissed her shoulders where it was curled under with an iron (my hair was tangled and curly). She lived in a small but modern mobile home that I coveted. There was a quiet, friendly Mennonite girl who wore a white cap and dresses every day. She had cords of flesh-colored scars down the left side of her face and body from a washbasin of boiling water that had fallen on her. Brother Ray, a brown-skinned boy, had no last name. His mother crocheted me a pair of red slippers one Christmas as thanks for the kindness I had shown her son. I have no memory of any cruelty toward him, but I know he was socially set apart from the rest of us. I don't know if it was his skin color, his quiet presence, or the strange moniker Brother.

There was my best friend Rhonda[†] whose father accidentally ran over and killed her two-year-old brother while backing out of their driveway, her name and coy smile forever bound to tragedy for me. (She never came to our cabin; friendships were played out at school since we all lived many slow, dirt-road miles from each other.) There was an older girl, new to the Ozarks, who my parents and I visited occasionally. Her relatively affluent mother, to save money, only let her drink powdered milk and have a single serving of dinner. She fell while doing a cherry drop from the trapeze bar on the playground swing set onto an exposed piece of plastic pipe and broke her back, leaving small drops of blood on the stark white pipe. In my memory they are all connected: restricted food and powdered milk and chalky broken bones. There were siblings I watched with curiosity, all with the same limp, oily hair, driven to school by their obese mother in a small Datsun truck. There were the seniors who were like grown men and women, the boys dressed like cowboys with tight jeans, big belt buckles, and blue Future Farmers of America jackets, the girls with feathered hair in blouses and jeans.

† Pseudonym

Socially, Rural Special was a success for us. It was, as much as I can really assess from this distance, a barebones education. We didn't learn about other countries that I can remember, or about much outside the basics of reading, writing, and arithmetic. ("Reading and writing and 'rithmetic, taught to the tune of a hickory stick!" we sang.) But when we got to our new school in the next town in the middle of third grade, I distinctly remember that I got in trouble for writing in cursive because the other kids hadn't yet learned it. However, when I asked my cousin Dave, the youngest of the three, if he felt he had received a good education graduating from Rural Special he said, "Where were you? Arkansas?? Prepared? College? From a school aptly named Rural Special? I think not."[16]

I don't know how the other students saw us. Two outsider girls? Just like everyone else? The girls with the hippy parents? (We weren't the only ones at the school.) I was rib skinny, with a dirty-blond rat's nest of curly hair that I hated having brushed, big gapped teeth, full lips I took from my father, and brown eyes. Katy was rounder with straight, black hair, green eyes, and ruddy cheeks. I was shy and self-conscious but dramatic and friendly as I grew comfortable. Katy was adoring and bold and not afraid to use bad words at school, but we were both good girls, dutifully sitting in our little desks, filling in our workbooks, and lining up for lunch. Katy dictated a letter to Granminnow through Momma in Head Start, "I love school so much and I'm right on everything."[17] I wrote Granminnow at the beginning of second grade:

> I Love school I'm
> leaning lost of things
> I Love My Teacher.
> The end[18]

Fourteen

PROGRESS

We're making progress as we define progress.
—Hillary Clinton about Arkansas in 1979 television interview[1]

Bill Clinton, just one month older than Momma, was sworn in as governor of Arkansas in January 1979. We were struggling with the usual winter cold and sickness in the cabin.

"Sorry about the lack of word from us [. . .] Everyone in the house has been sick but me!" Momma wrote to Granminnow.[2]

Granminnow wrote back at the end of the month between a flurry of activities—a play, church, a walk to the symphony with Irving, a parent enrichment course she was giving on how to keep your sanity in mid-winter, a Tuesday Tea at her house with thirty-two ladies, and a meeting of the Colonial Dames. She enclosed a small check and wrote, "When I think of all the supports a young mother has in the city, I wonder how you manage to keep from going stark raving mad! [. . .] I keep hoping I'll hear from you—your happy thoughts if there are any or your depressions. You sounded pretty depressed when I talked to you."[3]

I wish I could ask Granminnow what she was thinking at the time. Was she desperately worried? Or was she too accustomed herself to the hardship of adulthood, having been married to a workaholic alcoholic for most of her life? Although both she and Granpa Will shared the veneer of upper-class life from their pasts, on the salaries of a professor and a nursery-school teacher, they had often been broke. Her own experiences, I suspect, made her even more anxious for my mother.

"My thoughts are up and down," Momma wrote to allay her concerns, "You shouldn't worry about my thoughts. You've been my mother for 32 years and since when have I been one to tell *anyone* my thoughts unless I was *really* in the mood."[4]

Momma got a letter out to Chuck and Janey too, thanking them again for books and talking about gender issues:

The books are marvelous—Please don't ever stop the paperback presents—
It may last us through January even—*Warrior Woman* is excellent and
the Jean Stafford stories ditto—I noticed a preponderance of women's
writing—all very good—This is wonderful, because sometimes I get to
thinking that women were not meant to be writers (at a party—who tells
all the long involved stories—almost always the men, sigh)—Anais Nin is
the woman I unfortunately always think of when I think of women writers and I think she's a dreary novelist—But now I realize my thinking
was all hogwash—and I, as an aspiring woman novelist (In my dreams
only), have hope—
    I guess I'm living life now, not writing it—Plots abound is all I can say—[5]

Momma's communications were also hindered by a snow-soggy dirt
road. "Like one big long unfired clay pot" that was alternately freezing
and thawing, and impassable when not frozen solid.[6] Once again, we were
housebound and little mail was going in or out. Momma couldn't even get
to a neighbor's house for a phone call, a hassle even in the best of weather.
We still had no telephone in the cabin, relying on neighbors' phones for
emergencies and infrequent calls to family. Momma had mentioned in a
previous winter's letter to Granminnow that, should she need to call us
for an emergency, she could call the Sutterfields: "They are *old* + a fair
distance from us—But they can give Richard a message on his way to
work."[7] Daddy left his car on the highway and walked the three miles out
to it each morning for work, backpacking groceries in on his return home,
stopping for messages at the Bersches' or the Sutterfields'.[8]
    The harsh weather continued into February with a record nine inches
of snow.[9] We stayed home from school for much of it. The bus couldn't
make it down our road to our usual stop, and we couldn't walk to the main
highway to catch it. Even our older cousins were unable to traverse the
road on some days, the snow melting into mud several feet deep.
    The county graded our road occasionally, usually around election time.
There were open discussions in fields and on porches during election season of the buying, selling, and trading of votes, Daddy never seeing but
hearing of five-dollar bills passing between hands. All talk of politics was
basically local: Does the county maintain my road regularly? Do all the
school board members support the girls' basketball team (the most popular entertainment in Fox)? The only political talk Daddy remembers that
wasn't local was when locals said they weren't voting for Clinton in 1980

because he raised auto-license fees. But the area was so poor that voters found it worth it to sell a vote for goods or cash, democracy less important than food on the table.

A gravel truck rumbled down the road one year with the county judge up for reelection following close behind. The two vehicles pulled up out front, and the judge walked toward the cabin looking to sway my parents' vote with a bit of gravel. He'd been the county judge for years, an important local man with grey hair, a wrinkled face, and the local drawl. Katy and I slipped out from behind the cabin buck naked to see who had come visiting, generating laughter all around. They left us with smooth creek gravel from local rivers that car tires simply spit to the side or ground deep into the mud. They did not get my parents' vote.

Photographs throughout the years show even in dry weather a road deeply rutted with tire tracks, like wagon ruts. The Warshauers came up from Mountain View to visit us in their Volkswagen bug when a deluge turned the road to a thick, viscous soup. They were just able to swim the small car through the brown river and back to the highway.[10] Daddy kept chains, a Hi-Lift jack, and a come-along in his pickup to winch and pry the truck out of mudholes, the county seasonally awash with mud. Even I, as a child passenger, remember that getting unstuck from earth and water was a common part of driving in that life, like pulling over to get gas is for a suburban commuter, with the addition of cursing, the search for objects for traction, and the slow climb and lurch out of a hole.

Cloistered at home that winter of 1979, Katy and I slid off the porch on baking sheets into deep snowdrifts and drizzled hot molasses across cold snow that froze into candy. The mailman made it to our mailbox to deliver one of Granminnow's coveted care packages for Valentine's Day. She had filled it with paper plates and cups, oddments for crafting, clothes, and carrot bread. "We had a little Valentine party for us and [Rhett and the boys], and it was a big success," Momma wrote to thank her.[11]

But it wasn't exactly an idyll of winter snugness with three children in an isolated 700 square feet.

"I would like to kill my children and they would like to kill me," Momma wrote.[12]

Daddy and Miriam in the cabin addition around 1979.

"The girls loved [Old Maid and Candyland]," she had written in February, "but they fought horribly over who would win—Katy seems to be the luckiest—Sarah snatched her bald-headed in one game—She literally pulled a chunk of hair out of Katy's head—giving Katy an Uncle Chuck look—We have put the games away for a brief cooling off period."[13]

Katy infuriated me because she stole the Old Maid card, which we mistakenly thought was the winning card. She hid it under her butt. I grabbed her hair and pulled it as hard as I could, shocked when it came out in my hand. My usual weapon of choice was my sharp tongue; I was otherwise a coward. I jumped up to run. Katy was sweeter than I but braver and more physical. She cornered me across the room and beat Daddy's steel toe work boots onto my hunched back.

Between muddy roads and our fighting, Momma got a washer *and* a dryer that winter and, at last, a real, almost-working toilet that flushed through a pipe to the woods in back of the house (later to a septic tank).[14] The toilet was salvaged from a job site, cast off because it had no tank. It was flushed with buckets of water from the bathtub.

All toilet paper had to be collected in a wastebasket rather than flushed:

*Katy and me in front of the cabin about 1979. The washer
on the left is probably the one Momma got that winter.*

By the way, we still have a few grapefruit lying around from your Florida
shipment—They were delicious—The beautiful basket is now my bathroom wastebasket—A great help to prevent toilet paper from spilling
everywhere, since we don't put it down the toilet—What a joy that bathroom has been this winter—Don't know how I ever did without.[15]

Most of our garbage made its way to the chickens and pigs and compost,
but the dirty toilet paper was burned along with other small amounts
of trash we accumulated. Anything we couldn't burn was taken to the
county dump, a flat clearing constantly being bulldozed where the truly
poor of Stone County lingered to collect usable goods from the heaps. I
was awestruck, standing on a dirt precipice above a great sea of plastic
bags and junk. There was a dump in Timbo too, just a razed patch in the
woods, and locals dug holes on their land or dumped wherever there was
a ravine. And many drivers reflexively hurled trash from car windows.

The first of March brought even deeper mud. While Daddy trekked
backed out to his truck, Momma hunkered down with us into laundry
and novels and picture books and drawings, comforted to have an indoor

toilet. Soon another hard winter was behind us, and it was suddenly "everywhere green instead of white."[16]

Tornadoes were the great dread of my early life (alongside nuclear war), and the green wet of spring was their favorite hour. On gray days when the sky bore down on us with heavy voluptuous clouds, the air thick with moisture and tension and the surrounding vegetation glowing, the undersides of leaves would flicker silver in the wind like a warning light. I felt the burn of fear and longed for a storm cellar.

My cousins, Katy, and I boarded the school bus on a stormy morning that spring. After an hour's drive, we pulled over to pick up one last student. The bus idled in the quiet, charged air as a series of tornadoes came racing and rolling across the field on our left. I watched pine trees along the highway begin to fall. The boy we had stopped to pick up ran as a small stone hit his face; he flung himself through the open bus doors and up the steps and joined the rest of us, now crouched on the floor between our seats. A dark twisting cone continued to move toward us like a black wraith. As it lifted off the asphalt, a giant skip on its run through the countryside, the bus tilted dangerously on two wheels and an electric line behind us fell. My older cousins laughed, but I hunched paralyzed with fear against the edge of the vinyl seat.

As the bus righted itself, Scotty, the driver, pressed his foot to the gas pedal and rushed us through wind and rain to the school where my teacher, Mrs. Anderson, herded us under desks and tables shoved together on one side of the room. The classroom's linoleum floor had buckled and cracked and was shiny with rain. The windows were wide open, the curtains torn and blowing wildly as if to free themselves from their restraints of cold metal.

Later that afternoon, Daddy passed the house where we'd picked up the boy. A plantation of pine trees had stood between the house and the road. There were several hundred trees, each about forty feet tall, all laid out on the ground pointing in the direction of the tornado's path, the limbs stripped like a sprig of rosemary between your fingers.

For a few years after, I kept a small chunk of cedar Mrs. Anderson had given each student as a reminder of the large tree outside our classroom that had split and toppled from the great wind. A tornado dream from childhood still visits me: My panic mounts as a dark funnel cloud approaches. But then great relief washes over me as I suddenly realize, I just have to climb in bed and throw the covers over me and I'll be safe! Then I wake up and realize it was a dream and that covers provide no such assurance.

In April, Momma's letters hinted at a sprouting restlessness unfurling with the spring buds. Daddy was beginning to explore the idea of starting a wood products business, and Momma was imagining great changes in our living situation, writing to Granminnow:

> Your mention of possible financial help on building our house from your end was much appreciated—I *do* want you to save money for the kids to go to college. [This did not happen.] I feel that's *very* important, and more importantly, I don't want you to use up your capital for your own medical problems, etc.—If you should ever have a windfall, however, which you can spare at that moment, I would like to *borrow* over a long, long term enough to bulldoze away the cabin and put some new sleeping quarters on for the girls. But we are really pretty comfortable at the moment or *at least* relatively so.[17]

The cabin was still rustic and unfinished, the walls in many places bare wood framing; the floors throughout plywood; the rooms filled with secondhand, intermittently serviceable, jury-rigged appliances, but it was more comfortable than it had ever been. We had three bedrooms, a kitchen, a living area, a bathroom with a toilet and a bathtub and a sink (the door a simple sheet), electricity, running hot and cold water, a gas cookstove, a washer, and a dryer. The living area was nearly complete, with the exception of duct tape running between the windows to stop drafts where the missing trim belonged and pink insulation exposed where Daddy had run out of the salvaged tongue-and-groove cherry, white oak, and butternut paneling he'd bought for fifty dollars and installed diagonally around the dining table and couch.[18]

The old wooden farm table Daddy had purchased at a flea market or auction sat by the entrance to the kitchen. It seemed hulking to me as a child, but it was actually quite small. The dining and living area was decorated with the art and furniture from my parents' past life, the art mats forever stained with Arkansas mold and grime. There was a long, mid-century couch from the Bersches upholstered in wide black and white houndstooth; a woven Mexican blanket and an African mud cloth covering more half-finished walls of insulation; an indigo-blue rug made from a carpet remnant; sky-blue sheets tied back with twine at the windows; and two ornate rockers next to the long bookshelf—the one from Momma's family and another, an antique carved, pink-upholstered one with gooseneck arms, from Daddy's. And there was a very efficient Warm Morning wood-heat stove against the north wall of the room. I still have a faint scar around my belly button from when I leaned too close on a cold morning.

And I had my own room. My sisters slept downstairs, and Momma and Daddy moved to their own room in the 1976 addition. I had the cabin loft to myself, with its red-painted plywood floor and three low windows into the kitchen, the ceiling pitched with the roof in the center and too low on the sides for even a child to stand. It was in that room that I solidified my feelings about Fox and our land, where I put away for the future both a deep, emotional nostalgia and a hardened black nugget that was the danger of poverty and squalor and unreliable weather.

From the front dormer window, I could see out to the south pasture and the woods leading to the pond. Just outside a little window over my bed facing west, sang a whippoorwill, right above a hallowed spot where Pappy once buried a half potato after rubbing it on my wart to get rid of it. I hid there when bottle rockets were lit on the Fourth of July. When rain beat out a deafening tune on the tin roof during violent storms, I peered nervously out the window at small trees and saplings bent close to the ground under the force of the wind, their leaves whipped violently, absorbing in that moment with a shiver of gloom that the world was fragile and capricious and that home was a refuge.

Later in the spring, Momma mentioned to Granminnow that they might use the $2,500 she had offered to get Daddy's wood workshop up and running, instead of making further changes to the cabin.[19] But then in early July their plans changed again. Momma wrote:

> He is considering a different possibility, which is to use that money to
> begin putting up the house of our dreams. He has read some books and

learned some things about solar technology plus from some of his recent building experience, he feels a small but adequate house can be built for $10,000 (with part owner labor of course)—That leads me to add several thousand—that is still cheaper than the $30,000 one would expect considering present building costs. Anyway, we will remain in limbo on the matter until Richard has some time to devote to it—(our present house would become his shop).[20]

The dream house idea quickly morphed into their just wanting to make smaller improvements to the cabin, with an immediate plan to cover the original dry-stone foundation with a mortared rock wall, install a better flue for the heat stove, and have Daddy's friend Jim Bob nail paneling up in the original cabin for added warmth. "I should like you to send the $2500 right away," Momma wrote to Granminnow. The money she felt would be so much more valuable to us than "plates or silver or clothes."[21]

Momma was also starting to consider working in the coming year, but she couldn't "bear to abandon" Miriam at so young an age.[22] She was again exasperated with me and Katy: "My oldest girls are equally adorable, but Lord, I have no patience with them—They seem like adults already—very loud, boisterous adults. I'm trying anyway to put up with it and Miriam too. School will be out shortly and then we'll see how my nerves survive."[23]

"Slug-a-bed, slug-a-bed, barley butt, your bum is so heavy you can't get up!" we teased Momma, reciting a rhyme from our *Granfa' Grig Had a Pig* book.[24] We pulled our stuffed animals into the yard and operated on them. We cut slits in their cotton, filling them with dough hearts, crudely sewn back up and sealed with a press from a brown, pink-rubber-tipped glue bottle. We pulled cigarette butts from car ashtrays in the yard. We chased the chickens. We wandered into the shed by the cabin and pulled open the rough tin door and peeked inside. Dozens of small, varied bottles, clear and blue and yellow, empty but for bits of hay and dried bugs, sat on a dark shelf. We upset a hornet's nest and fled the shadows of the shed wailing in front of a cloud of stinging wasps. Or we ran around the house with raucous singing and dancing and squealing:

> Glory, glory hallelujah
> Teacher hit me with a ruler
> I bopped her over the bean

with a rotten tangerine
and her teeth came marching out!

Meanwhile, my parents were by this time in debt for the land to Mammy and Pappy and for a truck and Daddy's business expenses to the bank. Daddy's dream of self-sufficiency was long gone, and we were creeping back to modernity.

Momma also wrote in her early July 1979 letter that the construction business was going well enough for Daddy to rent a small office in Mountain View—actually a storage unit—for thirty dollars a month with a place to store his tools, a phone and answering machine, a desk, and a sign. "So you can send us a message by phone anytime now—if you can't yet exactly reach us by phone," Momma wrote.[25]

Daddy had finished two houses and one remodel, was halfway through another, and about to start a fourth house, and Aunt Rhett had hired him to build a small addition on her house that fall. Most of the money went back into the business for equipment, so the profit was small.[26]

There were other problems. In March of that year, Momma had complained to Granminnow:

He is just finishing up a beautiful, beautiful home near Mtn. View—
Unfortunately, the owners are in an uproar because it cost too much—
But he waived his 10% because they were friends—and he designed
the house (to their specifications) and drew the plans for *free* and
participated in a million conferences without pay so that it would be
perfect—They made expensive changes as they went along—adding
this + that and then of course there were the usual delays + rises in
prices on materials so a $35,000 home turned into a $50,000 home.
It's a shame, but they were supposed to do a lot of the work to cut down
the price and they haven't done a thing—in short, we don't feel too sorry
for them (Richard's total profit over a 6 month period on the house
was something like $3,000—that is, those were his wages—big deal)—
Anyway, Richard lost sleep over that one.[27]

She wrote that Daddy "was very nearly crushed by this since it is not the 1st time he has had to deal with this type of person." He had gotten a better handle on how to price his work that year to cover all the overhead of tools and the extra running around required in building a house, but the construction business was a constant uphill battle. It was a business that ostensibly could have afforded our family a steady income and a comfortable home, but the weather and the local economy were against him, and Daddy was too inexperienced—in construction and business—to make it work. He was "flying blind" as he told me recently, naïve about bidding a job and with little experience and no training or mentors in the industry. Even his carpentry skills were relatively new, but he was a quick study and had figured he could make a go of it.

In October 1979, Aunt Sarah visited again, a "pleasant, happy interlude" for Momma.[28] I hovered eagerly on these visits as she opened and went through her suitcase, filled with silk scarves and perfume and bright blouses. We made cookies with her for Halloween using cutters Granminnow sent in one of her activity boxes, and then she disappeared back across the sea.[29]

The warm and windy days of that Indian summer turned to rain and then ice in December. "An ice storm—very beautiful since the freezing rain makes icicles in the trees and everywhere, but absolutely miserable," Momma wrote mid-month.[30]

Six days later, we drove to the warmth of South Carolina and Mammy and Pappy's house where we spent Christmas. We met Other, Daddy's maternal grandmother (so named because she had been the "other" grandmother), for the first and last time and slept in quiet awe in the hardwood-floored, paneled bedroom that had been Daddy's. Everything felt spacious and suburban, and our father had been a boy there. Momma and Daddy were quietly unhappy and counted the days till our departure. The words on a plaque hanging in their breakfast nook that Momma had once found funny now rankled: Rebel Spoken, Yankee Understood.

"Richard's family is more than he can stand and ditto for me," she wrote to Granminnow, "his father is an angel, but his mother is a hopeless alcoholic—and very annoying too."[31] Pappy was no angel and made Daddy tense with his silent disapproval, but Momma couldn't see past the fact that he did everything his wife asked.

Sometime between that summer and winter, Granpa Will surfaced as well, in a rare letter (undated). He was holed up in his own cabin in the mountains of Colorado with his books and drifts of crumpled paper, an open cistern of drinking water full of mosquito larvae, depression, and the regular call of his old foe alcohol. He was still teaching sociology at the University of Colorado in Boulder and still puttering at the margins of an alternative lifestyle:

> After my book is finished and the house bills paid down, anyway, I'm probably going to do something like that in the communal and coopera-tive movement—this will be my last book (and I couldn't do better!) and after that anything further in sociology at CU would be a drag.
>
> I'm already in close touch with an important group just north of you—at Tecumseh, Missouri—which is trying to do the same thing. They are about 65 people, an offshoot of the most famous modern commune (Twin Oaks, in Virginia), and part of a movement more or less called Walden Two communes. Serious, no heavy religion or dope, rational organization, but having a hell of a lot of fun.[32]

Nothing ever came of these plans, but it was interesting for me to read—especially compared to Daddy's parents—how like-minded and receptive Granpa Will was to my parents and their generation. (His early academic colleagues called him "Wild Bill.") He had had some young people living with him in a cooperative sense in 1975, but he became disillusioned with the idea when he found it too hard to find motivated, serious roommates. "I won't live here alone any more but have had some bad experiences with strangers in connection with the crafts co-op I tried to start," he wrote Momma, so reminiscent of Daddy's constant plans, including his own crafts co-op in Colorado.[33]

The Tecumseh, Missouri, group Granpa Will wrote of was the East Wind Community, started in May 1974, an intentional community farm that still exists (supported by selling nut butters and the Utopian Rope Sandal).[34] East Wind was loosely based on the principles in the 1948 uto-pian novel *Walden Two* written by the famous psychologist B. F. Skinner.[35] The idea for the book had come to Skinner while lamenting the thought of soldiers—like Granpa Will—returning from the war to the same old soci-etal "ruts."[36] Granpa Will had feared these very ruts, once telling Momma that on returning from the war he had wanted to go to the woods and live simply. But the book didn't become successful until my parents' genera-tion found it.[37] Skinner's novel told of a community of a thousand people living together in harmony. He believed in the power of nurture over nature and that science, or "behavioral technology"—basically positive reinforcement—could create a better society, a society based on Thoreau's ideas of simplicity and self-reliance in *Walden* but applied on a larger more communal scale.[38] This would have been a very appealing idea to my sociologist grandfather, who had himself written in his 1964 book *Formal Theories of Mass Behavior* an entire chapter, "On the Logic of Addiction," filled with mathematical equations to explain addiction. In 2020, though still running, East Wind was roughly the same size it had been in 1979, not exactly a roaring success.[39] And a 2005 *National Geographic* article on East Wind that exposes solidarity problems, drinking, and an inability to build equity and move on makes me doubt Granpa Will would have been able to escape the usual human problems on its acres, much as we hadn't been able to on Fox Mountain.[40]

January of 1980 brought another, more crippling ice storm, every branch and blade of grass encased in watery glass. But the vicissitudes of the season soon ushered in the sun and warm winter days, allowing Momma to once again hang clothes out to dry on the line when the "new" dryer broke.[41]

Daddy, despite his recent successes, abandoned his construction business that winter, finally defeated by the struggle to keep it going. He started a promising new job with the Meadowcreek Project, started by the environmentalists and educators David and Will Orr. Meadowcreek was a nonprofit formed to serve as a self-sustaining, model community and education research center with an organic farm, solar-heated buildings, sustainable forestry, and other examples of ecological living. The Orr brothers hoped the project "would serve as a model of how human settlements in the future might both exist in harmony with their surroundings and offer meaningful lifestyles to their inhabitants."[42] The Orrs had sold their homes and put all the money they had into buying 1,500 acres of neglected Stone County land and moved there with their families in 1979. (David's son Danny was my third-grade crush.) They surveyed the land and decided on economic activities that would make exclusive use of the property and its natural resources: a wood business and an organic farm. They hoped to eventually have housing for up to twenty-five families that would be sunlit and sun-heated and solar-powered and have composting toilets and gray water–irrigated basement greenhouses for year-round vegetables. Grants would help fund the project while they waited for it to be self-supporting.[43] David Orr later told a writer something that my parents could have said, or have said in perhaps less eloquent form: "The transition from being in a place where self-congratulation ruled to living in the fifth poorest county in the second poorest state in the union was for me an indelible and incredible experience. [. . .] going to the periphery of the society was absolutely essential. It changed everything. The eleven years in that valley in Arkansas were to me the most informative of my life."[44]

Daddy was hired at Meadowcreek, Momma wrote, "to manage and start a wood products industry, fueled completely by steam engines, including a sawmill. Of course, this is what he has wanted to do all along but didn't have the capital to do. We are very excited, especially since our income has exactly doubled—$10,000 a year, which isn't much, but gives us hope."[45] She rejoiced to Granminnow:

> Thank God, we aren't living *below* the poverty level anymore—now we are at the poverty level! It's amazing to me that what would have been a good salary when Richard and I married ($10,000 a year) is now necessity for a family of 5—But thanks to living here and to help from you—and to making do—we can get by a lot better than some. Sarah + Katy think we are such poor folk.[46]

I was too young then to understand how truly privileged we were. I knew I had more than kids who were barefoot, but other locals seemed rich to me in their brick ranch houses or modern trailers. I was very conscious of our poverty, especially when we visited relatives. The obvious difference between our life and theirs fed my insecurities.

Katy still remembers asking Momma once, "Are we hillbillies?"

"Yes, you are," she told Katy, joking and unaware that Katy took it to heart. ("Thank God for Mississippi" we would learn to say—at least Mississippi was ranked poorer and worse off than Arkansas.)

Granminnow paid for us to fly as a family to Colorado for Uncle Jock and Aunt Liza's wedding on March 21, the day after my parents' own ninth anniversary.[47] Daddy wore hand-me-down pants and a suit jacket from Irving (Granminnow's husband) that Aunt Rhett had altered for him, and Momma wore a long, blue embroidered Mexican skirt with pink shoes she bought for seven dollars.[48] Katy and I were the flower girls. I remember feeling like a princess as I walked down the aisle of my great-great-grandfather's church in a long, pink dress and white gloves carrying

A postcard Momma sent to Granminnow in November 1976.
The printed info on the back says, "Hillbilly Family in the Ozarks Most
modern-day hill people are quite industrious and some are even moderately
prosperous. But this family helps maintain the reputation of the more easy-
going breed of natives. While the husband spends most of the day resting,
his wife is kept busy from early 'till late cooking, washing clothes, cutting
wood, fixing fences, carrying water and mending the seat of her
husband's overalls." OZARK POSTCARD PUBLISHERS, MISSOURI.

a white basket of flowers, slightly inebriated on the faint scent of baby's breath and carnations.

I was happy when Jock and Liza visited us in Fox weeks later on their honeymoon. My sisters and parents, the secluded cabin, Rural Special, Granminnow and Irving, Aunt Sarah, and Jock and Liza were the center of my world. It was a rich, though sometimes confusing, mélange of life-styles and personalities.

When Katy and I had begun learning to write in the late seventies, Granminnow sent us our own small supply of embossed letterhead on brightly colored paper. Letter writing was a rite of passage. I knew it was an important connection to our extended family, if an also sometimes

Aunt Liza with Miriam in front of our pasture in 1980.

onerous task. Most of my early letters were a dull list of thank yous. But by the time I was eight, I was writing in cursive and attempting all the conventions of greeting and closing and the formality of names. I referred to my parents as I heard other adults do. I wrote that spring:

April [3], 1980

Dear Granminnow and Irving

How are you doing. Wendy and Richard are god parents for a friend of ours baby. Her name is Jessica erin Bishop. And she has to sisters named Lisa Bishop who is (14) years old. And the other sisters name is Angela Bishop who is (12) years old. And her mother and fathers names are Mr. and Mrs. Randolph and doris Bishop. I got stung to day three times on the back. The wasp had gotten under my shirt. Tell Jock and Liza that we will send there pictures we made them soon.

Love
Sarah

The week after Easter—just days before winter gave a swan song of eight inches of snow to blanket the blooming redbuds, dogwoods, plums, and peaches—we had a big party on the land for Daddy's thirty-sixth birthday, and Katy and I were writing again:

April 14, 1980

Dear Granminnow and Irving

Richard is to lazy to thank you for the therty seven dollars so you might not have a thank you letter for a while. We just had a huge snow storm today. We had a huge Party for Richards birthday. A bunch of kids came to his birthday Party. And we had a fight girls against boys I got scratchs and david got on top of me and took his hand and slapt me on the chest and I was sor all over and I was crying. Hugs to everbody.

Love
Sarah

Dear Granminnow and iriving

I hope you are having a good time in Colorado I am having a good time in Arkanasas we had a party and The Girls and The Boys had a fight and The Girls and my cousin kicked me in the knee to times and It hurt me and after that I was on The Donkey and my Freind was hol[d]ing onto The Donkey and she let go of It and It Started to run and I fel off It and The Boys laughed at me in The Party my neighbor let me use her autoharp It was fun at The Party we had a Band and I was in It I had a fun time there and we had The Party at my house It was Richards Birthday the children got the Cake frst We had a nice dinner at The Party Wendy made The Best dinner

[Katy]

Despite all the changes around us—the renovations and modernizations to the cabin, the new salaried job for Daddy—Momma was still in downtown Mountain View in early June, "waiting for [her] 'WIC' app't. with a dozen other hot bedraggled mothers + children—They give anyone with children under 5 who qualifies by income milk, eggs, juice + cereal—Another gov't. freebee which is sometimes annoying—but a big help on the grocery bill—(about $40 a month of free stuff)."[49]

Incongruously, Daddy traveled to New York in July on behalf of Meadowcreek to a woodworking conference in Westchester, after which he ended up in Brooklyn.[50] He met a man there who was one of the many characters who passed through our lives in Fox, a stamp collector who specialized in stamps related to Wolfgang Amadeus Mozart.

"I technically live in a tiny town in Arkansas called Mozart," Daddy said, "but it doesn't really exist anymore, so we just say Fox."

The man "went absolutely nuts," Daddy told me. He knew of the town (if it can even be called that) and had searched for information. Daddy's old business partner Dean May's parents had been the postmasters of Mozart back in the forties or fifties when it still had a post office. The stamp collector—a pudgy, flamboyantly gay man with a thick New York accent—came to Fox soon after, staying with the Bersches, to meet Dean and dig through the May belongings to find an old Mozart postmark, to no avail. He left suddenly the way many a strange visitor did.

Katy and I were preparing to leave for Colorado again and made giddy by the last-minute arrival of a postcard from Granminnow: "I'm sitting in the sun drying my hair—I'm hoping I'll look elegant tonight for the opera!"[51] Momma had written Granminnow back in March, "We told the girls yesterday it would be about 90 days until they saw you. Today Katy said 'Mother, it's only 89 days 'til we go back to Granminnow's.'"[52] By June we could barely wait another minute for our trip: "Sarah thinks Colorado is the most beautiful + perfect place in the world."[53]

Colorado meant Granminnow most of all, the epitome of perfection and comfort to me, enveloped in the intoxicating smell of L'Air du Temps perfume and Wrigley's Doublemint gum. The pearls Momma inherited after her death years later were still sweet with her scent. She was always the nursery-school teacher, fascinated by our every word, never raising her voice, always calm and full of stoic good cheer. There was never a dull moment but never too much stimulation when we were with her. But she was also assertive and determined beneath her quiet, smiling exterior, and anxious, and measured in manner, so she orchestrated our days together carefully to avoid tension and overexcitement, hers and ours. She had quiet control. I adored her.

Colorado also meant trips to the opera (Tosca and Verdi's *Requiem* I remember), art classes at the museum, swimming at the country club with carrot sticks and tuna sandwiches, Granminnow's elegant home with a view of Pikes Peak from the living room window, and honey chicken and yogurt pops and one scoop of Häagen-Dazs after dinner. Colorado was an upstairs aerie just for us, encircled with windows and lined with old books (*The Five Little Peppers*, *The Borrowers*, the Thornton Burgess animal stories). And it was Aunt Ruth's old antique dollhouse stored on the shelves of an eighteenth-century corner cupboard, filled with miniature oil paintings, a real silver tea set, minuscule scissors and knives and books and photo albums. Our relatives all wore silver and turquoise jewelry; said witty things with glamorous voices like Katharine Hepburn; and lived in houses with heavy drapes (not sheets) and artwork, including gilt-framed portraits of our ancestors. With these inconsistencies, how could I not be confused about my place in the world. Was I poor? Was I fancy?

Colorado was also drier and neater; it was the smell of pine and after-noon rain on dry earth. It was not oppressively humid and dense like Arkansas, matted as the Ozarks were with the green of vine and weed and bush. In 1901, my great-great-grandmother, Miriam, a transplant from New York City, wrote of her adopted home in Colorado Springs, "We all can rejoice in the clear air, and the radiant sunshine" and "Surely the Mesa road, hung between earth and sky, is unique in the world."[54] It was on this Mesa Road hilltop that Uncle Chuck and Aunt Janey built their home, a home I visited and loved almost as much as Granminnow's. Colorado was a breath of fresh, dry air that gave me room to breathe, and on my return to Arkansas, I always looked healthier, my skin tan from the Rocky Mountain sun, the circles less pronounced under my eyes.

Katy and I flew to Colorado alone for two weeks in mid-July 1980, escaping temperatures on the farm as high as 110°F.[55] The Midwest and southern US were trapped under an extreme ridge of high pressure, and seventeen hundred people died that summer.[56]

"Almost all the creeks are dried up. Rock Hole is smelly," Momma wrote to us in Colorado where we were playing in a manmade lake at the coun-try club.[57] Swimming in local creeks that carved their way through sand-stone cliffs and trees was one of the great reliefs to the summer heat in Stone County.

Katy and I were back home by the end of the month. A day of rain, the air a thick, misty coat of stagnant heat and moisture, broke the drought, but within a few days the dry heat returned. We piled in a car, and Daddy drove us all to the one swimming hole that hadn't dried up or become unsanitary—Roasting Ear Creek ("Roce-near" to the locals):[58]

How lovely it was. The water is spring fed, so it is absolutely clear and 55°—That's refreshing, it cools you down right to the marrow. Unfortunately, last night Miriam came up with a high fever, so now I must assume that that water is unclean too, without any rain to keep it flowing. Everyone in the county is beset with ear infections, etc. from swimming in creeks that haven't got enough water coming in. This is the worst drought in years.[59]

The swimming cooled us down, but misery was always one workday or bad-weather day away. Before Katy and I returned from Colorado, heat exhaustion had dulled Daddy's senses back at work. "He caught the butt end of an oak tree on the mouth, dislocating some teeth and breaking off one tooth—We hope he won't have lost the teeth he dislocated, then he'll have to have root canal work—which would be terrible. At the moment, he is on a liquid diet, which makes him miserable," Momma wrote.[60] He would eventually have ten root canals over the next twenty years from that accident.

It's a miracle there were no tragic accidents. Daddy drove his tractor from a repair shop in Timbo up the steep incline of Fox Mountain towards home another afternoon. He tried to downshift using the hand clutch as the grade increased, but he couldn't get it back in gear. The tractor rolled backwards. Daddy jumped out as it came to the sharp curve at Devil's Elbow, before it went tumbling over the side of the mountain and landed upside down in a tree. A highway crew was down below and cut the tree down to get to the tractor. The Timbo mechanic came up with a wrecker and pulled it off the side of the mountain and back to the repair shop.

"I am very definitely interested in going back to school on a part-time basis this fall. I have just written a local university (c. 60 miles away) for information. I want to get a teaching certificate for French and Spanish," Momma wrote on the first of August 1980.[61] My parents had been in Arkansas for over seven years, but the rush of ever-changing plans discussed in the letters between 1979 and 1980 made it clear that times were changing, that the momentum of the cabin and the farm had run its course. My parents' ambitions were pushing them both in another direction. Daddy was also spending his workdays immersed in the exciting innovations and goals of Meadowcreek, which must have played at least some part in his restlessness, in spurring him forward.

A week later, the world outside Stone County beckoned again. Aunt Sarah wrote from Maputo, Mozambique:

Momma and me (on the left) cooling off at a local creek.

Daddy on his tractor.

You also mention that Moz. is trying to mechanize [while] in Fox you are reverting to traditional energy methods. This is a very serious and important problem here. [. . .] I showed Richard's project to the National Director for Forestry and Fauna (Allende's (Chile) former Minister of Agriculture, now a refugee) and he was quite interested, as was also the Director of Rural Electrification from Electricity of Mozambique. Does Richard have any more written information? Please send as much as you can. If you guys ever want an international contract, in a few years, organizations like the UN will be ready for you.[62]

She added, "We even had news in the Maputo *Noticias* (newspaper) about the heat in Little Rock." Arkansas was big enough for an international stage, and even tiny Fox, if only in my aunt's imagination.

Just like the move to Arkansas and the third baby, school happened quickly after Momma wrote about wanting to do it in her letters. In addition to a small loan my parents took out, Granminnow agreed to help. By September, Momma was enrolled at the University of Central Arkansas and driving an hour and a half to Conway three days a week. Susie Warshauer came to the cabin and watched two-year-old Miriam, taking countless beautiful black-and-white photographs of her playing in the yard in diapers and little dresses.[63] Katy and I were at school all day, but Susie's soft presence sheltered Miriam from Momma's sudden absences.

Entering the halls of the university, Momma saw more Black students than she'd ever seen, a comforting sign that she was back in the world. And in her French and Spanish courses she made real friends again with women who could understand her, women who loved foreign language and conversation. It was a break from the construction world around Daddy and backwoods barbecues with mountain man hippies.

Three manic, long, heavily researched typewritten letters also arrived from Granpa Will that fall, each signed with tragicomic introspection "Will (depressive) or Bill (manic)," about starting a wood products business with him in Colorado. In early November 1980, Momma wrote Granminnow:

> Of course I know you will be appalled at the thought of Richard + Dad going into business together—and logic would dictate against it— *However,* Dad (+ Jock) share certain goals with us which make it a very strong possibility—i.e. (1) a small wood products business producing 1 or 2 or more highly marketable commodities (i.e. specialty chairs or tables) (2) living in S.W. Colorado which *really* appeals to me—the remoteness of Arkansas combined with the climate of Colorado—and no long winters such as there are in Allenspark—also it is fairly well removed from the hippie life of Allenspark—which seems pretty corrupt and

dull to me—(3) we both have *some* capital—it remains to be seen how
much—Richard does not want to go into debt at all for this business, but
whether that's possible I don't know—I *am* very excited, I hope you are
too (at least at the thought of having your grandchildren nearby) [. . .]
I am now thinking it might be a year from now, possibly longer, when we
do this. Richard says this is to be our last move so he wants everything
just right—Also this is his big chance to establish a successful business
of his own and he doesn't want to blow it—I know he has the skills, the
imagination, and the leadership ability—but one never knows how the
rest will turn out—I have great hopes.[64]

Momma was one minute excited about her new college classes and the
thought of working again, and the next talking of a wild plan in Colorado
where locations with "the remoteness of Arkansas" appealed to her. It's
hard to grasp where her head was. Homesickness maybe made Colorado
look so good she could imagine anything there.

Daddy had grown disillusioned with parts of the management of
Meadowcreek, feeling he had no control but that any problems would
be blamed on him. More importantly, he did not want to leave our farm
behind to live there, as his boss had now requested for the sake of the
community. The tensions between them escalated to just shy the point
of physical altercation. Daddy's tolerance was worn thinner by the three-
and-a-half hours he spent undergoing "horrible medieval things," Momma
wrote, in a dentist's chair that month in Little Rock, his gums peeled back
and cleaned due to periodontal disease discovered after his post-accident
root canal (his parents helped pay the $1,000 it cost).[65]

Even I was suddenly feeling unsettled that fall and wrote to tell
Granminnow and Irving:

School is the pits this year because its to strict. I got me a thermos and
lunch box. We are going to have little puppies pretty soon.

Love Sarah[66]

Granminnow sent more money in October to pay for a camper shell
for our truck so we could drive to Colorado for Christmas to attend Aunt
Sarah's wedding to her first husband.[67] And we went to a little traveling circus set up in a field outside Mountain View. We came early in the
day to watch them raise the big circus tent—outsized elephants pulling
their ropes to raise the giant canvas, people running to-and-fro, old cars

parked pell-mell in the grass. I had written Granminnow with exaggerated excitement that we were "going to the Circus wich has the biggest circus tent in the world."[68] Katy wrote that there would be "50 elethants and the bigest tent in Arkansas."[69] It was a grand day out in the woods.

The circus was an auspicious day of un-Foxlike entertainment. Two weeks into November, Momma wrote Granminnow, "Richard quit Meadowcreek and we are formally trying to sell our house. [He] will finish his contract at Meadowcreek and be paid through Jan. 1 [. . .] After that he will have to get some other work until we leave, that is until we sell our house. As you can see, we are living in limbo for the moment."[70] The very next day, she confirmed, "we are trying to sell our house, move to Colorado, preferably directly to southwestern Colorado where I think we will be happiest," and "We are both so excited we can hardly stand it. Richard is thrilled at the idea of having his own shop—and designing his own products."[71]

And that was it. The last letter to or from Fox. Then we were gone. We drove to Colorado as planned for Aunt Sarah's wedding to a Swede a few days before Christmas, but the next letter does not go out until early February 1981, and the return address is in Mt. Vernon, Arkansas, where we lived for the next two-and-a-half years. All I remember is the wedding; maybe the trip to Colorado and the excitement of my new pink flower girl dress and a wedding drowned out any sadness of leaving. And perhaps I still thought we were moving to my beloved Colorado. But we did not move to Colorado, Daddy did not start a wood products business, and Granpa Will's obsessive and heavily researched letters stopped and faded into a strange memory. John Weaver, our longtime neighbor, bought our cabin and the land, and I never saw it again.

Fifteen

THE END

> Nothing happened—and that's the way to tell a true story
> from a made-up one. A made-up story always has a neat and
> tidy end. But true stories don't end, at least until their heroes
> and heroines die, and not then really, because the things
> they did, and didn't do, sometimes live on.
> —Elspeth Huxley, *The Flame Trees of Thika*[1]

We left the cabin in late January of 1981. I know we were still there on Sunday, January 25, when I turned nine, because I know I was in that living room with its blue-sheet curtains and unfinished cherry paneling, sitting on the houndstooth couch, when we heard on the radio that the fifty-two Americans held hostage at the US Embassy in Iran had returned to United States' soil. It's the only birthday from childhood I have any memory of, because of that fact. National Public Radio had infiltrated our isolation and brought the drama of the world into my anxious brain. We moved to a country town called Mt. Vernon, an hour south of Fox along Highway 36, roughly on the way to Little Rock, with rolling hills, countless Baptist and Church of Christ churches, and more contemporary living.

No letter exists to mark our departure—except that early February letter with a new return address—or to explain the sudden change of plans. My parents can no longer recall what happened in those last few months between looking at a move to Colorado and what would become a move to another small Arkansas town. Daddy remembers that he had become more disillusioned with the failure of his business, pressures at Meadowcreek, and the impossible local economy, but he remembers nothing about Colorado, except that it was perhaps just too expensive. Momma does remember feeling an unexpected panic during our trip to Colorado for Aunt Sarah's wedding at the reality of living so close to family—particularly at the thought of living under their watch with her difficult husband. And what they could afford there seemed even more desolate than Arkansas. She was annoyed, but relieved, when Daddy announced a different move from the land that was as precipitous as the one to it.

But my parents don't remember how their plans changed so drastically. It seems we were all anesthetized. I have not a single memory of the move. Not of leaving third grade in the middle of the year and the only home I'd ever known. Not of packing up the cabin. Not of driving to our new home and moving in. Not of the first day at a new school.

After our rustic cabin, the gaudy double-wide trailer we rented—with its mottled brown wall-to-wall carpeting and faux-gilded mirrors—seemed grand, as did the small farmhouse that came later. In a photo from 1981, my parents' transformation from the heirloom dress and hippy chic of their wedding was complete: Momma and Daddy and my sister Miriam stand in front of the trailer by a charcoal grill, Daddy in a CAT ball cap and cut-off jeans, a Pabst Blue Ribbon on the card table, and Momma overweight and dowdy.

The community of Mt. Vernon—slightly more prosperous, less remote, more attached to propriety—was far less kind and forgiving than the mountain folk of the Ozarks, and we were eyed suspiciously from the beginning (Momma was again "a Yankee"). It is here that all my idyllic memories of childhood get mangled up like sheets in a washer with the hateful memories of what it was like to be a newcomer, and not Baptist, in a rural town in Arkansas. I had never felt like an outsider in Fox—we were raised there alongside the other children, and there were others like us. But in Mt. Vernon we were renters, we spoke with strange diction, and we held ourselves all wrong.

In fact, as I read and transcribed and Momma's letters came to an end, I was sad to see the world of Fox go, yet again. I was overwhelmed by a sense that Mt. Vernon was the more depressing part of this story. We left the woods to escape its shortfalls for what? For the bleak and banal setting of Mt. Vernon? I suspect as a child, however, I was just happy to move into the "fancy" trailer and then the more modern farmhouse and have an old garage to dig around in and a pond to play in and a cherry tree to hang out underneath. But did my parents feel they had failed in Fox? No. Momma has since told me (and Daddy agreed), "We don't think like that. It instead gave us a tremendous push to start our new lives. It probably gave us confidence since we achieved a good deal even though we were so inexperienced."[2] Although Momma had just started to adjust to life in the woods, the move to Mt. Vernon was an exciting fresh start—for both of my parents. For Daddy, the move meant a job in construction management with a large, established contractor and generally more opportunity. For Momma, it meant being closer to the University of Central Arkansas in Conway. Eight months after moving to Mt. Vernon, Momma wrote her maternal aunt, "[Richard] is also going to school—1 course at a time to get a construction engineering degree—He is now cursing himself for belonging to the drop out generation and not finishing when he was young + free—*But* such is life—would that I had gotten a teaching certificate the 1st time through."[3] Daddy quickly gave up on the construction degree, but Momma would go on to get her teacher certification in French, Spanish, and Social Studies and be teaching high school French within three years. This was something she had thought about as far back as the summer of 1969—she had written her mother then from Boston that she was "getting very excited about the thought of teaching" French or history—so she was finally back on track.[4]

I have always believed the hardship of Fox was the primary wedge between my parents—the source of their conflict and eventual divorce. Eight years of voluntary poverty and living outside the mainstream, resume-building world delayed my parents' entry back into this world and lay a foundation of continual struggle that eroded their marriage and at times risked our health and education. But their troubles really began the moment they moved in together. I now feel that the woods—at least initially—saved their marriage. Building a home gave them a common, life-affirming, daily struggle. The peripatetic, two-working-parent life that started in Mt. Vernon destroyed the marriage. Momma would soon be coping with the strain of being a paycheck-to-paycheck working mother, most of the demands of home falling to her. We would move from Mt. Vernon, to Little Rock, to—a little over five years after leaving the woods—the golden hills and tract houses and bustle of northern California.

We moved to a suburban military town and settled into a sixties tract house with a bedraggled palm and an orange tree and a blooming agave wrought in aluminum on the front screen door. That first summer of 1986 we binged on California—we went to Napa wineries, ate grilled oysters on Drakes Beach, and made a pilgrimage to Big Sur and met Henry Miller's old friend Emil White. Everything seemed to be looking up. But six years after, with only Miriam left at home, Momma asked for a divorce. There were tears all around—my father the most devastated, crying to us girls in a way so unprecedented, I didn't know what to think or do with it— followed by a few short-lived attempts at reconciliation, and then a quiet, amicable split.

Without Fox, would my parents have had fewer financial struggles? Most likely. But they cared little when they set out for Arkansas for traditional notions of security. I can't predict now whether without the woods my father would ever have gone back to college or whether my mother would ever have actually gone to UC Berkeley. Or what they would have done even if they had. But I'm not sure it matters. My parents came together at a young age when they were both reeling from lost love, war, the cultural revolution, and difficult home lives. They were a product of their times and their experiences, and they made certain decisions and they lived them.

Those decisions led to me and my sisters and to an unconventional journey, a life lived against the grain. Despite Granminnow's occasional efforts, I lost some of the middle/upper-middle-class security and experience I could have had: piano and summer camps, SAT prep and college tuition and inheritance, visits to college campuses, college-bound friends. But generational poverty and situational poverty are two very different things. Our poverty was buffered by the privilege of generational wealth, by educations and family financial support (however small). Both my parents are in stable, if slightly precarious, financial situations now. The characters that run through this book helped us all, my mother most in the end. Granminnow, Mammy, Pappy, Aunt Ruth, Nana, Uncle Chuck and Aunt Janey, and Aunt Sarah have all been a financial support to our family in small and large ways over the years. My sisters and I all eventually graduated from college, even if it took us longer and we paid for it ourselves. And the journey Momma and Daddy took us on gave us a long, slow look outside the bubble we could have been born to; confidence in diverse environments; respect for those in poverty and a "there but for the grace of God go I" sensibility; and a gothic childhood of magic and strangeness that I treasure.

As I read and compiled and listened and meditated on our years in the Ozarks, I was consumed with conflicting emotions. One minute I felt angry with my father and his selfishness and annoyed with my mother and her propaganda and her stoicism. Most days, I felt I could barely tolerate my current life. I was too deep into the woods and our long-ago alternative lifestyle. I felt contemptuous of soccer games and piano lessons and summer-camp conversations. I felt a wistful affection and pride for my parents' hard work and determination to create something out of the ordinary for themselves and for us. I also felt a creeping, mournful feeling of how really absurd it all was. I wanted to break down and cry for my mother at times. Every discussion I have with her about those years carries at least tinges of bitterness. Daddy willfully threw us into abject poverty and toil, a life by luck of birth they could have avoided. But I know there is more to life than purely practical choices. And another luxury of their birth was to be able to choose, to grasp at something more than convention dictated. I don't know if it was the right decision, but I know that even Momma, with her old anger still a glowing ember, feels like she gained something priceless. She is grateful for the skills and strength she gained, the fall from her naïve ivory tower, and for the wild freedom she gave her children. She feels to some extent that these major decisions were made *for* her, that her life was not fully hers, but she also recognizes the role her own personality played. When I openly worked through my frustrations with her while writing this—her lack of agency that nagged at me—she admitted, "It's just how I am. I don't know why. I can't explain it. It's a problem I have." She was resigned and accepting—of herself and of my frustration.

I find myself isolating the experience into two realms: the one that is the story of a selfish, demanding husband and the other that is the story of a man who cannot be tamed, for the good of us all. I feel an almost shameful relief that it happened, even if a part of my mother was the sacrifice. Despite all the hard work and danger, life had been easy and joyous too. Music and woods and play define those years for me. The cabin was the structure I would call home the longest of any other until I reached my late thirties. My parents' determination to avoid a bourgeois life and their laissez-faire and youthful sense of adventure gave us a freedom I can never give my son. And I can thank their generation for the fact that things like whole-grain bread and yogurt are mainstream products, that I can now easily mimic my farm diet with organic produce and meats and grass-fed milk from the grocery store. I can cringe at their earnestness, their folly, but I can't help but be moved by what one writer wrote in a book about the movement: a return to the farm "meant less a going-backwards than a going-forwards, a way to meet the challenges of the modern era."[5]

Our life on the land was certainly not sustainable, however. It was fed by Daddy's outside labors, a steady supply of checks from family, and food stamps—and debt. Momma had seen clearly that self-sufficiency was impossible, the locals' inability to do it the most damning evidence. "Looking around us, we see that the people here work like dogs to pay for their land and to make their land pay," she wrote her grandmother in our first summer in Arkansas.[6] While doing research for this book, I came across a column on Ozark living in a 1975 issue of *Mother Earth News*, a bible for back-to-the-landers. If it had only been written a few years before, perhaps Daddy would have read it, although I doubt it would have changed much. The writer had become alarmed by the starry-eyed responses he'd received for a listing of Ozark land. He warned those who would dare venture into "deep country" that "it's a myth that a person can settle in the depths of the country and maintain himself there [. . .] Only the rich can lead full, beautiful lives in a really wild area. Most others are enslaved to endless drudgery and penny-pinching. Think hard and realistically before you make the leap."[7]

Daddy did not build the most innovative, green, or architecturally interesting cabin either. It was meant to be a temporary shelter, and it was rustic and naïve. (Louisa May Alcott's father said in 1843 of his short-lived utopia, Fruitlands: "The present buildings being ill placed and unsightly as well as inconvenient, are to be temporarily used, until suitable and tasteful buildings in harmony with the natural scene can be completed."[8]) But the cabin was competently built, inexpensive, and it housed us well. Momma was not a master of the perfect garden or a homemaker par excellence, but she was stoic, incredibly hardworking, and unafraid. And, as the locals would say, "If you got a bucket of shit to eat, there ain't no sense nibbling." She tackled pigs' heads and chicken killing and old-fashioned diaper washing with strength, if not gusto. She was also overtaken to an extent by Daddy's single-minded, obsessive drive for his interests and knew only how to make the best of any situation. She never fell apart, at least not permanently, under the sheer weight of all the work, but trudged on, in part fueled by her own drive for a clean, honest life. There was a storm brewing under her dogged determination to move forward each day, but it would take years to surface with any force of action. She found a happiness of sorts in her babies and healthy meals accomplished and a garden planted and pride in hard work that did really matter to her.

Nor was it all pastoral indulgence for Daddy. It may have been his dream, but he was most surely worn down on occasion by the pressure to support a family of four, then five, and long, hard days of manual labor in a relentless climate. But he, far more than Momma, found fulfillment and passion despite the physical demands and mostly tuned out the panic that three children and a dissatisfied wife at home might stoke, rendered deaf and dumb to it by his own narrow focus. It wasn't an entirely calculated act but an earnest love, of family, of building things, of being with animals and in nature. A project to quench a racing brain.

My father now lives near my sister Katy on the Central Coast in California, having divorced the woman he married after my mother. He's retired from a career in construction as an estimator. He lives simply in a tiny rented house on a semi-rural property surrounded by relatively few possessions, still excited by his passions. He keeps his binoculars close, photographs wildflowers, travels California giving talks on condors and helps with their restoration in Pinnacles National Park, and works on myriad other pet projects related to the wild. We stay in regular contact—me calling, emailing, texting with questions on the minutiae of Arkansas or his past or with a construction question—but he is often absorbed in his own world, which is not always easy to penetrate.

Momma met another man after the divorce and lived with him for a few years but never remarried, mostly content to face life on her own terms. She retired ten years ago from teaching high school Spanish in the Bay Area. She moved to Portland, Oregon, to be near my sister Miriam and me and our families. She owns a condo above a coffee shop, minutes from downtown, and lives on a modest but comfortable fixed income. This is thanks in part to the generosity of her childless uncle Chuck and aunt Janey, who left her a part of their estate. She also tutors children around the city, reads and writes, goes to the theater on weekends, and cares for her grandchildren. She and I live five minutes from each other and still talk on the phone too long about family gossip and books and television shows.

My mother, my father, my two sisters, and I have grown "civilized." Our days of hatchet and stump, of gravel road and wooded path are for stories and dreams. I taught my son, Lewis, to shoot the furry heads off stems of ribwort plantain. I will continue to make him pork chops and collards, but he will never get to eat them at an old farm table bought at auction in a tiny room in a tiny cabin in a great wide forest. He will never see butchering blood drip into the rocky dirt. He will never see the squirrels in the backyard laid bare on his dinner plate. He will never sit desperately wishing in vain for some beautiful, sweet confection that seems as far away as the moon. He will never feel the shame of being a poor relation.

We do not hike or camp regularly as a family; I am not an avid outdoor enthusiast. I do not want nature's hot breath too nearly on me, rubbing up against me with its fetid wet flora, spitting its ticks and snakes and chiggers on me, trapping me under its demands. I am not squeamish—I still carry some of that good farm girl grit in my bones—but I know all too well what lurks in its charming shadows.

But nature at a distance—a smell of flowers or greenery wafting by; a vista of mountains or sea or gently rolling hills suddenly before me; or a cool, earth-laden breeze on a warm day—fills me with sentimental longing. It is a whisper of the past and of mortality and is, in some convoluted way, what I pay homage to in my love of home and garden. My home is my playhouse among the trees, my burrow, a part of the natural landscape. It is the little cabin in the woods that kept us warm and dry between 1973 and 1981 being created again and again.

I find, in fact, that there is much of the woods left in me. I am still transported by the music, by the smell of dirt on potatoes or the spit-sweet scent of sycamore trees and algae on river rocks. The map of the land is like a recurring dream. A little voice in my head still says "nekkid" and "holler." I dig and sweat and forget my hair in my urban garden. There is often dirt under my short, uneven fingernails from spring through fall. My designer jeans are stained with mud and the knees blow out too soon. And I'm not so different from my young self, once identifying hickories and labeling leaves. I walk with my friends or my husband or my son and call out the plants I see. "That's a beautiful stewartia!" "Look at that arbutus!" "That's purslane." I still require quiet cabin-like seclusion, days of reading and music and housework. I will never take my prosperity, my comfort, and the relative ease of my life for granted.

And as time takes me further and further away from the woods, I worry that I will forget. I sense it somehow matters, that those years speak to who I am. But the whippoorwills and crystal-clear creeks and country roads in my memory have become more a condition of the soul than a geographical place. I realize that nothing will be lost. The woods are inside of me forever, a chiaroscuro of forces creating a beautiful whole. Momma and Daddy's experiment was a success: here I am at fifty, and I'm still mulling it over, still smelling the pond and the trees and the poke-weed leaves, still thrilled by the sound of the banjo and the mandolin, still wandering in my mind's eye through the cabin and its surrounds, still enchanted by the magic of that childhood.

I stepped out of the shower one morning and thought I heard a whip-poorwill and froze and listened to hear it again, my heart inexplicably racing. It was only the dry metal gears in my neighbor's casement window rubbing against each other as she opened it. I hadn't heard a whippoor-will in years—not since I left Arkansas at fourteen. Yet it still called out in the humid Ozark air of my mind.

NOTES

All letters and audiocassettes quoted in this book come from the author's personal collection, unless otherwise noted. All information in the book not cited here comes from my own memories and many conversations with my parents over a period of years via phone, text, and email.

Shortened names used in the notes

Wendy	Caroline Wendell Neidhardt/McPhee
Richard	Richard Neidhardt
Minnow	Miriam Emery McPhee Howbert, "Granminnow"
Nana	Eleanor Washburn Emery, Minnow's mother
Chuck	Charles Francis Emery Jr., Minnow's brother
Cooie	Eleanor Emery Harper, Minnow's sister
Schlesinger Library	Papers of the Washburn, Emery, McPhee, Harper Family, 1841–2006 (inclusive), 1915–1989 (bulk), at the Arthur and Elizabeth Schlesinger Library on the History of Women in America, Radcliffe Institute for Advanced Study, Harvard University.

Prologue

1. Jeffrey Jacob, *New Pioneers: The Back-to-the-Land Movement and the Search for a Sustainable Future* (University Park: The Pennsylvania State University, 1997), 3.

Chapter 1

1. Joseph Mitchell, "A Place of Pasts," *New Yorker*, February 16, 2015, 32.
2. Richard to Wendy, July 3, 1970.
3. Nana to Cooie, February 6, 1971, Schlesinger Library.
4. Richard to Wendy, July 9, 1970.
5. Richard to Wendy, June 25, 1970.
6. Richard to Wendy, July 10, 1970.
7. See, e.g., Bernard R. Berelson, Paul F. Lazarsfeld, and William N. McPhee, *Voting: A Study of Opinion Formation in a Presidential Campaign* (Chicago: The University of Chicago Press, 1954); William N. McPhee and William A.

Glaser, eds., *Public Opinion and Congressional Elections* (New York: Free Press of Glencoe, 1962); William N. McPhee, *Formal Theories of Mass Behavior* (New York: Free Press of Glencoe, 1963); Columbia250, "William McPhee," Columbia University, http://c250.columbia.edu/c250_celebrates /your_columbians/william_mcphee.html; and Jill Lepore, *If/Then: How the Simulmatics Corporation Invented the Future* (New York: Liveright Publishing Corporation, 2020).

8. Wendy to Minnow, March 14, 1975.
9. William McPhee to Wendy, December 27, 1967.
10. Chuck to Wendy, February 23, 1968.
11. Chuck to Wendy, February 23, 1968.
12. Wendy to Diana Harper, August 5, 1968.
13. Wendy to Minnow, July 28, 1969.
14. Wendy to Minnow, July 28, 1969.
15. Wendy to Minnow, August 25, 1969.
16. Claire Kirch, "Chinook Bookshop Closing," *Publishers Weekly*, April 19, 2004, https://www.publishersweekly.com/pw/print/20040419/27127-chinook -bookshop-closing.html.
17. Richard to Wendy, June 16, 1970.
18. Wendy to Minnow, July 7, 1970.
19. Wendy to Minnow, July 23, 1970.
20. Wendy to Minnow, July 7, 1970.
21. Wendy to her family, August 17, 1970.
22. Wendy to William McPhee, July 23, 1970.
23. Richard to Wendy, July 9, 1970.
24. Richard to Wendy, July 10, 1970.
25. Richard to Wendy, June 17, 1970.
26. Richard to Wendy, July 13, 1970.
27. Richard to Wendy, July 13, 1970.
28. Richard to Wendy, June 17, 1970.
29. Richard to Wendy, June 23, 1970.
30. Richard to Wendy, June 25, 1970.
31. Richard to Wendy, July 13, 1970.
32. Richard to Wendy, June 18, 1970.
33. Richard to Wendy, June 21, 1970.
34. Richard to Wendy, June 17, 1970.
35. Richard to Wendy, June 18, 1970.
36. Wendy to Minnow, July 23, 1970.

Chapter 2

1. Henry Miller, *Big Sur and the Oranges of Hieronymus Bosch* (New York: New Directions, 1957), 17.

2. Virgil, *The Georgics*.

3. Jan Marsh, *Back to the Land: The Pastoral Impulse in Victorian England, 1880–1914* (Quartet Books, 1983).

4. Jeffrey Jacob, *New Pioneers: The Back-to-the-Land Movement and the Search for a Sustainable Future* (University Park: The Pennsylvania State University, 1997), 18.

5. Eleanor Agnew, *Back from the Land: How Young Americans Went Back to Nature in the 1970s and Why They Came Back* (Chicago: Ivan R. Dee, 2004), 4.

6. Michael Bryan, Federal Reserve Bank of Atlanta, "The Great Inflation 1965–1982," accessed December 11, 2020, https://www.federalreservehistory.org /essays/great-inflation#:~:text=The%20Great%20Inflation%20was%20the ,Fed%20and%20other%20central%20banks; Scott Horsley, "Think Inflation Is Bad Now? Let's Take a Step Back to the 1970s," *NPR, Weekend Edition*, May 29, 2021, https://www.npr.org/2021/05/29/1001023637/think-inflation -is-bad-now-lets-take-a-step-back-to-the-1970s; and Bureau of Labor Statistics, US Department of Labor, "Consumer prices up 9.1 percent over the year ended June 2022, largest increase in 40 years," *The Economics Daily*, July 18, 2022, https://www.bls.gov/opub/ted/2022/consumer-prices-up-9-1 -percent-over-the-year-ended-june-2022-largest-increase-in-40-years.htm.

7. Minnow to Cooie, July 8, 1971, Schlesinger Library.

8. Minnow to Cooie, July 8, 1971.

9. Charles A. Reich, "Reflections: The Greening of America," *New Yorker*, September 26, 1970, 42.

10. Richard to Wendy, June 16, 1970.

11. *Oxford Public Ledger*, August 3, 1899, 1.

12. Wendy to Minnow, July 15, 1975.

13. Wendy to Minnow, July 15, 1975.

Chapter 3

1. Brooks Blevins, *A History of the Ozarks, Volume 1* (Champaign: University of Illinois Press, 2018), 13.

2. Blevins, *A History of the Ozarks, Volume 1*, 22, 122–123.

3. Although Quapaw Indians lived around this new Mississippi River outpost, the word "Arcansas" that the French used actually came from the more northern Native American language Illini or Miami-Illinois. Blevins, *A History of the Ozarks, Volume 1*, 3.

4. Blevins, *A History of the Ozarks, Volume 1*, 29–36.

5. Leslie Stewart-Abernathy, Arkansas Archeological Survey, Russellville, "Cherokee," accessed January 15, 2021, https://encyclopediaofarkansas.net /entries/cherokee-553/; Blevins, *A History of the Ozarks, Volume 1*, 66.

6. Brooks Blevins, *A History of the Ozarks, Volume 2* (Champaign: University of Illinois Press, 2019), 241.

7. Blevins, *A History of the Ozarks, Volume 1*, 74–76.

8. US Department of Commerce, Bureau of the Census, "Population of States and Counties of the United States: 1790–1990," March 1996, Population of Counties—Arkansas: 1890–1990, https://www2.census.gov/library /publications/decennial/1990/population-of-states-and-counties-us-1790 -1990/population-of-states-and-counties-of-the-united-states-1790-1990 .pdf.

9. Blevins, *A History of the Ozarks, Volume 1*, 4.

10. Blevins, *A History of the Ozarks, Volume 2*, 242.

11. Brooks Blevins, *Hill Folks: A History of Arkansas Ozarkers and Their Image* (Chapel Hill: The University of North Carolina Press, 2002), 128.

12. Donald Harington, *The Architecture of the Arkansas Ozarks* (New York: Harvest/HBJ, 1987), 229–230.

13. Blevins, *A History of the Ozarks, Volume 1*, 6–7.

14. Wendy to Aunt Ruth, February 24, 1973.

15. Wendy to Minnow, March 14, 1973.

16. Wendy to Minnow, March 14, 1973.

17. Wendy to Minnow, February 15, 1973.

18. Wendy to Minnow, February 15, 1973.

19. Wendy to Nana, February 11, 1973.

20. Wendy to Ruth Washburn, February 24, 1973.

21. Wendy to Ruth, February 24, 1973.

22. Wendy to Ruth Washburn, May 3, 1973.

23. Wendy to Minnow, February 15, 1973.

24. Wendy to Minnow, June 3, 1973.

25. Wendy to Minnow, May 4, 1973.

26. Wendy to Minnow, February 15, 1973.

27. Wendy to Minnow, February 15, 1973, April 15, 1973, March 14, 1973.

28. Sarah McPhee to Wendy, February 4, 1973, March 1–2, 1973.

29. Wendy to Minnow, May 4, 1973.

30. Wendy to Ruth Washburn, May 3, 1973.

31. Wendy to Minnow, May 4, 1973.

32. Wendy to Ruth Washburn, May 3, 1973.

33. Wendy to Minnow, May 4, 1973.

34. Wendy to Minnow, February 15, 1973.

Chapter 4

1. Henry Miller, *Tropic of Cancer* (New York: Signet/Penguin, 1995), 23.

2. Wendy to Minnow, April 15, 1973.

3. Wendy to Minnow, April 15, 1973.

4. Brooks Blevins, email to author, September 29, 2021.

5. Wendy to Minnow, March 22, 1973.

6. Wendy to Minnow, April 15, 1973.

7. Wendy to Minnow, April 15, 1973.

8. Wendy to Minnow, March 22, 1973.

9. Wendy to Minnow, June 3, 1973.

10. Wendy to Ruth Washburn, July 3, 1973.

11. Wendy to Ruth Washburn, July 3, 1973.

12. Wendy to Minnow, June 3, 1973.

13. Wendy to Minnow, June 3, 1973.

14. Nana to Cooie, June 30, 1973, Schlesinger Library.

15. Nana to Cooie, June 30, 1973.

16. Ruth Washburn to Wendy, July 10, 1973.

Chapter 5

1. Wendy to Minnow, April 15, 1973.

2. Minnow to Nana, July 31, 1973.

3. Wendy to Ruth Washburn, May 3, 1973.

4. Wendy to Minnow, August 29, 1973.

5. Wendy to Minnow, April 30, 1974.

6. Wendy to Minnow, July 19, 1973.

7. Wendy to Nana, August 26, 1973.

8. Wendy to Minnow, August 29, 1973.

9. Nana to Wendy, undated, summer 1973.

10. Wendy to Minnow, August 29, 1973.

11. Wendy to Minnow, August 29, 1973.

12. Wendy to Nana, August 26, 1973.

13. Wendy to Minnow, August 29, 1973.

14. Wendy to Minnow, December 10, 1973.

15. Wendy to Minnow, December 10, 1973.

16. Wendy to Minnow, August 29, 1973.

17. Wendy to Minnow, October 7, 1973.

18. Wendy to Minnow, November 9, 1973.

19. Wendy to Minnow, November 9, 1973.

20. Wendy to Minnow, November 9, 1973.

21. Wendy to Minnow, November 27, 1973.

22. Wendy to Minnow, December 5, 1973.

23. Wendy to Minnow, December 5, 1973.

24. Wendy to Minnow, February 3, 1976.

25. Wendy to Minnow, May 6, 1975.

26. Wendy to Minnow, December 10, 1973.

27. Wendy to Chuck, November 5, 1974.

28. Wendy to Minnow, December 28, 1973.

29. Wendy to Minnow, February 13, 1974.

30. Wendy to Minnow, February 13, 1974.

Chapter 6

1. John Steinbeck, *The Grapes of Wrath* (New York: Penguin, 2006), 234–235.

2. Wendy to Minnow, February 13, 1974.

3. Wendy to Minnow, March 20, 1974.

4. Ruth Stout, *How to Have a Green Thumb Without an Aching Back: A New Method of Mulch Gardening* (New York: Cornerstone Library, 1979), 99.

5. Wendy to Minnow, April 30, 1974.

6. Wendy to Minnow, January 14, 1980.

7. Wendy to Minnow, April 30, 1974.

8. Federal Emergency Management Agency, "Major Disaster Declaration: Heavy Rains and Flooding," declaration DR-435-AR, May 31, 1974, https://www.fema.gov/disaster/435; Federal Emergency Management Agency, "Major Disaster Declaration: Severe Storms & Flooding," declaration DR-437-AR, June 8, 1974, https://www.fema.gov/disaster/437.

9. Minnow to Cooie, undated, mid-June 1974, Schlesinger Library.

10. Sarah McPhee to Wendy, June 15, 1974.

11. Wendy to Minnow, July 5, 1974.

12. Wendy to Minnow, July 14, 1974.

13. Wendy to Minnow, July 5, 1974.

14. Wendy to Minnow, July 5, 1974.

15. Wendy to Chuck and Jane Emery, July 14, 1974.

16. Wendy to Minnow, July 14, 1974.

17. Wendy to Minnow, July 25, 1974.

18. Wendy to Minnow, July 14, 1974.

19. Wendy to Chuck and Jane Emery, July 14, 1974.

20. Wendy to Minnow, July 25, 1974.

21. Nana to Cooie, July 14, 1974, Schlesinger Library.

22. Wendy to Minnow, July 25, 1974.

23. Wendy to Minnow, September 9, 1974.

24. US Bureau of the Census, "General Social and Economic Characteristics, 1980," Arkansas Census Data, Educational Attainment by County—1980, Universe: Persons 25 and Over.

25. Chris Kraus, *After Kathy Acker* (South Pasadena: Semiotext(e), 2017), 123.

26. Wendy to Nana, September 28, 1974.

27. Wendy to Minnow, September 9, 1974.

28. My mother's letters (September 28, 1974, to Minnow and Nana) say the addition was 10' × 12', but my father, who built it, has confirmed multiple times that the main cabin and the addition were each 8' × 10'.

29. Wendy to Nana, September 28, 1974.

30. Wendy to Minnow, September 9, 1974.

31. Wendy to Minnow, September 28, 1974.

32. Wendy to Minnow, November 19, 1974.

33. Wendy to Minnow, April 4, 1974.

34. Wendy to Minnow, March 20, 1974.

35. Wendy to Minnow, November 19, 1974.

36. Wendy to Chuck, November 5, 1974.

37. Wendy to Minnow, March 14, 1975.

38. Wendy to Minnow, August 29, 1973.

39. Wendy to Minnow, August 29, 1973.

40. Wendy to Minnow, October 16, 1974.

41. Wendy to Minnow, November 13, 1974.

42. Wendy to Chuck, November 5, 1974.

43. Wendy, email to author, September 30, 2021.

44. Martha Weinman Lear, "What do these women want? The Second Feminist Wave," *New York Times Magazine*, March 10, 1968, 24, https://www.nytimes.com/1968/03/10/archives/the-second-feminist-wave.html; Sascha Cohen, "The Day Women Went on Strike," *Time*, August 26, 2015, https://time.com/4008060/women-strike-equality-1970/; and Constance Grady, "The waves of feminism, and why people keep fighting over them, explained," *Vox*, July 20, 2018, https://www.vox.com/2018/3/20/16955588/feminism-waves-explained-first-second-third-fourth.

45. Wendy to Minnow, November 19, 1974.

46. Wendy to Minnow, November 19, 1974.

47. Recording of Mammy and Pappy visit, June 1975, side 2, audio, 6:45.

Chapter 7

1. Wendy to Minnow, May 4, 1973.

2. Richard Neidhardt, interview with the author; Elliott Hancock, interview by Brooks Blevins in Mountain View, Arkansas, *Creation and Development of the Arkansas Folk Festival and Ozark Folk Center—An Oral History Project*, Lyon College Regional Studies Center, June 25, 2003, https://home.lyon.edu/mslibrary/rcol/hancock.htm.

3. US Bureau of the Census, "Census of Housing: 1970-Volume 1 Part 5, Housing Characteristics for States, Cities, and Counties," Arkansas, Chapter A, General Housing Characteristics, Arkansas. Table 29-Selected Characteristics for Counties: 1970.

4. Eileen Schwartz, "A Q&A with Tony Joe White," *Texas Monthly*, December 2002, https://www.texasmonthly.com/articles/a-qa-with-tony-joe-white/.

5. Richard Neidhardt, interview with author; David Holt, "Jimmy Driftwood's

Hometown Hits," *David Holt's State of Music*, YouTube, June 1, 2020, video, 0:58, https://www.youtube.com/watch?v=_RWmH-RMghA.

6. Tommy Simmons, interview by Brooks Blevins in Mountain View, Arkansas, *Creation and Development of the Arkansas Folk Festival and Ozark Folk Center—An Oral History Project*, Lyon College Regional Studies Center, September 28, 2003, https://home.lyon.edu/mslibrary/rcol/simmons.htm.

7. Blevins, *Hill Folks*, 252–258.

8. "Singer Believes Deaths Were Murder, Suicide," *El Dorado Times*, October 12, 1967, 30.

Chapter 8

1. Harington, *The Architecture of the Arkansas Ozarks*, 56.

2. Ken Rudin, "A Dog of a Different Color," *Political Junkie with Ken Rudin*, NPR, July 23, 2009, https://www.npr.org/sections/politicaljunkie/2009/07/a _dog_of_a_different_color.html. Momma wrote Uncle Chuck on November 5, 1974: "Stone Co. voted itself dry for yet another 2 years—sigh—It's a little odd for a westerner to understand politics in the Solid South—Can you imagine living where the *democratic* primary *is* the election?"

3. Wendy to Chuck and Jane Emery, May 17, 1973.

4. Wendy to Chuck, November 5, 1974.

5. Wendy to Alpha Phi Chapter, Gamma Phi Beta Sorority, Colorado College, October 4, 1966.

6. Sarah Neidhardt, *My Life*, Joe T. Robinson Middle School, 1983–84 school year, Little Rock, Arkansas.

7. Wendy to Minnow, April 14, 1974.

8. Although Vance Randolph, the chronicler of Ozark culture, was an Episcopalian from Pittsburg, Kansas.

9. Wendy to Minnow, February 13, 1978.

10. "A Short History of the Church of the Good Shepherd," Church of the Good Shepherd Columbia website, accessed October 8, 2021, http://www.good shepherdcolumbia.org/about-us/short-history-of-the-church-of-the-good -shepherd/.

11. *Wilmington Messenger*, Wilmington, North Carolina, December 27, 1889, 4.

12. Chuck to Wendy, July 7, 1975.

13. Patricia Ann Sutterfield Buck, note to RogersDNA.com listing for Marvin Taft Sutterfield, June 20, 2001, accessed February 24, 2015, http://www .rogersdna.com/geddna/individual_detail.php?id_fam, website deactivated.

14. Theresa Marie Van Orman, "Folk From 'Off'—The Role of Outsiders in the Preservation, Creation, and Perpetuation of Traditional Craft and Music in Stone County, Arkansas" (MA thesis, Goucher College, 2014), 44–45.

15. Wendy to Minnow, August 15, 1978.

16. Wendy to Minnow and Irving Howbert, March 22, 1979.
17. Wendy to Minnow and Irving Howbert, March 22, 1979.
18. Wendy to Minnow, March 14, 1973.
19. John "Jock" McPhee to Wendy, April 11, 1975.

Chapter 9

1. Marcel Proust, *Remembrance of Things Past. Volume 1: Swann's Way, Within a Budding Grove*, trans C. K. Scott Moncrieff and Terence Kilmartin (New York: Vintage, 1982), 48–51.
2. Wendy to Nana, September 28, 1974.
3. Wendy to Ruth Washburn, May 3, 1973.
4. Wendy to Minnow and Irving Howbert, June 24, 1977, and March 25, 1980.
5. Wendy to Minnow, February 27, 1980.
6. Author to Santa, December 1977.
7. Wendy to Minnow, August 3, 1975.
8. Wendy to Nana, September 28, 1974.
9. Richard to Minnow, October 20, 1975.
10. Wendy to Minnow, June 4, 1977.
11. Eliot Wigginton, ed., *The Foxfire Book: Hog dressing, log cabin building, mountain crafts and foods, planting by the signs, snake lore, hunting tales, faith healing, moonshining, and other affairs of plain living* (Garden City, New York: Anchor Books, 1972), 203.
12. Fox [Rural Special] Head Start Newsletter, October 1977.
13. Recording of Sarah and Katy for Granminnow, side 1, audio, 7:04.
14. Wendy to Minnow, April 29, 1980.
15. Wendy to Minnow, July 5, 1974.
16. Wendy to Minnow, July 25, 1977.
17. Brooks Blevins, email to author, September 29, 2021; Richard Neidhardt, text to author, September 30, 2021.
18. Euell Gibbons, *Stalking the Wild Asparagus* (Chambersburg, Pennsylvania: Alan C. Hood & Company, Inc., 1962), 90–91.
19. Wendy to Minnow, September 30, 1976.
20. Wendy to Minnow, December 9, 1975.
21. George Bersch to Wendy and Richard, July 21, 1992.
22. Recording for Mammy and Pappy, Christmas 1978, side 2, audio, 4:30.
23. Recording for Mammy and Pappy, 10:49.
24. Buddy Gough, "Out for blood," *Arkansas Democrat-Gazette*, July 16, 2012, https://www.arkansasonline.com/news/2012/jul/16/out-blood-20120716/.
25. Wendy to Minnow, November 19, 1974.
26. Dave Roberts, email to author, October 30, 2019; Richard Neidhardt, interview with author.

Chapter 10

1. Wendy to Ruth Washburn, January 11, 1975.
2. Wendy to Minnow, January 11, 1975.
3. Wendy to Minnow, January 11, 1975.
4. History.com editors, "'Wheel of Fortune' premieres," History.com, September 18, 2019, https://www.history.com/this-day-in-history/wheel-of-fortune -premieres-nbc; "Television," *New York Times*, January 6, 1975, 53.
5. Wendy to Minnow, March 14, 1975.
6. Wendy to Minnow, March 14, 1975.
7. Wendy to Minnow, September 28, 1974.
8. Recording of Sarah and Katy for Granminnow, November 1977, side 2, audio, 18:58.
9. Wendy to Minnow, April 4, 1975.
10. Wendy to Minnow, May 9, 1975.
11. Wendy to Minnow, June 3, 1975.
12. Wendy to Nana, May 9, 1975.
13. Wendy to Nana, May 9, 1975.
14. Wendy to Minnow, July 15, 1975.
15. Recording of Mammy and Pappy visit, June 1975, side 1, audio, 7:57.
16. Wendy to Minnow, August 3, 1975.
17. Wendy to Minnow, September 6, 1975.
18. Wendy to Minnow, August 3, 1975.
19. Wendy to Minnow, August 18, 1975.
20. Wendy to Minnow, August 18, 1975.
21. Wendy to Minnow, September 6, 1975.
22. Wendy to Minnow, August 18, 1975.
23. Wendy to Minnow, September 6, 1975.
24. Wendy to Minnow, September 18, 1975.
25. Wendy to Minnow, October 1, 1975.
26. Richard to Minnow, October 20, 1975.
27. Wendy to Minnow, November 16, 1975.
28. Wendy to Minnow, December 9, 1975; Wendy to Nana, January 3, 1976.
29. Wendy to Minnow, January 3, 1976.
30. Wendy to Nana, January 3, 1976.
31. Wendy to Minnow, February 3, 1976.
32. Wendy to Minnow, February 24, 1976.
33. Wendy to Minnow, February 24, 1976.
34. Wendy to Minnow and Sarah McPhee, June 2, 1976.
35. Charles Fiske Emery, email to the author, February 25, 2015.
36. Wendy to Minnow and Sarah McPhee, June 19, 1976.
37. Wendy to Minnow and Sarah McPhee, June 2, 1976.
38. Wendy to Minnow, September 23, 1976.

39. Wendy to Minnow, September 23, 1976.

40. Wendy to Minnow, September 30, 1976.

41. Wendy to Minnow, April 4, 1975.

42. Ruth Wendell Washburn, *Children Have Their Reasons* (New York: D. Appleton-Century Company, Inc., 1942), ix.

43. Wendy to Minnow, June 3, 1975.

44. Wendy to Minnow, September 23, 1976.

45. Wendy to Minnow, November 27, 1976; Wendy to Minnow, February 2, 1977.

46. Sarah McPhee, email to author, October 9, 2014.

Chapter 11

1. I have since learned that he got this from a song called "Dead Armadillo" by the Lost Gonzo Band on their 1976 album *Thrills*.

2. Wendy, email to author, December 8, 2007.

3. Wendy to Ruth Washburn, January 11, 1975.

4. Wendy to Minnow, April 23, 1975.

5. Jackson depicts some of the harshness in her short story "The Renegade," written around the same time as "The Lottery," in which Mrs. Walpole—another city woman who feels out of place in the country—is informed by a neighbor one morning that her dog has been killing chickens. As she makes her way around the village doing her errands, everyone she meets has heard the rumor, and all kinds of gruesome solutions are offered: tying a dead chicken around the dog's neck, letting a mother hen scratch out the dog's eyes, or—most horribly—forcing the dog to run while wearing a spiked collar, so that it cuts off her head.

6. Katy Neidhardt to Jock and Liza McPhee, April 29, 1980.

7. Recording for Mammy and Pappy, Christmas 1978, side 1, audio, 4:40.

8. Richard Neidhardt, email to author, December 11, 2007.

9. Recording for Mammy and Pappy, Christmas 1978, side 1, audio, 6:32.

10. Recording for Pappy's birthday, November 1978, side 2, audio, 2:06.

11. Recording for Pappy's birthday, 5:41.

12. Wendy to Minnow and Irving Howbert, September 24, 1978.

13. Wendy to Nana, September 28, 1974.

14. "Eddie" to Richard, June 9, 1977.

15. Brooks Blevins, email to author, September 29, 2021.

16. Wendy to Minnow, November 13, 1974.

17. Wendy to Minnow, August 29, 1973.

18. Wendy to Minnow, November 27, 1976.

19. Wendy to Minnow and Irving Howbert, December 31, 1976.

20. Wendy to Minnow and Irving, December 31, 1976.

21. Wendy to Minnow, March 9, 1977.

22. Wendy to Minnow, March 1, 1977.

23. Wendy to Minnow, May 3, 1977.
24. Wendy to Minnow, April 26, 1977; Wendy to Minnow, March 25, 1977.
25. Wendy to Minnow, May 18, 1977.
26. Wendy to Minnow and Irving Howbert, June 24, 1977.

Chapter 12

1. Sir Philip Sidney, *The Countess of Pembroke's Arcadia (The Old Arcadia)* (New York: Oxford University Press, 1999), 14.
2. Wendy to Minnow, June 4, 1977.
3. Wendy to Minnow, June 4, 1977.
4. Wendy to Minnow, July 25, 1977.
5. Wendy to Minnow, August 9, 1977.
6. Wendy to Minnow, May 18, 1977.
7. Wendy to Minnow, September 5, 1977.
8. Wendy to Minnow, September 5, 1977.
9. Recording of Sarah and Katy for Granminnow, November 1977, side 2, audio, 5:25
10. Recording of Sarah and Katy for Granminnow, 5:13.
11. Recording of Sarah and Katy for Granminnow, 26:13.
12. Recording of Sarah and Katy for Granminnow, 28:55.
13. Wendy to Minnow, September 5, 1977.
14. Wendy to Minnow, December 2, 1977.
15. Chuck to Wendy and family, December 27, 1977.
16. Wendy to Minnow, January 3, 1978.
17. Wendy to Minnow, January 3, 1978.
18. Wendy to Minnow, January 3, 1978.
19. Wendy to Minnow, June 3, 1975.
20. Wendy to Minnow, February 13, 1978.
21. Wendy to Minnow, February 13, 1978.
22. Wendy to Minnow, June 6, 1976.
23. Wendy to Minnow, April 26, 1977.
24. "heritage hustlers": Blevins, *Hill Folks*, 227.
25. Wendy to Cooie, July 20, 1978.
26. The business appears to have stayed open at least another year. I found an article in the Mountain Home, Arkansas, *Baxter Bulletin* from the following summer announcing the new business, despite Momma's announcing of it being postmarked summer 1978. Craig Ogilvie, "Mountain View businessmen found Outdoor Center, Inc.," *Baxter Bulletin*, June 14, 1979, 62.
27. Wendy to Minnow, August 15, 1978; Wendy to Minnow and Irving Howbert, September 7, 1978.
28. Wendy to Minnow, August 25, 1969.

29. Wendy to Minnow and Irving Howbert, October 16, 1978.
30. Wendy to Minnow, November 16, 1975.
31. Wendy to Chuck, November 5, 1974.
32. Wendy to Minnow, April 30, 1974.
33. Sarah McPhee to Wendy, undated, about May 1978.
34. Sarah McPhee to Wendy, February 5, 1977; Sarah McPhee to Wendy, undated, sometime in summer 1980.
35. Sarah Neidhardt, *My Life*, Joe T. Robinson Middle School, 1983–84 school year, Little Rock, Arkansas.
36. Wendy to Minnow, August 15, 1978.
37. Wendy to Minnow and Irving Howbert, September 24, 1978.
38. Recording for Pappy's birthday, November 1978, side 1, audio, 16:45.
39. Recording for Mammy and Pappy, Christmas 1978, side 1, audio, 0:48.
40. Recording for Mammy and Pappy, Christmas 1978, side 2, audio, 11:53.
41. Wendy to Minnow and Irving Howbert, January 4, 1979.
42. Michael Warshauer, emails to author, May 20, 2015, and May 22, 2015. Mountain View was written up in the *New York Times* in 1987, and Michael's bakery was mentioned: Mitchel L. Zoler, "Folk Arts are Reborn in the Ozarks," *New York Times*, May 3, 1987, https://www.nytimes.com/1987/05/03/travel/folk-arts-are-reborn-in-the-ozarks.html.
43. Wendy to Minnow and Irving Howbert, January 4, 1979.
44. Minnow to Cooie, February 19, 1984, Schlesinger Library.
45. Wendy to Minnow and Irving Howbert, January 4, 1979.
46. Sidney, *The Countess of Pembroke's Arcadia*, 14.
47. Wendy to Minnow, October 7, 1977.
48. Recording for Mammy and Pappy, Christmas 1978, side 2, audio, 21:36.
49. Recording for Mammy and Pappy, 21:01.
50. Wendy to Ruth Washburn, May 3, 1973; Richard to Minnow, October 20, 1975; Wendy to Nana, January 3, 1976; Wendy to Minnow, July 20, 1978.
51. Wendy to Minnow, May 18, 1977.
52. Wendy to Minnow, July 20, 1978.
53. Wendy to Minnow, March 1, 1977; Wendy to Minnow, July 20, 1978.
54. Recording for Mammy and Pappy, Christmas 1978, side 2, audio, 22:05.

Chapter 13

1. Paul Durand, "Advice on Ozarks Homesteading," *Mother Earth News,* May/June 1975.
2. Rural Special Head Start newsletter, November 1977.
3. Wendy to Minnow, September 6, 1975; Kenneth Rorie, "Fox (Stone County)," CALS Encyclopedia of Arkansas, last updated May 21, 2021, https://encyclopediaofarkansas.net/entries/fox-stone-county-8997/.

4. Blevins, *Hill Folks*, 208, 297n54.

5. Wendy to Minnow, September 6, 1975. Eight years later, Hillary Clinton helped make foreign languages and art mandatory in Arkansas schools as chair of the Arkansas Blue Ribbon Commission, authorized by The Quality Education Act of 1983.

6. Wendy to Minnow, October 7, 1977.

7. Wendy to Minnow, October 7, 1977; Fox [Rural Special] Head Start Newsletter, October 1977.

8. "Ten in First Headstart Class," *Colorado Springs Gazette-Telegraph*, September 29, 1965, 37; 1966 letters between Minnow and Cooie, Minnow and Chuck and Jane Emery, and Cooie and Nana, Schlesinger Library.

9. Wendy to Minnow and Irving Howbert, October 16, 1978.

10. Wendy to Minnow and Irving, October 16, 1978.

11. Recording of Sarah and Katy for Granminnow, November 1977, side 1, audio, 13:41.

12. Recording of Sarah and Katy for Granminnow, November 1977, side 2, audio, 3:47.

13. Recording of Sarah and Katy for Granminnow, side 2, 17:44.

14. Wendy to Minnow, September 5, 1977.

15. Wendy to Minnow, October 7, 1977.

16. Dave Roberts, Facebook message to author, October 24, 2019.

17. Katy Neidhardt to Minnow, undated, about 1978.

18. Author to Minnow, September 11, 1979.

Chapter 14

1. "Hillary Rodham Clinton interview, 1979," YouTube, AlphaX News, accessed November 3, 2022, https://www.youtube.com/watch?v=bg_sEZg7-rk, video, 22:00.

2. Wendy to Minnow and Irving Howbert, January 4, 1979.

3. Minnow to Wendy, January 21, 1979.

4. Wendy to Minnow, March 1, 1979.

5. Wendy to Chuck and Jane Emery, January 4, 1979.

6. Wendy to Minnow, February 19, 1979.

7. Wendy to Minnow, December 9, 1975.

8. Wendy to Minnow, March 1, 1979.

9. Wendy to Minnow, February 9, 1979.

10. Michael Warshauer, email to author, October 21, 2007.

11. Wendy to Minnow, February 19, 1979.

12. Wendy to Minnow, March 1, 1979.

13. Wendy to Minnow, February 9, 1979.

14. Wendy to Minnow, March 1, 1979.

15. Wendy to Minnow, February 9, 1979.

16. Wendy to Minnow and Irving Howbert, March 22, 1979.

17. Wendy to Minnow and Irving Howbert, April 25, 1979.

18. Wendy to Minnow and Irving Howbert, November 21, 1979.

19. Wendy to Minnow and Irving Howbert, April 25, 1979.

20. Wendy to Minnow and Irving Howbert, July 2, 1979.

21. Wendy to Minnow, July 10, 1979.

22. Wendy to Minnow and Irving Howbert, July 2, 1979.

23. Wendy to Minnow, May 7, 1979.

24. Wallace Tripp, ed. and illus., *Granfa' Grig Had a Pig and Other Rhymes Without Reason* (New York: Little, Brown and Company, 1976), 29.

25. Wendy to Minnow, July 10, 1979.

26. Wendy to Minnow, July 10, 1979.

27. Wendy to Minnow, March 22, 1979.

28. Wendy to Minnow and Irving Howbert, November 1, 1979.

29. Wendy to Minnow and Irving Howbert, November 3, 1979.

30. Wendy to Minnow and Irving Howbert, December 12, 1979.

31. Wendy to Minnow, January 14, 1980.

32. William McPhee to Wendy, undated, sometime in 1979.

33. William McPhee to Wendy, May 21, 1975.

34. Mike Mariani, "The New Generation of Self-Created Utopias," *New York Times Style Magazine*, January 16, 2020, https://www.nytimes.com/2020/01/16/t-magazine/intentional-communities.html; "History," East Wind Community, accessed October 18, 2021, https://www.eastwindblog.co/?page_id=56.

35. Thomas Michael Kersen, *Where Misfits Fit* (Jackson: University Press of Mississippi, 2021), 144, Kindle.

36. Richard Todd, "'Walden Two': Three? Many More?," *New York Times*, March 15, 1970, 229, https://www.nytimes.com/1970/03/15/archives/walden-two-three-many-more-walden-two.html.

37. Todd, "'Walden Two': Three? Many More?"

38. Todd, "'Walden Two': Three? Many More?"

39. Mariani, "The New Generation of Self-Created Utopias."

40. Maria Stenzel and Alan Mairson, "ZipUSA: Tecumseh, Missouri," *National Geographic Magazine*, August 2005, 114.

41. Wendy to Irving Howbert, January 14, 1980.

42. The Mother Earth News Editors, "The Meadowcreek Project: A Model of Sustainability in the Ozarks," *Mother Earth News*, March/April 1982, https://www.motherearthnews.com/nature-and-environment/sustainability-model-zmaz82mazglo.

43. The *Mother Earth News* Editors, "The Meadowcreek Project." According to an email from David Orr to the author, Meadowcreek "hit its stride during our time, around 1983–90, with the completion of the Conference center and dorm facilities. We had a constant stream of people coming and going for events

including the first conference for New York Foundations on sustainability, the first conference for bankers and climate scientists (co-sponsored with Gov. Clinton), annual events for environmental educators with Brown University, January terms for college students, a Russian exchange program, gifted and talented programs, Elder Hostels, programs for local colleges, events on religion-economics-environment etc. In all we averaged in those years ~2000+ conference guests, students, and visitors and every event featured local music, outdoor activities, basketball, local story-tellers, and local foods. As an educational venture it drew on the thinking of Maria Montessori, John Dewey, Rudolf Steiner, the Highlander Center etc . . . aiming to connect head, hands, and heart in every event. I hear that it still goes on under local management and is doing interesting things on food, music, and well-being." (David Orr, email to author, October 15, 2021.) The Orrs left Meadowcreek in 1990, and David Orr went to Oberlin College where he was the Paul Sears Distinguished Professor of Environmental Studies and Politics and senior advisor to the president of Oberlin College. While at Oberlin, he was instrumental in all aspects of the building of the Adam Joseph Lewis Center, which was named by an AIA panel in 2010 as "the most important green building of the past 30 years." (Oberlin College, https://www.oberlin.edu/david-orr.) He is a respected and prolific author, now retired from Oberlin, and currently a Professor of Practice at Arizona State University working on democracy/climate issues.

Meadowcreek has continued under various forms and owners. According to Rachel Reynolds, who runs the current Meadowcreek Learning and Retreat Center, it is now a land-based art and culture site with a community-based library, a lodge, an artists-in-residence program, and a CSA garden and food pantry that serves 425 families last count in three counties. They have hosted a concert series in their historic barn, including the state old-time fiddle contest in 2021. They plan to scale up next year and work on building renovations. (Rachel Reynolds, email to Brooks Blevins, October 29, 2021.)

44. Carl N. McDaniel, *Wisdom for a Livable Planet: The Visionary Work of Terri Swearingen, Dave Foreman, Wes Jackson, Helena Norberg-Hodge, Werner Forn* (San Antonio: Trinity University Press, 2011), 199, 201.
45. Wendy to Minnow and Irving Howbert, February 2, 1980.
46. Wendy to Minnow, February 27, 1980.
47. Wendy to Minnow and Irving Howbert, March 10, 1980.
48. Wendy to Minnow and Irving Howbert, March 12, 1980.
49. Wendy to Minnow and Irving Howbert, June 4, 1980. The Women, Infants, and Children (WIC) program was started by the federal government in 1972 to provide supplemental nutritional support to low-income families.
50. Wendy to Minnow and Irving Howbert, June 18, 1980.
51. Minnow to Katy Neidhardt, July 5, 1980.
52. Wendy to Minnow and Irving Howbert, March 25, 1980.

53. Wendy to Minnow and Irving Howbert, June 4, 1980.

54. Miriam Storrs Washburn, "Colorado Springs from a Woman's Standpoint with Greetings to the Year 2001," July 1901, Colorado Springs Century Chest Collection, Ms 0349, Transcription 66, Tutt Library Special Collections Department, Colorado College, Colorado Springs, Colorado.

55. Wendy to Minnow and Irving Howbert, August 1, 1980.

56. "Heat: A Major Killer," National Weather Service website, accessed October 11, 2021, https://www.weather.gov/oax/heatsafety. "In 1980 the nation saw a devastating heat wave and drought that claimed at least 1700 lives and had estimated economic costs $15–$19 billion in 1980 dollars."

57. Wendy to Minnow, Sarah, and Katy, July 18, 1980.

58. Brooks Blevins, email to the author, September 29, 2021.

59. Wendy to Minnow and Irving Howbert, August 1, 1980.

60. Wendy to Minnow, Sarah, and Katy, July 18, 1980.

61. Wendy to Minnow and Irving Howbert, August 1, 1980.

62. Sarah McPhee to Wendy, August 10, 1980.

63. Wendy to Minnow and Irving Howbert, September 22, 1980.

64. Wendy to Minnow, November 2, 1980.

65. Wendy to Minnow, November 13, 1980.

66. Author to Minnow and Irving Howbert, September 1980.

67. Wendy to Minnow and Irving Howbert, October 26, 1980.

68. Author to Minnow, October 9, 1980.

69. Katy Neidhardt to Minnow, October 7, 1980.

70. Wendy to Minnow and Irving Howbert, November 12, 1980.

71. Wendy to Minnow, November 13, 1980.

Chapter 15

1. Elspeth Huxley, *The Flame Trees of Thika* (New York: Penguin Books, 1982), 105.

2. Wendy McPhee, email to author, September 30, 2021.

3. Wendy to Cooie, October 6, 1981.

4. Wendy to her family, June 16, 1969.

5. Dona Brown, *Back to the Land: The Enduring Dream of Self-Sufficiency in Modern America (Studies in American Thought and Culture)* (Madison: University of Wisconsin Press, 2011), back-cover synopsis.

6. Wendy to Nana, August 26, 1973.

7. Paul Durand, "Advice on Ozarks Homesteading," *Mother Earth News,* May/June 1975.

8. A. Bronson Alcott and Charles Lane, "Fruitlands," *The Dial* 4, no. 1 (July 1843): 135.

INDEX

Page numbers in italics refer to photographs.

Abbreviations used:
SN—*Sarah Neidhardt*
RN—*Richard Neidhardt, Jr.*
WM—*Wendy (Caroline) McPhee*

A

Abbie (dog), 163, 165, 166
Aberli, Ray, 61
abortion, 22
Acadia (Prendergast), 30
Adams, Miriam Washburn (Aunt
    Minnie), 83, 136, 178
Addams, Charles, 188
Adventures of the Wilderness Family,
    The (film), 37n
After Kathy Acker (Kraus), 93
Agnew, Eleanor, 34
agricultural school, 54, 71, 81, 91, 100
Ain't You Got a Right to the Tree of Life
    (Carawan), 188
Aladdin lamp, 84
alcohol prohibition, 66–67, 116, 250n2
Alcott, Louisa May, 33, 238
Alexandria Quartet, The (Durrell), 188
"Alice's Restaurant Massacree"
    (Guthrie), 15
Allenspark, Colorado, 38–39, 147,
    230–31
American Mountain People (National
    Geographic Society), 105
Andersen, Hans Christian, 3, 184, 190
Anderson, Mrs. (first grade teacher),
    205, 214
Angell, Roger, 190
animal butchery. *See* butchery

animals. *See* dead animals; farm ani-
    mals; pets; *and specific animal*
Animals Should Definitely Not Wear
    Clothing (Barrett), 184
Ant and Bee (Banner), 184
Arcadia, 197
Architecture of the Arkansas Ozarks,
    The (Harington), 47
Arnold Cave, 179
Arnow, Harriette, 188
arts-and-crafts movement, 47
Ashton-Warner, Sylvia, 159
auctions, 39, 79, 200, 215. *See also* sale
    barns
Aunt Ruth (great aunt of WM). *See*
    Washburn, Ruth Wendell
Aunt Sarah (aunt of SN, sister
    of WM). *See* McPhee, Sarah Eddy
Aunt Minnie (great aunt of WM). *See*
    Adams, Miriam Washburn
autoharp, 105, 225

B

"Babes in the Wood, The" (anonymous),
    112
Back from the Land (Agnew), 34
back-to-the-land movement: and
    books of, 35, 40, 90; and counter-
    culture movement, 8, 11, 17, 34, 93,
    128–29, 220–21; and East Wind

back-to-the-land movement (*cont.*)
Community, 220–21; in film, 37; and
folk music, 34, 105, 123; and goats,
170; and historical perspective of,
33, 47; and impact of in society,
237–38; and impetus for, 34–35;
and industries of, 35, 125–26, 128,
220; and locals, 52, 116; and modern
version, 33–34; in Ozarks region,
46–47; and physical appearance
in rural setting, 130–31; and RN,
35–36, 90; and school buses, 125,
128–29; and SN's perspective on, 71,
236–41; in Stone County, Arkansas,
36, 84, 90, 120, 123, 124, 125, 128–
31; and WM, 38–39, 90. *See also*
class; counterculture movement;
homesteading; Fox, Arkansas: and
SN's perspective on childhood in;
Meadowcreek Project
"Baldheaded Lena" (The Lovin'
Spoonful), 111
banjos, 105, 106–7, 111, 123, 173, 241
Banner, Angela. See *Ant and Bee*
Barbie, 5, 161, 180
barn construction, 60, 99, 157
barrel stave manufacturing, 92
Barrett, Judi. See *Animals Should
Definitely Not Wear Clothing*
Bass, Lisa, 206
Batesville, Arkansas, 61
bathroom facilities, 178, 182–83; and
additions and renovations to in
cabin, 159, 176, 182–83, 191, 212–14,
215; and bathing, 48, 68, *96*, 101,
106, 182, 191, 215; and chair-toilet,
5–6, 182–
83; and Granminnow's complaints
about, 67, 182; at Key Place, 58, 59,
182; in rental house, 48; at Rural
Special public school, 154–155,
204–5; and toilet paper, 189, 212–13.
See also outhouses

"Battle of New Orleans" (Driftwood),
109
Beardsley, Aubrey, 188
bears, 129
Beatles, The, 110
Beauvoir, Simone de, 101
Becker, Marion Rombauer. See *Joy of
Cooking*
Beecher, Henry Ward, 122
Bemelmans, Ludwig. See *Madeline*
Ben Franklin (store), 48, 157
Berkeley, California, 27, 37, 50–51
Berry, Webb, 173
Bersch, George, 120–21, 123, 144, 175,
176, 182, 185, 196, 210, 216, 226
Bersch, Mollie, *186*, 203. *See also*
Bersch, George
Bersch, Mary, 120, *186*
Bersch, Tom, 120
biscuits and gravy, 140
Bishop family (Jessica, Lisa, Angela,
Randolph, Doris), 224
blackberries, 143
Black Elk Speaks (Neihardt), 188
Blanchard Shirt Factory, 91, 92
Blanchard Springs Caverns, 91, 186
Blevins, Brooks, 170, 201–2
blister beetles, 81
Blowing Spring Cave, 179
Blueberries for Sal (McCloskey), 184
Boericke, Art. See *Handmade Houses:
A Guide to the Woodbutcher's Art*
Bonds, Toby, 206
Borrowers, The (Norton), 226
Boston, Massachusetts, 24–25, 26, 38,
189, 235
Boston Mountains, 47, 49
Brahman bulls (Brimmers), 58, 63
Brand, Stewart. See *Whole Earth
Catalog, The*
Branscum, Scotty, 165, 214
Brantingham, James M., 28
Brautigan, Richard, 188

bread, homemade, 140

Brewer, Jimmy, 206

Broad River, 41

Brooklyn, New York, 122, 225

Brother Ray (classmate of SN), 203, 206

Brown, Edward Espe. See *Tassajara Bread Book*

Brown v. Board of Education, 19

Burgess, Thornton, 226

burritos, 139

butchery, 102–3, *103*, 137–38, 139, 144, 145–46, 156, 193, 240

buttercups, 6

butter, home-churned, 140

C

cabin construction, 50, *53*, *55*, 60, 72, *73*, *86*, *181*; and additions and renovations to, *xiv*, 88, 99, 159, 175–76, 191, *192*, *212*, *213*, 215, 216–17; finances and, 77–78; and initial plan for, 68, 82, 84, 238; and kitchen, 83, 94–97, *95*, *134*, *192*; and location on land, 83; and main structure, 82–83, 248n28. *See also* bathroom facilities; electricity; farm/land build-out; outhouses

cabin furnishings, 11, 70, *134*, 178, 215–16

cabin, move in to, 82–84, *85–86*, 87–89

California king snake, 12

California, move to, 235–36

capitalism, 34

Carawan, Guy and Candie. See *Ain't You Got a Right to the Tree of Life*

Carter family, 108

cassette recordings: of cousins, 144, 165–68, 193–95, 198, 200; for Granminnow, 18–19, 140, 150, 179, 204; of Katy, 140, 152, 167, 179, 191; for Mammy and Pappy, 19, 10̇3–4, 152, 165–68, 191–92, 193–96; of

Pappy, 152; of SN, 140, 150, 152–53, 166, 179, 191, 204; of Rhett, 167, 194, 200; of RN, 192, 193, 194, 195–96, 200; of John Weaver, 125, 194, 195, 200; of WM, 150, 191, 193, 194, 195, 199, 200, 204

catfish, 173

cattle auction. *See* sale barns

cats, 164, 165. *See also* Kitty Hanya

caves/caving, 35, 178–79, 185, 196

Celestial Seasonings teas, 140

Celotex, 118

Centennial wood cookstove, 39, 83

chair-toilets, 5–6, 182–83

chamber pots, 182

Charlotte's Web (White), 173

Cherokee, 46

Chevy sedan, 77, 149, 157, 170, 198, 199

chicken houses, 91, 92, 99, 119, 144, 172

chickens, 8, 34, 102, 105, 174, 217; and breeds of, 172; and butchering of, 137, 238; at cabin, 54, 71, 72, 81, 169, 172, 213; and catching of as job, 92; and dogs killing, 165, 253n5; and eggs, 81, 98, 123, 172; and factory farming, 98, 172; and hypnotizing of, 137; for manure, 69, 80. *See also* chicken houses

Chigger (dog), 163, 164, 166

childbirth, 61–62

childhood amusements, 3–10, 180, 184, 189–90, 217

children's rhymes, 111, 112, 125, 140, 184, 217–18

children's songs, 122

Children's Workshop, 159

chiles rellenos, 140

Chinook Bookshop (Colorado Springs), 24, 25–28, 35, 90, 188

Christmas celebrations: in cabin, 175, 180, 196, 197; in Colorado, 147, 231, 232; at Key Place, 76; and letter to Santa, 135; in Little Rock, Arkansas,

Christmas celebrations (*cont.*)
156–57; and mass at Bersches', 175;
at Rhett's house, 144, 193–96, 198,
200; in South Carolina, 42, 219
church services, 118–19, 120–21, 123, 196
Chuck (uncle of WM). *See* Emery,
Charles F., Jr.
civil rights movement, 14, 101, 117
Clark, Kenneth and Mamie, 19
class: and back-to-the-landers, 34–35,
52, 125; and cousins' (Roberts) life
before Fox, 193; and dichotomies of
in Neidhardts' Fox life, 70, 81, 84,
93, 147, 158–59, 176, 178, 188, 187–91,
197, 202, 209, 215–16, 226–27; and
divide between Neidhardt family
and locals, 118, 130, 161; and educational advantages of, 20, 159, 184,
187–91, 202, 203, 236; of Fox life
compared to developing world, 190;
and impact of self-imposed poverty,
222, 236, 237, 240; and privilege
and self-imposed poverty, 34–35,
52, 54, 92–94, 107–8, 141, 159, 236;
of RN and WM, 11, 13, 19–20, 97,
209; and SN's childhood confusion
about, 222, 226–27; and SN's perspective on in her life, 178, 188, 189,
202, 209, 236. *See also* financial
support; Head Start program; welfare; Women, Infants, and Children
(WIC) program
Claude (French boyfriend of WM), 27,
29, 30
Clinton, Arkansas, 70, 149, 188
Clinton, Bill, 209, 210–11
Clinton, Hillary, 209, 256n5
Clinton State Bank, 200
Cohan, Ray. See *How to Make it on the
Land*
collard greens, 138
Colette, 188
Colonial Dames, 209

Colorado Springs, Colorado. *See*
Colorado
Colorado, 43, 52, 59, 71, 100, 107, 158,
168; and Celestial Seasonings, 140;
and Denver, 20, 25; and Head Start
programs, 203; and Pikes Peak, 30,
37, 226; and possible move to after
Arkansas, 230–31, 232, 233; and
RN before marriage, 16–17, 25–26,
28–30, 108, 165; and visits to, 147,
161, 222–23, 226–27, 231, 232; and
WM and RN's married life in, 35–36,
37–38, 39–40, 42, 55, 70, 82, 188;
and WM before marriage, 20–23, 24,
25–26, 30; and WM's family church,
122. *See also* Chinook Bookshop;
Colorado College; Howbert, Miriam
Emery McPhee; McPhee, William N.
Colorado College, 18, 20, 21, 22, 24
Columbia, South Carolina, 13–16, 17,
40–41, 122
communes, 33, 36, 128, 220–21
Compton, Os, 68
Congaree River, 41
Connor, Ray: and Arkansas, first
visit to, 36; and Arkansas, move
to, 42–43, 45; and cabin construction, 82; as co-landowner, 39; and
departure from Arkansas, 42, 67,
68–69; and financial help, 52, 54; as
gardener, 68–69; and living arrange-
ments, 48, 49, 57; and personality
of, 68; and physical appearance of,
130; and preparations for move to
Arkansas, 39; and sale of land, 69;
and working the land, 48–49, 52, 55
Connor, Sunshine, 43. *See also* Connor,
Ray; Connor, Susan
Connor, Susan, 42–43, 48–49, 52, 57,
68, 168. *See also* Connor, Ray
Conway, Arkansas, 45, 70, 230, 235.
See also University of Central
Arkansas

Cooie (aunt of WM). *See* Harper, Eleanor Emery

cookbooks, 135

cookstoves, 133, 215. *See also* woodstoves

copperheads, 60, 168–69

coral mushrooms, 142

corporal punishment, 203, 204–5

cottonmouths, 168, 169

counterculture movement, 8, 11, 17, 93, 130–31; and communes, 220–21; and drop out generation, 235; and impetus for, 34–35. *See also* back-to-the-land movement; Stone County, Arkansas: and back-to-the-land movement

Country Joe and the Fish, 112

Country Life movement, 47

Country Living, 188

country roads. *See* dirt roads

cousins. *See* Roberts, David; Roberts, Edward; Roberts, Richard

cows: Angus-Holstein, 99, 171; and butcher, 138; and cream, 140; and deaths of, 8, 163; and Granminnow's complaints about, 67; and loading chutes, 157; Mama Cow, 99, *167*, 172, 175; for milk, 99, 171–72; and pastureland, 80; and purchase of, 99; and salt blocks, 6. *See also* milking cows

Craft Guild, The (Manitou Springs), 17, 28

creamed onions, 145, 174, 175

crescent rolls, 135, 145, 175

crypto operator (US Army), 15–17

Curious George (Rey), 158

D

Daddy. *See* Neidhardt, Richard, Jr.

Daddy Tom (great-grandfather of RN). *See* Taylor, Thomas George

Danny (classmate of SN), 206. *See also* Orr, Daniel

dandelion greens, 143

Datsun trucks, 199–200, 206

David (cousin of SN). *See* Roberts, David

Davis, Adelle, 88, 90, 97–98, 99, 140

dead animals, 8, 70, *103*, 163, 164, 165, 166, 253n5

debt: and chicken houses, 91; and construction business, 218; and cow, 99; and education expenses, 230; for land, 67, 69, 218; and pressure of, 198; and RN's before Arkansas, 50; for rototiller, 80; and self-sufficiency, 238; for vehicles, 156, 199–200, 218

deer, 138, 145

deer season, 165, 204

Deliverance (film), 115

delta blues, 110

Democratic primary, 250n2

dental work, 93–94

Denver, Colorado, 18, 20, 25, 190

departure from cabin, 232–35

desserts, 135, 196

Devil's Elbow, 9, 49, 228

Dew Drop Inn, 163, 172, 187

dirt roads, 9, 34, 69, 72, 82, 129, 200, 241; to cabin, 120, 149, 163, 188, 201, 210–11; and initial repairs to on land, 49, 51–52; at Key Place, 59, 63; and mud, 49, 109, 210–11, 212, 213

Disney, 184

Dittmer, Katy. *See* Neidhardt, Katherine

Dodge van, 199

dogs, 162, 163, 164, 165. *See also* Abbie; Chigger; Junior; Old Belle; Tiny

Dollmaker, The (Arrow), 188

domestic animals. *See* dead animals; farm animals; pets; *and specific animal*

donkeys, 225

Dooly and the Snortsnoot (Kent), 184

Driftwood, Cleda, 109, 110

Driftwood, Jimmy, 109–11, 113
Drop City, 36
drop out generation, 235
dry county, 66–67, 116, 250n2
dryer, 212, 221
dulcimers, 36, 105, 123
dung beetles, 6, 10
Durrell, Lawrence, 188

E
earthworms, 6, 142
Easter celebrations, 118–19, 176
East Wind Community, 220–21
education and school, 119, 154–55,
    201–7, 230. *See also* Rural Special
    public school
Edward (cousin of SN). *See* Roberts,
    Edward
elderberries, 9, 141
electricity, 5, 36, 76, 88, 89–90, 94, 96,
    135, 148, 158, 173, 215
Eloise (Thompson), 184
embossed stationery and envelopes, 81,
    223–24
Emery, Charles Fiske (cousin of WM),
    158
Emery, Charles F., Jr. (Uncle Chuck):
    and book giving, 88, 90; and career,
    101; and Colorado home, *21*, 23–24,
    227; and financial support from,
    236, 239; and importance of to WM,
    75, 236, 239; and letters to WM,
    23–24, 123, 180; and possibility of
    visit to Arkansas, 75–76; and wed-
    ding anniversary, 26. *See also* letters
    from WM to Chuck
Emery, Eleanor Washburn (Nana): and
    autograph book of, 190; and death
    of, 178; and financial support from,
    54, 75, 157, 236; and furniture from,
    178; and health concerns about
    Neidhardts, 98–99; and letter from
    Granminnow, 65–68; and letters

from WM, 97, 138, 157, 169; and
    letters to Cooie, 62, 91; and letter to
    WM, 70; and phone call from, 62; on
    RN, 18, 62; on role of women, 120;
    on vaccinations, 99; and Katherine
    Sergeant White/Roger Angell, 190
Emery, Jane Aycrigg (Aunt Janey): on
    back-to-the-land movement, 33;
    and Chinook Bookshop, 25, 90; and
    Thanksgiving tradition, 174. *See also*
    Emery, Charles F., Jr.
Emery, Jean Jackson (Aunt Jean), 158
Emery, John Wendell (Uncle John), 158
Emma (family maid of RN), 117–18
energy crisis, 34, 43
enslaved people, 41–42
Episcopal church, 14, 20, 120–22, 186,
    250n8 (chap. 8)
Etta (neighbor; pseudonym), 123

F
Fairfield Bay, Arkansas, 153
family pets, 162–66. *See also* Abbie;
    Chigger; Junior; Kitty Hanya; Old
    Belle; Tiny
farm animals, 163, 169–73. *See also* dead
    animals; pets; *and specific animal*
farm labor. *See* barn construction;
    cabin construction; dirt roads: and
    initial repairs to on land; farm ani-
    mals; farm/land build-out; fence
    building; gardens; milking cows;
    household labor; pond; wells
farm/land build-out, 49–50, 51–52,
    69, 71, 148, 182–83. *See also* barn
    construction; dirt roads: and initial
    repairs to on land; farm animals;
    fence building; pond; wells
farm-to-table diet, 135–39
Farris, Everil, 119
fauna. *See* dead animals; farm ani-
    mals; pets; snakes; *and specific
    animal*

Fayetteville, Arkansas, 47
Feminine Mystique (Friedan), 101
feminism, 81, 99–101, 102, 210
fence building, 54, 71, 151, 172–173
fiddle, 105, 106, 111, 257–58n43
financial support, 236, 238, 239; for
    cabin and land building, 54, 77–78,
    159, 216–17; for education, 230; for
    general needs, 54, 154; for travel, 75,
    160, 147, 231. *See also* welfare; *and
    individual family member names:
    and financial support of*
Fine Woodworking, 188
firearms, 145
fireflies, 10
Fisher, Dorothy Canfield, 160
fish farming, 173. *See also* pond
fishing, 6, 173. *See also* pond
Fish is Fish (Lionni), 184
Five Acres and Independence (Kains),
    35, 90
Five Little Peppers, The (Sidney), 226
Flatt, Lester, 108
flea markets, 39, 215
fleas, 62
flies, 70, 74, 137
folk music, 15, 34, 105–7, 108, 109, 110,
    112–13, 123
food memories, 135–36, 138–46
food stamps, 8, 77, 91, 92–93, 148, 238.
    See also welfare; Women, Infants,
    and Children (WIC) program
foraged foods, 136, 141–42, 143
foreign language education, 202,
    256n5. *See also* McPhee, Caroline:
    and foreign languages
Formal Theories of Mass Behavior
    (McPhee), 221, 243–44n7
Fossil Rock Bluff, 83, 166
Fountain Valley School, 30–31
Four Strong Winds (Ian & Sylvia), 112
Fox, Arkansas: and *American
    Mountain People*, 105; and Aunt

Rhett, 127; as back-to-the-land
    utopia, 36; first visit to, 35–37; and
    gossip, 92, 106, 189; in international
    context, 53, 229; and locals' houses,
    107–8, 107, 123, 222; and Mozart,
    Arkansas, 47–48, 225–26; and
    murder/shooting of friends, 130; and
    musical get-togethers, 105–7, 108;
    and Pentecostal church, 119; and
    radio stations, 189; and SN's per-
    spective on childhood in, 8–9, 11–12,
    50–51, 93–94, 113, 216, 234–41; and
    Ticer's Market, 92, 136; and Tony
    Joe White, 108–9. *See also* Rural
    Special public school; Stone County,
    Arkansas
Foxfire books, 40, 90, 138
Fox Mountain, 49, 50, 88, 109, 149,
    221, 228
fried green tomatoes, 137
Friedan, Betty, 101
frogs, 6, 40
from off. *See* outsiders
Fruitlands, 33, 238
Fujikawa, Gyo, 112
fundamentalist religions, 118–19
furniture, childhood, 178, 188
furniture factory, 158–59
Future Farmers of America, 206

G
garbage dumps, 213
"Garden of Paradise, The" (Andersen),
    190
gardens, *80*; and failures, 88, 137; and
    first garden, 68–69; and first garden
    after Connors left, 79–81; and moon
    cycles, 79; and vegetables and fruits
    in, 60, 137, 142, 151, 153, 158; and
    WM's dread of, 80, 175
gas stoves, 133, 215
Geraldo, Lewis. *See under* Neidhardt,
    Sarah: son

GI Bill, 54, 71, 91

Gibbon, Euell, 90, 141–42

goats, *4*, 8, 72, 81, 102–3, *103*, 145–46, 169–71, *171*, 180

goldenrod, 3, 6

Good, Jim Bob, 217

Gourmet Cookbook (*Gourmet* magazine staff), 135

government assistance. *See* food stamps; welfare; Women, Infants, and Children (WIC) program

grandparents (of SN). *See* Howbert, Irving (step); Howbert, Miriam Emery McPhee; McPhee, William N.; Neidhardt, Adelaide Taylor; Neidhardt, Richard F., Sr.

Granfa' Grig Had a Pig and Other Rhymes Without Reason (Tripp), 184, 217

Granminnow (grandmother of SN). *See* Howbert, Miriam Emery McPhee

Granpa Will (grandfather of SN). *See* McPhee, William N.

grasshoppers, 142–43

Great Big Ugly Man Came up and Tied His Horse to Me, A (Tripp), 184

great-grandmother (of SN, Nana). *See* Emery, Eleanor Washburn

Great Inflation, 34

Great Timbo Valley, 49

"Greening of America, The" (Reich), 38

"Greenwood Side" (Ian & Sylvia), 112–13

grits, 133, 139

grocery shopping, 135–36

Guardian, The, 189

guinea fowl, 172

guitars, 14, 17, 30, 51, 103–4, 105, *106*, 108–9, 111

Gullah culture, 118, 188

guns, 145

Guthrie, A. B., Jr., 25

Guthrie, Arlo, 15

H

Haggard, Merle, 107

Handmade Houses: A Guide to the Woodbutcher's Art (Boericke/ Shapiro), 88

Harington, Donald, 47, 115

Harper, Eleanor Emery (Cooie), 9, 62, 66, 68, 187

Hart, Shirley, 108

Harvey, Paul, 189

Harvey's Hideout (Hoban), 184

Hastings-on-Hudson, New York, 20

Head Start program, 139, 154–55, 201, 203–4, *205*, 207

HearthStone Bakery, 196

heat stoves, 59, 74, 107, 158

heat waves. *See* hot weather

Heidi (Spyri), 5

heritage hustler, 187

Highlights, 188

hillbillies, 11, 36, 47, 222, *223*

Hill Folks (Blevins), 201–2

hippies, 18, 26, 27, 33, 62, 77, 106, 129, 130–31, 138, 230–31

Hoban, Russell. See *Harvey's Hideout*

hog-nosed snakes, 169

hogs. *See* pigs

Holm, Hanya, 18

homesteading: and advice on in Ozarks, 187, 201, 238, 255n1; and conditions of in Stone County, 84, 129; and economics of, 72, 107–108, 147–48, 178, 198, 216–17, 221, 234; and history of in Arkansas, 47, 108; and homestead widows, 49; and homesteading seminars, 187; and illness and injury as impediment to work, 148, 151, 177; and isolation, 48–49, 73, 155; and marriage,

197–98; and modern movement, 34; and Ozark Folk Center State Park, 110; and pioneer remnants of, 4–5; and women's plight, 62, 102. *See also* back-to-the-land movement; barn construction; bathroom facilities; cabin construction; childhood amusements; dead animals; dirt roads; farm animals; farm/land build-out; fence building; Fox, Arkansas: and SN's perspective on childhood in; gardens; household labor; Howbert, Miriam: on Fox living conditions; letters from WM to Chuck; letters from WM to Granminnow; McPhee, Caroline; Meadowcreek Project; music and parties; Neidhardt, Richard, Jr.; pets; pond; running water; self-sufficiency; wells

hot weather, 6, 60–61, 67, 69, 70, 86–87, 88–89, 90, 154, 177, 227–28, 230, 259n56

hound dogs, 109, 149, 163

household labor: and children, 62, 81, 153, 159, 161, 187; and chopping wood, 94, 99, 179, 193, 100; and cooking, 67, 87, 119, 133–46, 175; and decorating, 59, 67; and demands of, 69, 89, 99, 159, 175, 179, 197–98, 223; and division of, 99–101, 119–20, 151; and feeding animals, 72, 81, 100, 169–70; and feminist concerns, 99–101, 102, 119–20; and firewood, 158–59; and freezing food, 137, 141, 159; and hauling water, 6, 89, 94, 100, 102, 198; and lack of hot water, 68, 74, 133, 149, 153; and laundry, 57, 67, 68, 76, 77, 100, 115, 187, 212, 221; and local women, 59, 100, 102, 119; and tools of, 59, 68, 133, *134*, 135; and washing dishes, 83, 84,

187; and WM as back-to-the-lander, 238–39; and wood stoves, 74–75, 76, 77. *See also* butchery; gardens; letters from WM to Chuck; letters from WM to Granminnow; milking cows; woodstoves

Howbert, Irving, 161, 209, 222. *See also* Howbert, Miriam Emery McPhee

Howbert, Miriam Emery McPhee (Granminnow, Minnow): and activity boxes from, 184, 211, 219; and Arkansas visits, 65, 84, 185, 196; and career, 20, 101, 203; and carrot bread, 135, 211; and Chinook Bookshop, 90; and Christmas celebrations with Neidhardts, 147, 231, 232; and Christmas gifts from, 76, 156–57, 175, 176, 180, 196–97; and death of, 19; and dollhouse, 226–27; and Easter gifts from, 176; and Europe trip, 65; and film footage of as child, 39; and financial support from, 37, 153, 159, 183, 191, 209, 215–17, 222, 230, 231, 236; and Florida trip, 196–97; on Fox living conditions, 65–68, 84, 197; and gift of car, 200; and Head Start programs, 203; and health concerns for SN and the family, 84, 91, 98; and importance of to SN, 223, 226; and letter from RN, 155–56; and letters from Katy, 207, 225, 232; and letters from SN, 142, 207, 224, 225, 231, 232; and letters to sister (Cooie), 37, 197; and letter to Nana, 65–68, 84; and letter to WM, 209; and magazine subscriptions from, 188; on marriage of WM and RN, 37–38, 175; and marriage to Irving Howbert, 161; and parenting style of, 20, 160, 209, 226; and personality of, 160, 226; and physical

Howbert, Miriam Emery McPhee (Granminnow, Minnow) (*cont.*)
appearance of, *39*, 65, *66*, 161, 185, *186*; and religious beliefs and practices, 20, 121–22; and rheumatic fever, 98; and RN, 38; and Ruth Washburn Cooperative Nursery School, 20, 203; and Valentine's Day gifts from, 211, 212; and visit from SN and Katy, 226. *See also* cassette recordings: for Granminnow; letters from WM to Granminnow
How to Have a Green Thumb Without an Aching Back (Stout), 81, 90
How to Make it on the Land (Cohan), 90

I
Ian & Sylvia, 112
ice storms, 219, 221. *See also* winter weather
"I-Feel-Like-I'm-Fixin'-to-Die Rag" (Country Joe and the Fish), 112
Illini/Miami-Illinois, 245n3 (chap. 3)
illness, 148–50
I Married Adventure (Johnson), 35
inflation, 34, 102
insect infestations, 69, 70
International Scout, 102, 198
Iran hostage crisis, 233
Irving (step-grandfather of SN). *See* Howbert, Irving
In the Night Kitchen (Sendak), 184
Inside Llewyn Davis (film), 82n

J
Jackson, Helen, 156
Jackson, Shirley, 165, 253n5
Jacob, Jeffrey, 34
Janey (aunt of WM). *See* Emery, Jane Aycrigg
Janus Pit, 185

Jean (aunt of WM). *See* Emery, Jean Jackson
"Jelly, Jelly" (White), 104
Jew's harp, 105
Jimmy (classmate of SN), 206. *See also* Brewer, Jimmy
Jimmy Driftwood Barn, 110
Jock (uncle of SN, brother of WM). *See* McPhee, John Washburn
John (uncle of WM). *See* Emery, John Wendell
John Deere tractors, 9, *229*
Johnson, Osa, 35
Joy of Cooking (Rombauer), 135
june bugs, 10
Junior (dog), 163–64, 166

K
Kains, Maurice G. *See Five Acres and Independence*
Katy (mule), 170
Katy (sister of SN). *See* Neidhardt, Katherine
Kennedy, Robert, 24
Kent, Jack. *See Dooly and the Snortsnoot*
Key Place: and bathroom facilities, 58, 59, 67, 182; and Christmas celebration, 76; and commuting to land from, 72, 79, 81, 82; and descriptions of house and conditions, *58–59*, 65, *66*, 67, 76, 88; and farm animals, 70; and fire in house, 74; and kitchen, 57, 59; and local murder, 130; and owners of, 58, 59–60; and radio station reception, 189; and vehicles, 157, 199
kindergarten. *See* Head Start program
King, Martin Luther, Jr., 24
Kingston, Maxine Hong. *See Warrior Woman, The*
Kingston Trio, 15, 111, 112

KitchenAid mixer, 133
kitchen memories, 6, 57, 59, 94–96, 133–48, 162, 176, 191, 215–16
Kitty Hanya (cat), 18, 163, 165
Klemmedson, Judy, 36, 123–24
Klemmedson, Kevin, *53*
Kraus, Chris, 93
Ku Klux Klan, 14

L

La cuisine et un jeu d'enfants (Oliver), 135
L'Air du Temps perfume, 226
LaJeune, Ruby, 124–25
LaJeune family, 124, 172
lamb's-quarter, 143
Land of Opportunity (Arkansas state nickname), 36
Larry (friend of RN), 35–36
laundromats, 76, 77, 115, 187. *See also* household labor
Laura (once-enslaved person), 41–42
laying chickens. *See* chickens
Leaves of Grass (Whitman), 40
Lee, Garther and Flossie, 107
Lee, Lonnie, 105–7, 108, 110, 119
Lee, Neda Merle, 107
Leslie, Arkansas, 178
Let's Eat Right to Keep Fit (Davis), 90, 97–98
letters from WM to Chuck (and Janey): on books, 88, 90, 188, 209–10; on equality of the sexes, 99–101, 210; on food/environment, 98; on homesteading, 76, 88–89, 99–101, 101–2; on locals, 100, 102, 115, 116–17; and requests for visit, 75–76; on Stone County politics, 250n2; on swimming holes, 88–89; on writing, 210
letters from WM to Granminnow: on back-to-the-landers, 130–31; on bathroom facilities, 182, 213;

on birth control, 177; from Boston before marriage, 24–25, 187, 235; on Children's Workshop, 159; on Christmas celebrations, 76, 175, 196; on church services, 118–19, 121, 175; on cigarette smoking, 140; on college and return to in Arkansas, 228; on Colorado trips, 75, 90–91, 102, 147, 226; on cousins, 126, 211; on deaths of animals, 164; on departure from Arkansas, 232; on dieting, 140; on Easter, 176; on electricity, 89; on feelings, 209; on financial concerns/needs, 54, 75, 77–78, 147–48, 154, 176, 183, 198, 215, 216–17, 225; on flower girl dresses, 180; on food supply, 67, 81, 138; from France before marriage, 26, 27, 29–30; on furniture from family, 30, 178; on garden, 69, 79, 80, 81, 175; on government assistance, 77, 225; on hauling water, 89; on Head Start program, 154, 203; on health concerns, 52, 91, 97, 209, 227–28; with health food suggestions, 97–98, 99, 156; on homesteading, 71, 90–91; on isolation, 48–49, 73; on Katy's concussion, 87; on living conditions, 57, 215; on locals that were friends, 59, 61, 71, 73, 106; on married name, 81; on mosquitoes, 70; on musical get-togethers, 105–6, 177; on parenting, 48–49, 52–53, 61, 69, 73, 76, 78, 87, 90, 155, 160, 184, 211, 212, 217; on "pleasure trip," 153–54; on pregnancy, 177, 179; on preparing for new baby, 52–53; on public school (Rural Special), 202, 203, 205; on rattlesnakes, 168; and reading material, importance of, 189; and recipes, 140–41, 143; on relaxing/leisure time, 177, 187, 197;

letters from WM to Granminnow (*cont.*)
on renovations to cabin, 191, 213,
216–17; on Rhett and the boys, 126,
211; on RN's carpentry work, 55,
77; on RN's construction business,
150, 153, 184, 218; on RN's family,
41–42, 74, 77, 152, 219; on RN's
health, 86, 231; on RN's injuries, 151,
228; on RN's irritability, 49, 150;
on RN's job at Meadowcreek, 222,
232; on roads, 51–52; on running
water, 153; on Rural Special school,
154, 155; on selling cabin, 232; on
stationery, 81; on swimming holes,
227–28; on teaching, 159, 202, 228,
235; on Thanksgiving Day, 145; on
Valentine's Day, 211; on vehicles, 102,
199; on visits from family, 65, 75,
158; with vitamin requests, 97; on
weather, 70, 87, 214, 219, 227–28; on
wedding for Lewis and Mindy, 182;
on wood products business idea,
230–1, 232; on workload, 175, 187.
See also hot weather
letter-writing, 19, 81, 223–24
Lewis (son of SN). *See also* Geraldo,
Lewis; Neidhardt, Sarah Taylor: son
Lewis (uncle of SN, brother of RN).
See Neidhardt, Lewis
Lewis, C. S., 188
Lick Fork Creek, 4, 83
Lionni, Leo. See *Fish is Fish*
Lipchitz, Jacques, 19
Lisa (classmate of SN), 206. *See also*
Bass, Lisa
Little Richard (cousin of SN). *See*
Roberts, Richard
Little Rock, Arkansas, 152, 153–54,
155, 156, 161, 196, 230, 235
livestock auctions. *See* sale barns
Living the Good Life (Nearing), 35,
90

Liza (mule), 79–80, 170, *171*
Liza (aunt of SN). *See* Vander Veen,
Lizabeth
lizards, 163
local elections, 210–11
locals. *See* Fox, Arkansas; letters from
WM to Chuck: on locals; letters
from WM to Granminnow: on locals
that were friends; McPhee, Caroline:
and locals; Neidhardt, Richard F.,
Jr.: and locals; Stone, County,
Arkansas; *and individual names*
Lomax, Alan, 107
Louisiana Purchase, 46
Lovin' Spoonful, The, 111
Lurleen (maid of RN neighbor), 117

M
MacDonald, Betty. See *Mrs. Piggle-
Wiggle*
Madame Alexander Sweet Tears dolls,
175
Madeline (Bemelmans), 184
mad squirrel disease, 145
maggots, 70, 137
male-female relationships, 99–101,
119–120
Mama Cow (cow), 99, *167*, 172, 175
Mammy (grandmother of SN). *See*
Neidhardt, Adelaide Taylor
mandolin, 105, 241
marijuana, 4, 77, 101, 116, 220
Marshall, Arkansas, 178
May, Dean, 178, 226
McCloskey, Robert. See *Blueberries
for Sal*
McPhee, Caroline Wendell (WM,
Wendy, Momma): as actress, 20, 21,
22, 27, 121; and ancestry of, 20, 38,
222; in Arkansas, first time, 36–37;
and Arkansas, move to, 42–43, 45;
and back-to-the-land experience

in retrospect, 234–35, 237; and back-to-the-land movement, 38–39; and back-to-the-landers/hippies in Stone Co., 128–29; and birth and childhood, 20, 136; and birth of daughters, 31, 61–62, 119, 185; in Boston, 24–25, 38; in California as young adult, 19–20; and California, move to, 235–36; and Chinook Bookshop, 24, 25–26, 27; and civil rights movement, 101, 117; at Colorado College, 21–22, 24; and Colorado visits, 75, 102, 147, 160, 161, 169, 198, 222–23, 232; and departure from cabin, 232, 233–35; and dieting, 140; and divorce, 236; and father, 21, 23, 147, 160; and feminism, 99–101, 102, 119–120; and foreign languages, 19, 27, 88, 159, 178, 188, 202, 228, 230, 235, 239; in France, 17, 26–29; and French boyfriend, 27, 29, 30; and guns, 145, 168; and handwriting of, 19; and health concerns, 97–99, 149–50, 168–69; and health food interest, 97–99, 135, 204; on homesteading, 50, 69–70, 71–72, 86, 89–90, 97; and Key Place, move to, 57–59; and killing cat, 165; and letter from Granminnow to Nana about, 37–38; and letter from Nana, 70; and letter from Sarah (sister), 84, 86; and letters from father, 23, 220; and letters from RN, 26, 28, 29; and letters to Cooie, 187, 235; and letters to Nana, 70, 71, 97, 138, 157, 169, 238; and letters to Ruth, 50, 54, 61, 133, 147, 164; and letters while in France, 26, 27, 28, 29–30; and letter-writing, 19; on local school, 154–55, 202–4; and locals, 52, 59, 71, 81, 115, 116–17, 118–20, 123; and marijuana, 77,

116; and marital conflict, 20, 36–37, 37–38, 71–72, 74–75, 150, 170, 175, 197–98, 199, 233–34, 235–36, 237; and marriage of, 30–*31*; and milking cows, 151; and outdoors, feelings about, 38–39, 70; and papers and photos owned, 17, 18, 19; and parenting style of, 61, 155, 160–61, 178, 193; and personality of, 21, 30, 37–38, 58, 91, 149–50, 160, 165, 193, 197–98, 209, 237; and physical appearance of, 20, *21*, *22*, 27, *31*, 48, 72, *73*, *80*, *85*, *96*, *127*, *134*, *167*, *171*, 185, *229*, 234; and "pleasure trip," 153–54; and politics of, 33; and post-Arkansas life, 239–40; and pregnancy, 22–24, 31, 38, 48, 52–53, 61, 177, 179, 182; and purchase of land, 36–37, 67, 69; and reading choices of, 35, 90, 187–90; and recipes, 139, 140–41; and religious beliefs and practices, 119, 120, 121–22; and return to school, 228, 230, 231, 235; and RN before marriage, 26, 27–31; on RN's family, 219; and South Carolina visits, 42, 183–84, 192; and stillbirth, 23; and teaching, 159, 235, 239; and teaching experiment, 159; and University of California–Berkeley, 27, 30, 37, 50–51; and vitamins, 97, 99; as "Yankee," 115, 234; and young adult years, 21–24. *See also* cabin, move in to; cassette recordings: of WM; Christmas celebrations; debt; Easter celebrations; gardens; household labor; letters from WM to Chuck; letters from WM to Granminnow; milking cows; music and parties; self-sufficiency: problems with; Thanksgiving Day celebrations; woodstoves

McPhee, John Washburn (Jock), 224;
and Arkansas visits, 84–85, 134, 156,
173; and father, 147; and importance
of to SN, 190, 223; and letters from
abroad, 190; and letter to WM, 131;
and physical appearance of, 21, 84,
85, 134; and request for visit to, 75;
and wedding of, 222–23; and wood
products business, 230

McPhee, Sarah Eddy (Aunt Sarah):
and Arkansas visits, 161–62, 173,
219; on back-to-the-land experiment, 53, 86, 162; in Europe, 73; and
importance of to SN, 161, 190, 223,
236; and letter from Brazil, 190;
and letter from Mozambique, 190,
228–30; and letters from France, 53,
84, 86; in Sweden, 190; and travel
postcards, 190; and wedding of, 231,
232, 233

McPhee, William N. (Granpa Will),
209; and alcoholism, 21, 220, 221;
in Allenspark, Colorado, 38–39, 147,
219–20; and career of, 20, 21, 101,
147, 220, 221, 243–44n7; and counterculture movement, 220–21; and
letters to WM, 23, 220; and manic
depression, 147, 230; and parenting
style of, 20, 23, 160; and personality
of, 147, 160; and physical appearance
of, 147; and religious beliefs and
practices, 121–22; and visit to, 147;
and wood products business idea,
230–31, 232; and World War II, 23,
220

Meadowcreek, Arkansas, 201, 221–22

Meadowcreek Learning and Retreat
Center, 257–58n43

Meadowcreek Project, 221–22, 225,
228–9, 231, 232, 233, 257–58n43

Mike (mule), 170

Milagro Beanfield War, The (Nichols),
188

milking cows, 140, 151, 167, 167, 171–72,
179

Miller, Henry, 33, 35, 57, 188, 236

Milne, A. A., 140

Mindy (aunt of SN). See Morrell,
Mindy

Minnow. See Granminnow

Miriam (sister of SN). See Neidhardt,
Miriam Adelaide

Miriam Bypass, 185

Mississippi, 222

Miss Mill (great-grandmother of RN).
See Taylor, Mildred Kennon

Mize, Seth, 106–7

mobile homes. See trailers

Modern Farmer, 34

moles, 163

Momma. See McPhee, Caroline
Wendell

Moody, Dalton, 52, 89, 124, 128, 163,
172

moonshine, 68

morel mushrooms, 142

Morrell, Mindy, 103, 127, 156, 180,
182

Morris, Earl and Bobbie, 58, 59–60,
70, 91, 93, 99, 153, 157, 170

Morrison, Luther, 109

Morrison's Gas Station, 109

mosquitoes, 67, 70, 219

Mother Earth News, 201, 238

Mother Goose, 184

Mountain View, Arkansas, 47–48;
and bakery (HearthStone), 196,
255n42; and barbershop, 192; and
blank checks, 200; and butcher,
138; and construction business,
218; as county seat, 45, 115; and
Dew Drop Inn, 163–64, 172, 187;
and folk music, 105, 109; and grocery shopping, 77, 136, 225; and
hospital/medical care, 87, 185; and
location of, 45, 47; in New York

Times, 255n42; and public libraries, 188; and real estate agents, 36; and rental house, 48, 52, 55, 61, 163; and Sears distribution center, 182; and shirt factory, 92, 100; and shopping, 48, 77, 157; and social welfare services, 225; and tourism, 105, 185, 187, 254n26, 255n42; and traveling circus, 231–32. *See also* Stone County, Arkansas

mouthbow, 105

Mozambique, 190, 228–30

Mozart, Arkansas, 47–48, 120–21, 201, 226

Mozart, Wolfgang Amadeus, 225

"Mr. Noah" (Van Ronk), 82

Mrs. Piggle-Wiggle (MacDonald), 184

Mt. Massive (Colorado), 27, *28*

Mt. Vernon, Arkansas, 232, 233, 234–35

muddy roads. *See* dirt roads

mules, 54, 79–80, 102, 165, 170, *171*

mushrooms, 6, 9, 141, 142, 149

music and parties, 102–13, *103, 106,* 173, 177, 224–25

N

Nana (grandmother of WM). *See* Emery, Eleanor Washburn

National Geographic, 188, 190, 221

National Geographic Society, 105

National Public Radio (NPR), 184, 189, 233

Native Americans, 46, 245n3 (chap. 3). *See also* Cherokee; Illini/Miami-Illinois; Osage Indians; Quapaw Indians

Nearing, Helen and Scott. See *Living the Good Life*

Neidhardt, Adelaide Taylor (Mammy): and accent of, 73, 152; and alcoholism, 219; and Arkansas visits, 41, 73–74, 94, 125, 151–53, 155, 172, 187;

and Bible story collection, 122; and cassette recordings of, 103, 165–67, 193–96; and Christmas celebration, 219; and financial support from, 69, 218; and love of music, 14, 152; and parenting style of, 13, 152; and personality of, 74; and physical description of, 73–74; and politics of, 13, 152; at South Carolina Eye Bank, 151

Neidhardt, Katherine Storrs (Katy): and baptism of, 185, *186*; and behavior, 217; and birth of, 61–62, 119; and birthday, 176; and butchery, 102–3, 137, 146; and caves/caving, 178–79; and college, 236; and concussion, 87; and cousins (Roberts), 126–27, 193; and departure from cabin, 233–35; and drawings of, 151, 189, 203; as flower girl, 161, *181,* 182, 185, 222–23; and "hillbilly" concept, 222; and letters to Granminnow, 207, 224–225; and letter-writing, 223–25; and personality of, 67, 160, 207, 212; and physical appearance of, *4,* 67, 69, *85, 96, 127, 134, 174, 192,* 207, *213*; and playhouses, 5–6, 184; and pocketknives, 182; and post-Arkansas life, 239; and postcard from Granminnow, 226; and rattlesnakes, 168, 169; and reading choices of, 135, 184, 188–90; and sibling conflicts, 212; and tricycle riding, 176; and Vacation Bible School, 119, 122; and Tony Joe White, 109. *See also* cassette recordings: of Katy; childhood amusements; Christmas celebrations; Colorado: and visits to; Easter celebrations; letters from WM to Chuck; letters from WM to Granminnow; McPhee, Caroline; music and parties; Neidhardt, Richard F., Jr.; Neidhardt, Sarah; Rural Special public school

Neidhardt, Lewis, 193; and music, *106*;
and physical appearance of, 76, *103*,
127; and pocketknives, 182; and visits from, 76–77, *103*, *136*; and visits
to in Little Rock, 154, 156; and wedding to Mindy, 180, 182; and WM's
feelings about, 77

Neidhardt, Miriam Adelaide, 187,
199, 217, 227, 234; and baptism of,
185, *186*; and birth of, 185; and cave
name, 185; and college, 236; and
divorce of parents, 236; and physical appearance of, *127*, *186*, *212*,
224; and post-Arkansas life, 239;
and Susie Warshauer, 196, 230.
See also Christmas celebrations;
Colorado: and visits to; letters
from WM to Chuck; letters from
WM to Granminnow; McPhee,
Caroline; Neidhardt, Richard F., Jr.;
Neidhardt, Sarah

Neidhardt, Richard F., Jr. (RN,
Daddy): and accent, 15, 42, 115–116;
and accidents and injuries, 151, 159,
228; and allergies as child, 150; and
ancestry, 20, 41–42; in Arkansas,
first time, 36–37; and Arkansas,
move to, 42–43, 45; and back-to-
the-land movement, 35–36; and
back-to-the-landers/hippies in
Stone Co., 128–29; and birth and
childhood, 13–16, 17, 40–42, 136;
in Brooklyn, New York, for work,
225–26; and California, move to,
235–36; and carpentry work, 5, 39,
40, 55, 60, 75, 99, 150, 178, 183, 192,
219; and caves/caving, 178–79; as
cheerleader, 13, *14*; and childhood
desk, 188; at Chinook Bookshop,
25–26; and civil rights movement,
14, 117; and climbing, 17, 27, *28*, 30;
and college, 14, 15; and Colorado,

move to, 17; and construction business, 91, 92, 100, 119, 148, 150, 153,
178, 183–84, 192, 218–19, 221; and
construction management job,
235; and construction schooling,
235; and craft guild, 17, 28; and
departure from cabin, 233–35;
and divorce from WM, 236; and
drop out generation, 235; and drug
use, 3, 15, 16, 18, 30, 35, 101; and
the Factory (New York City), 15; as
folk singer, 15, 17, 30, 106, 108; and
food interest, 18, 146; in Germany,
16–17; and GI Bill, 54, 71, 91; and
handwriting of, 17; and health of, 86,
177, 198, 231; and Key Place, move
to, 57–59; and letters to WM, 26,
28, 29; and letter to Granminnow,
155–56; and locals, 70, 115–16, 117,
118–19, 123, 124, 128, 130–31, 144–
45; and love of nature, 12–13, 40–41,
239; and marriage (first), 16; and
marriage (third), 239; and marriage
to WM, 30–*31*; and Meadowcreek
frustrations, 231, 234; and music,
14–15, 17, 18, 103–4, 105, *106*, 106–7,
108, 110, 111–13; in New York City
before marriage, 15, 116; and odd
jobs in Arkansas, 91, 92; and Ozark
Folk Center State Park cabin, 110;
and parental conflicts, 13, 17, 35, 74,
219; and parenting style of, 48, 157,
160–61, 178–79, 193; and personality
of, 12–14, 16, 17, 18, 28–29, 30, 36,
49–50, 68, 72, 77, 116, 142–43, 150,
160–61, 178, 191, 192, 193, 197–99,
239; and physical appearance of, 12,
13–14, *14*, *16*, 17–18, 27, *28*, *31*, *42*,
72, *73*, *96*, *103*, *106*, *127*, *211*, 130,
164, *171*, *174*, 185, 192, *229*, 234;
and "pleasure trip," 153–54; and
politics of, 33; and post-Arkansas

life, 12–13, 239; and preparations for move to Arkansas, 39–40, 42–43; and purchase of land, 36–37, 67, 69; and race, 14, 42, 117–18; and reading choices of, 35, 90, 187–90; and religious beliefs and practices, 20, 120, 121–22; and salary at Meadowcreek, 222; and snakes, killing, 168, 169; and snakes, love of, 12, 41, 169; and South Carolina visits, 17, 42, 117, 219; and surgery, 155; and tourism business job, 185, 187; and Vietnam War enlistment, 15–17, *16*, 35; and WM before marriage, 26, 27–31; and wood products business, 215, 216, 222, 225, 228, 230–31, 232; and young adult years, 15, 17–18, 35, 194–95. *See also* agricultural school; barn construction; butchery; cabin construction; cabin, move in to; cassette recordings: of RN; chicken houses; Christmas celebrations; Colorado: and visits to; debt; farm/land build-out; Easter celebrations; fence building; garden; letters from WM to Granminnow; McPhee, Caroline: and marital conflict; Meadowcreek Project; milking cows; music and parties; pond; sale barns; self-sufficiency: problems with; Thanksgiving Day celebrations; wells

Neidhardt, Richard F., Sr. (Pappy): and Arkansas visits, 94, *95*, 125, 151–53, 187; and career, 94; and cassette recordings of, 103–4, 152, 165–67, 191–96; and childhood in Ohio, 137; and Christmas celebration, 219; and financial support from, 69, 218; and hypnotizing chickens, 137; and love of music, 14, 152; and parenting style of, 13, 17, 152, 219; and personality of, 94; and physical appearance of, 94, *95*; and politics of, 13, 152; and Strom Thurmond, 152; and voice of, 152; and wart cure, 216

Neidhardt, Sarah Taylor (SN): and animals, 163; in Arkansas, first time, 36–37; and baptism of, 185, *186*; and behavior, 217; and birth of, 31; and birthdays, 48, 233; and butchery, 102–3; and cabin bedroom, 216; and California, move to, 235–36; and caves/caving, 178–79; and college, 236; and Colorado, love of, 226–27, 232; and cousins (Roberts), 126–27, 193; and departure from cabin, 233–35; and divorce of parents, 236; and drawings of, 151, 189, 203; and Jimmy Driftwood, 109; and education and school, 116, 119, 154–55, 179, 201–7, 214, 230; and family papers, 17, 18–19; and fears as a child, 116, 189, 214–15, 216, 233; as flower girl, 161, *181*, 182, 185, 222–23, 232; and friendships, 205–7; and health of, 8, 42, 52, 61, 91, 97, 149, 227; and IOU from father, 48; and letters to Granminnow, 142, 207, 224–25, 231, 232; and letter to Santa, 135; and letter-writing, 223–25; and locals, 116, 205–7; and move to Key Place, 57–59; on murder in Fox, 130; and music, 105, 111–13, 122–23, 237; on parents' marriage, 150, 197–98, 199; and personal essay of, 190–91; and personality of, 67, 150, 160, 205, 207, 212; and physical appearance of, *4*, *7*, *42*, *66*, *67*, *85*, *86*, *96*, *103*, *127*, *157*, *174*, *181*, *186*, *205*, 206, 207, *213*, *229*; and playhouses, 5–6, 184; and pneumonia, 149; and pocketknives, 182; and post-Arkansas life, 239–41; and postcard collection, 190; and

Neidhardt, Sarah Taylor (SN) *(cont.)*
postcard from Granminnow, 226;
and race, 117; and reading choices
of, 5, 135, 184, 188–90, 226; and religious beliefs and practices, 119, 121,
122–23, 201; and sibling conflicts,
155, 212; and son, 18, 51, 160, 237,
240; and South Carolina visits, 42,
117, 219; and talking in early years,
67, 69, 73; and swearing, 116; as a
toddler, 50; and tricycle riding, 176;
and Vacation Bible School, 119, 122;
and wanderlust of, 190–91, 196;
and wedding dress, 122. *See also*
back-to-the-land movement: SN's
perspective on; cassette recordings:
of SN; childhood amusements;
Christmas celebrations; class: SN's
perspective on in her life; Colorado:
and visits to; Easter celebrations;
Fox: SN's perspective on childhood
in; letters from WM to Chuck;
letters from WM to Granminnow;
McPhee, Caroline; music and par-
ties; Neidhardt, Richard F., Jr.;
Thanksgiving Day celebrations
neighbors, 123–31
Neihardt, John G., 188
Nelson, Willie, 189
newcomers. *See* outsiders
New Pioneers (Jacob), 34
New York City, 15
New Yorker, 11, 38, 175, 188, 189–90
New York Times, 34
Nichols, John, 188
Nin, Anaïs, 188, 210
Nixon, Mrs. (second grade teacher),
204–5
Nixon, Richard, 152
North Carolina, 41, 127
Norton, Mary. See *Borrowers, The*
Nu-Way Foods, 135–36

O
O'Brien, Ellen, 70
"Oh My Darling, Clementine," 112
Oh, What a Busy Day! (Fujikawa), 112
oil embargo, 34, 43, 133
okra, 142
Old Belle (dog), 109, 149, 163, *164*, 165
Old Farmer's Almanac, 79
Oliver, Michel, 135
Onia, Arkansas, 109
organic food, 34, 90, 98, 221, 237
Organic Gardening, 79, 90, 188
Orr, Daniel (Danny), 206, 221
Orr, David and Will, 221–22,
257–58n43
Osage Indians, 46
Other (grandmother of RN). *See*
Taylor, Adelaide Trehou
outhouses, 8, 34, 59, 107, 168, 182–83,
183
outsiders (newcomers): in early history
of Ozarks, 46; and murder of, 129;
and Ozark heritage tourism, 110,
185, 187; and perspective of locals,
60, 107, 115, 116, 118, 120, 130, 234;
in Stone County, 102, 123, 124,
125, 128–30, 196. *See also* McPhee,
Caroline; Meadowcreek Project;
Neidhardt, Richard F., Jr.
Oxford Public Ledger, 41
Oxford Smoking Tobacco Company, 41
Ozark Folk Center State Park, 110
Ozarks (Arkansas): and *American
Mountain People*, 105; as bohemian
mecca, 36, 47; and climate of, 36,
227; and folk traditions of, 107;
and geography of, 45–46, 47; and
glories of, 35; and history of, 46–47;
and music in, 35; and mythology
of, 47; and name of, 46, 245n3
(chap. 3); as retirement location,
120, 153; and Springfield Plain,

47; and stereotypes of, 36, 46–47, 115; and tourism in, 46–47. *See also* Boston Mountains; Fox, Arkansas; homesteading: and advice on in Ozarks; letters from WM to Chuck: on locals; letters from WM to Granminnow: on locals that were friends; McPhee, Caroline: and locals; Neidhardt, Richard F., Jr.: and locals; outsiders; Stone County, Arkansas

Ozark Outdoor Center, 187, 254n26

P

panfried pork chops, 139
Pappy (grandfather of SN). *See* Neidhardt, Richard F., Sr.
Parma, Arkansas, 201
Peachy, Mr. (sawmiller), 75
penicillin, 149
Pentecostal church, 118–19
persimmons, 143–44, 149
pets, 162–66. *See also* Abbie; Chigger; Junior; Kitty Hanya; Old Belle; Tiny
petting zoo, 176
Phillips, Wendell, 20
Pickle brothers, 128–29
pickup trucks. *See* trucks
pigs, 18, 138–39, 158, 167, 172–73, 193, 238
Pikes Peak (Colorado), 30, 37, 226
pinto beans, 139
pioneer homestead, 4–5
plantation agriculture, 41–42
planting systems, 79
playhouses, 5–6, 184
pleasure trip, 153–54
Plott hounds, 163
pneumonia, 149
pocketknives, 182
Pointer Sisters, 189
Point Richmond, California, 12

pokeweed (poke salat), 10, 143, 241
Polaroid Square Shooter, 65, *66*
politics, local, 115, 210–11, 250n2
"Polk Salad Annie" (White), 108, 143. *See also* White, Tony Joe
pollution, 34
pond, 5, 6–7, *7*, 149, 173, *174*, 241
pork chops, 139, 161, 240
Port Authority Bus Terminal, 15
Portland, Oregon, 239–40
possum-farmers, 144
possums, 138, 144
poverty. *See* class; food stamps; Head Start program; welfare; Women, Infants, and Children (WIC) program
Prendergast, Maurice, 30
Price, Mrs. Junior, 73
Pryor, David (governor), 110
public assistance. *See* food stamps; welfare; Women, Infants, and Children (WIC) program
public libraries, 188
public schools, 119, 154–55, 201–7. *See also* Rural Special public school
puff adders, 169
Purple Jesus, 195
pysanka, 126

Q

Quapaw Indians, 245n3 (chap. 3)
Queen Anne's lace, 6, 9

R

rabbits, 145, 172, 190
raccoons, 144, 187
racism, 14, 93, 117–18, 203
radio stations, 189
Randolph, Vance, 107, 250n8
Ranger Rick, 188
rat snakes, 169
Rattlesnake Hill, 52, 168

rattlesnakes, 7–8, 60, 144, 146, 164, 168, 169

Reich, Charles, 38

religious beliefs and practices, 161; and atheism, 121–22; and Baptists, 14, 116, 117, 120, 122, 178, 201, 233, 234; and Bible Belt, 123; and Catholics, 93, 120, 121; and Congregationalists, 122; and Episcopalians, 14, 20, 120–22, *186*, 250n8 (chap. 8); and Judaism, 14, 93, 121, 196; and Mennonites, 206; and Pentecostals, 118–19

Reverence for Wood, A (Sloane), 35, 90

Rey, H. A. and Margret. See *Curious George*

Reynolds, Rachel, 258n43

Rhett (aunt of SN, sister of RN). *See* Roberts, Henrietta

Rhonda (classmate of SN), 206

Rhus-ade, 141–42

ribwort plantain, 240

Richard (Daddy, RN). *See* Neidhardt, Richard F., Jr.

Richard Scarry's Cars and Trucks and Things That Go (Scarry), 184

roads. *See* dirt roads

Roasting Ear Creek, 227

Roberts, David (Dave), 126–27, *127*, 146, 187, 195, 196, 207, 211, 214, 225; and cassette recordings of, 144, 167, 168, 193

Roberts, Edward, 126–27, *127*, 187, 211, 214; and cassette recordings of, 144, 166, 167, 193, 195

Roberts, Henrietta (Rhett) Neidhardt, 169, 188, 195, 211; and accent, 126; and Arkansas, move to, 125, 187; and Arkansas, visits before move, 125; as artist, 125–126, 127, 187, 202; and cassette recordings of, 167, 193, 194, 200; and death of, 127; and family

papers of, 19; and government assistance, 93; and house in Fox, 125, 126, 193; and music, 125, 126, 127; and Miriam, 196; and North Carolina, 127; and personality of, 125, 126; and physical appearance of, 125, *127*; and SN's relationship with, 125, 127; and WM's relationship with, 126; 202, 218

Roberts, Richard (Little Richard), 126–27, *127*, 187, 199, 211, 214; and cassette recordings of, 144, 166, 167–68, 193, 194, 195, 198, 200

Rock Hole, 227

Rombauer, Irma S. See *Joy of Cooking*

Roosevelt, Theodore, 47

rose hip tea, 143

rototiller, 80

Ruminer (local man), 120

running water, 89–90, 94, 96, 153

Rural Special public school, 108–109, 119, 154–55, 179, 201–7, *205*, 214

Rushing, Arkansas, 201

Rushing, Rodney, *205*

Ruth Washburn Cooperative Nursery School, The, 203

S

S&H Green Stamps, 136

Sagan, Françoise, 188

sale barns, 17, 70–71, 72, 91, 99, 119, 170

salt blocks, 6

Salt Peter Cave, 179

Saturday Review, 189

sawmills, 75, 91, 92, 119, 222

Scarry, Richard. See *Richard Scarry's Cars and Trucks and Things That Go*

Schroeder, Pat, 99–100

Scotty (bus driver). *See* Branscum, Scotty

scrapple, 138–39
Scruggs, Earl, 108
Sears catalog, 154, 182
seed ticks, 8
Seeger, Pete, 107, 112
segregation, 117–18
self-imposed poverty, 92–94
self-sufficiency, 221–22; and food, 135–36, 138, 156; problems with, 54–55, 72, 218, 238. See also financial support
Sendak, Maurice. See In the Night Kitchen; Where the Wild Things Are
sexism, 60, 77, 99–100
sexual revolution, 22, 30
Shannon, Bookmiller, 106–7
Shapiro, Barry. See Handmade Houses: A Guide to the Woodbutcher's Art
Shepherd of the Hills, The (Wright), 46–47
shirt factories, 91–92, 100
Shit on a Shingle, 140
Sidney, Margaret. See Five Little Peppers, The
Sidney, Sir Philip, 177, 197
skinks, 163
Skinner, B. F., 220
sledgehammer incident, 198, 200
Sloane, Eric. See Reverence for Wood, A
Smith, Dorothy Hall. See Tall Book of Christmas, The
Smithsonian Institution Festival of American Folklife, The, 107
snakes, 5, 12, 41, 60, 138, 168–69. See also venomous snakes; and specific snake
snapping turtles, 138, 144
snow. See winter weather
social welfare services. See welfare
Society for the Prevention of Cruelty to Animals (SPCA), 165

solar technology, 216–17, 221
South Carolina: and accents in, 42, 74, 116, 126; and Christmas celebrations in, 42, 219; and cousins, 193; and electrical supplies from, 94; and Eye Bank, 151; and visits to, 42, 117, 219. See also Columbia, South Carolina; Neidhardt, Richard F., Jr.; Roberts, Henrietta (Rhett) Neidhardt
sows. See pigs
Space Trilogy (Lewis), 188
spelunking. See caves/caving
Spider's Web, The (NPR), 184
Springfield Plain, 47
Spyri, Johanna. See Heidi
squirrels, 144–45, 151, 166, 193, 240
Stafford, Jean, 210
Stalking the Wild Asparagus (Gibbon), 90, 141–42
stamp collectors, 225–26
"State of Arkansas, The" (folk ballad), 45
stationery, 81, 223–24
Steig, William. See Sylvester and the Magic Pebble
stock pond. See pond
Stone County, Arkansas: and animal abandonment, 165; and back-to-the-land movement, 36, 84, 90, 120, 123, 124, 125, 128–31; and Black people in, 117; and caves/caving in, 178–79, 185; and climate of, 36, 50, 88–89, 158; and colloquialisms of, 71, 73, 91, 92, 102, 115, 128, 143–44, 158, 169, 227, 238, 240; and county seat of, 45; and courthouse, 109; and drought, 70, 71, 89, 177, 227–28; and education level in, 92; and employment opportunities/economy, 91–92, 93–94, 107–8, 200, 222; and folk music in, 108, 109, 110, 123; and garbage dumps in, 213; and local

Stone County, Arkansas (*cont.*)
  population numbers, 46; and locals,
  115–16, 117, 118–19, 222; and medical
  care in, 52, 87, 93, 99, 148–49, 185;
  and music scene in, 35, 105–10, 143;
  and Ozark stereotypes, 47, 115; and
  plumbing in homes, 107, 108; and
  police in, 200; and politics in, 115,
  210–11, 250n2; and public schools
  in, 119, 154–55, 201–7; and spring
  flowers, 151; and tourism in, 109. *See
  also* alcohol prohibition; Fox; Great
  Timbo Valley; hot weather; laundromats; Meadowcreek; Meadowcreek
  Learning and Retreat Center;
  Meadowcreek Project; Mountain
  View; Mozart; Rural Special public
  school; Rushing; swimming holes;
  Timbo
storms, 82, 84, 87, 214–16. *See also*
  winter weather
Storrs, Richard Salter, 122
Stout, Ruth, 81, 90
stovepipe fire, 74
Student Nonviolent Coordinating
  Committee, 117
sugary treats, 135, 196
sumac, 9, 68, 69, 79, 83, 141–42
sumac juice, 141–42
Summer of Love, 21–22
sunfish, 173
sustainable communities. *See*
  Meadowcreek Project
Sutterfield, Taft and Mary, 123, 210
swearing, 29, 49, 72, 116, 201
swimming holes, 35, 88–89, 227–28,
  229, 241
"Swinging Doors" (Haggard), 107
Swiss Family Robinson, The (Wyss), 35
Sylvester and the Magic Pebble (Steig),
  184
Szyk, Arthur, 184

T
tadpoles, 163
Tall Book of Christmas, The (Smith), 180
tape recorder, 184, 193
Tapp, C. W., 170
Tassajara Bread Book (Brown), 135
"Tattooed Lady, The" (Kingston Trio),
  111
Taylor, Adelaide Trehou (Other), 219
Taylor, Lewis William, Jr. (reverend),
  122
Taylor, Lewis Nathaniel (reverend,
  father of Mammy), 122
Taylor, Mildred Kennon (Miss Mill), 41
Taylor, Thomas George (Daddy Tom),
  41
Teacher (Ashton-Warner), 159
Tecumseh, Missouri, 220
telephone access, 19, 62, 161, 179, 210,
  218
"Tennessee Stud" (Driftwood), 109
Thanksgiving Day celebrations, 102–3,
  145–46, 173–75
These Thousand Hills (Guthrie), 25
39 Whitehall Street, 15
Thompson, Kay. See *Eloise*
Thoreau, Henry David, 33, 220–21
Thumbelina (Little Tiny), 3
thunderstorms, 84, 87, 214–26
Thurmond, Strom, 152
Ticer, Mrs. (Fox grocer), 92
Ticer's Market, 92, 115, 136
ticks, 8, 10, 70, 163
Tiger's Milk, 140
Timbo, Arkansas, 109, 119, 165, 228
Timbo Market, 109, 136
Timbo School, 54, 71
Time to Keep, A (Tudor), 184
Tiny (dog), 163, 165
tobacco farming, 41
Toby (classmate of SN), 206. *See also*
  Bonds, Toby

toilet paper, 212–13
toilets. *See* bathroom facilities
tomatoes, 137, 142
tornadoes, 214–15
tortillas, 139
tractor accident, 228
tractors, 8, 9, 80, 153, *213*, 228, *229*
trailers, 108, 115, 123, 124, 222, 234
traveling circus, 231–32
Treat, Hollis, 109, 119, 136
trees on land, 9
tricycle riding, 176
Tripp, Wallace, 184
Trout Fishing in America (Brautigan),
 188
trucks, 42, 45, 198, 204, 231; and bear
 attack, 129; Datsun truck, 199–200;
 and financial support for, 218, 219;
 and muddy roads, 211, 213; and
 unreliability, 65, 67, 77; used trucks,
 54, 157, 161, 199. *See also* vehicles
Tucker Field, 49, 79
Tudor, Tasha, 184
turkey (food), 174–75
Turkey Creek, Arkansas, 201
turtles, 138, 144
Twin Oaks (Virginia), 220

U
Ukrainian Easter eggs, 126
unemployment rate, 34
University of California–Berkeley, 27,
 37, 50–51, 236
University of Central Arkansas, 228,
 230, 235
University of Colorado Boulder, 220
University of South Carolina, 14, 15

V
Vacation Bible School, 119, 122
vaccinations, 98–99
Valentine's Day, 211

Van Ronk, Dave, 82, 111
Vander Veen, Lizabeth (Liza), 156,
 222–23, *224*
vans, 45, 199
vehicles, 199–200; and debt, 156, 199–
 200, 218; and move to Fox, 42; and
 unreliability, 66–67, 77, 87, 198–99,
 200. *See also* Chevy sedan; Datsun
 trucks; Dodge van; International
 Scout; tractors; trucks; Volkswagens
venomous snakes, 7–8, 60, 144, 146,
 164, 168–69. *See also specific snake*
Vietnam War, 15–16, 34
vinegar, 139
Violet Hill, Arkansas, 170
visitors, 54, 65–68, 73–77, 84–*85*, 94,
 103, 151–52, 158, 180
vitamin requests, 97–98
Volkswagens, 161, 200, 211

W
Walden (Thoreau), 33, 220–21
Walden Two communes, 220–21
Walden Two (Skinner), 220
Walnut Acres, 136
Warm Morning wood-heat stove, 216
Warshauer, Michael and Susie, 196,
 197, 211, 230
Washburn, Miriam Storrs, 122, 227
Washburn, Ruth Wendell (Aunt Ruth):
 and antique dollhouse, 226–27; and
 book by, 160, 253n42; and childcare
 advice of, 62–63, 160; as child psychologist, 50, 62–63, 160; and death
 of, 156, 158, 159; and financial support from, 54, 78, 159, 160, 236; and
 homes of, 189; and importance of in
 family, 159–60, 189; and letters from
 WM, 50, 61, 133, 147, 164; and letter to WM, 62–63; and life partner
 (female), 160; and magazines from,
 160, 188–89

washing machines, 57, 83, 141–42, 187, 191, 212

washtub bass, 105

WASPs, 11, 24, 116, 150, 209

watercress, 6, 143

Watergate, 148, 152

water gravy, 107

water moccasin. *See* cottonmouths

water witching, 89

We Always Lie to Strangers: Tall Tales from the Ozarks (Randolph), 107

Weaver, John, 125, 128, 129, 170, 173, 193, 194, 195, 200, 232

welfare, 77, 91, 92–93, 136, 141, 148, 225, 238. *See also* food stamps; Women, Infants, and Children (WIC) program

wells: and distance from cabin, 89, 135; and dog's death in, 163; dug, 4, 123; with electric pump, 89, 94; and freeze prevention, 158; hand-drawn, 89; and lack of, 102; and pump house for, 158; and water line to house, 153; and water witching, 89

Wendy (Momma, WM). *See* McPhee, Caroline Wendell

Wheel of Fortune, 148–49

"Where Have All the Flowers Gone?" (Seeger), 112

Where the Wild Things Are (Sendak), 184

whippoorwills, 216, 241

Whitcomb, Johnny, 62, 119

Whitcomb, Joyce, 62, 119

White, Emil, 236

White, E. B., 173, 190

White, Katherine Sergeant, 190

White, Josh. *See* "Jelly, Jelly"

White, Tony Joe, 108–9, 143

Whitman, Walt, 35, 40, 65, 105, 165, 188

Whole Earth Catalog, The (Brand), 35

Wigginton, Eliot. See *Foxfire* books

wild game, 136, 138, 144, 145, 146. *See also* squirrels

Wilkie, Colin, 108

Williams, Robin, 128

winter weather, 49, 88, 99, 158, 210; and ice storms, 219, 221; and snow, 150, 156, 166, 183, 210, 211, 224–25

Wolf Pen Ridge, 7

Women, Infants, and Children (WIC) program, 136, 225, 258n49

Women's Strike for Equality March, 101

Woodbutcher's Art, The. See *Handmade Houses: A Guide to the Woodbutcher's Art*

wood sorrel, 142, 201

woodstoves: as back-to-the-lander staple, 8; for cooking, 6, 39, 59, 69, 83, 87, 96, 133, *134*, 191; for heat, 59, 61, 102, 108, 216, 217; for heating water, 68, 149; lighting of, 74–75, 76; in summer heat, 62, 69, 87

woodworking, 121

Woody (basket maker), 128

Woman Warrior, The (Kingston), 210

World, 188

World Books, 145

World War II, 23

worm pills, 8

Wright, Harold Bell, 46

Wyss, Johann David. See *Swiss Family Robinson, The*

Y

"You are My Flower" (Carter/Flatt/ Scruggs), 108, 11

Z

Zwinger, Jane, 31